AFTER AUTHORITY

SUNY series in Global Politics

James N. Rosenau, editor

AFTER AUTHORITY

*War, Peace, and Global Politics
in the 21st Century*

Ronnie D. Lipschutz

State University of New York Press

Published by
State University of New York Press, Albany

© 2000 State University of New York

For information, address State University of New York Press
State University Plaza, Albany, N.Y. 12246

Production by Michael Haggett
Marketing by Patrick Durocher

Library of Congress Cataloging-in-Publication Data

Lipschutz, Ronnie D.
    After authority : war, peace, and global politics in the 21st
century / Ronnie D. Lipschutz.
        p.   cm. — (SUNY series in global politics)
    Includes bibliographical references and index.
    ISBN 0-7914-4561-5 (hc : alk. paper). — ISBN 0-7914-4562-3 (pbk.
: alk. paper)
        1. World politics—1989–   2. War.   3. Peace.   I. Title.
II. Series.
D860.L55   2000
909.82'9—dc21   99-38551
                                                                          CIP

10 9 8 7 6 5 4 3 2 1

To Lee Grodzins

Contents

Acknowledgments

Once, it seems, we knew what to do.
　　—Bronislaw Szerszynski, "On Knowing What to Do"

This book has been a long time coming. It is the second in what I have come to think of as my "security triology." The first was *On Security* (Columbia, 1995), the third is tentatively entitled *Minds at Peace,* and it should appear sometime early in the next millennium. Although some of the preliminary thinking behind this volume occurred in the mid- to late-1980s, the ideas did not really germinate until I arrived at UC-Santa Cruz in 1990, and taught a senior seminar entitled "National Security and Interdependence." Looking at the literature, I began to think more was needed in international relations than just epistemological debate and more was needed in foreign policy than simply "redefining security." I tried, therefore, to write on globalization and national security during my first few years at UCSC, but the book refused to be written. Eventually, I gave up, and went on to other books and other projects. Sometimes, however, books come together quite unexpectedly, and when I returned to the project in 1997, I discovered that a number of papers and articles I had written, presented, and published fit together in what I thought (and what I hope *you* think) is an interesting and provocative way.

As is always the case with such books, they are the product of more than one person, although I take full responsibility for everything that appears here. In the course of thinking about and writing what appears here, I have incurred more debts to friends and colleagues than I am now able to recall. Among those who have, in one way or another, helped me along the way are Beverly Crawford, Ken Conca, Gene Rochlin, Peter Euben, Karen Litfin, James Rosenau, Hayward Alker (who suggested the title), Mary Ann Tetreault, and David Meyer (and, needless to say, many more). My wife, Mary, and my children, Eric and Maia, deserve the utmost thanks and love for showing such great forebearance in dealing with almost constant grumpiness. Finally, I dedicate this book to Lee Grodzins who, as my graduate advisor at MIT, saw that heavy-ion nuclear physics was not in my future.

Financial support for various parts of this book have come from a variety of sources, including: the Social Sciences Division and Academic Senate of UC-Santa Cruz, the UC Systemwide Institute on Global Conflict and Cooperation at UC-San Diego, the Center for German and European Studies at UC-Berkeley, the Pew Charitable Trusts, and the Lipschutz-Wieland Research Periphery.

Portions of chapter 2 originally appeared in Ronnie D. Lipschutz, "The Great Transformation Revisited," Brown Journal of World Affairs 4, no. 1 (winter/spring 1997): 299–318. Copyright 1997 Brown Journal of World Affairs, reprinted by permission.

Portions of chapters 3 and 4 originally appeared in Ronnie D. Lipschutz, "On Security," pp. 1–23, and "Negotiating the Boundaries of Difference and Security at Millenium's End," pp. 212–28, in Ronnie D. Lipschutz (ed.), *On Security* (New York: Columbia University Press, 1995). Copyright 1995, Columbia University Press, reprinted by permission of the publisher.

A different version of chapter 5 was published as Ronnie D. Lipschutz, "The Nature of Sovereignty and the Sovereignty of Nature: Problematizing the Boundaries between Self, Society, State, and System," in Karen T. Litfin (ed.), *The Greening of Sovereignty in World Politics* (Cambridge: MIT Press, 1998). Copyright 1998 MIT Press, reprinted by permission.

Portions of chapter 6 were originally published as Ronnie Lipschutz and Beverly Crawford, "Economic Globalization and the 'New' Ethnic Strife: What is to be Done?" San Diego: Institute on Global Conflict and Cooperation, UC-San Diego, (Policy Paper 25, May 1996). Copyright 1996 IGCC, reprinted by permission; Ronnie D. Lipschutz, "Seeking a State of One's Own: An Analytical Framework for Assessing 'Ethnic and Sectarian Conflicts'," in: Beverly Crawford and Ronnie D. Lipschutz (eds.), *The Myth of "Ethnic Conflict"* (Berkeley: Institute of International and Area Studies, UC-Berkeley, 1998). Copyright 1998 IIAS, reprinted by permission; and Ronnie D. Lipschutz with Judith Mayer, *Global Civil Society and Global Environmental Governance* (Albany: State University of New York Press, 1996), chap. 7.

Different versions of Chapter 7 appear in Jose V. Ciprut (ed.), "The State as Moral Authority in a Evolving Global Political Economy," *The Art of the Feud: Reconceptualizing International Relations* (Westport, CT: Greenwood Publishing, forthcoming 2000); and David Jacobsen, Mathias Albert and Yosef Lapid (eds.), "(B)orders and (Dis)Orders: The Role of Moral Authority in Global Politics," *Identities, Borders and Order* (Minneapolis: University of Minnesota Press, forthcoming 2000).

Chapter 8 draws on a number of sources, including Ronnie D. Lipschutz, "Reconstructing World Politics: The Emergence of Global Society," *Millennium* 21, no. 3 (winter 1992): 389–420 (published in revised form in Jeremy Larkins and Rick Fawn, eds., *International Society after the Cold War,* London, Macmillan, 1996). Copyright 1992, 1996, *Millennium* Publishing Group, reprinted by permission; Ronnie D. Lipschutz, "From Place to Planet: Local Knowledge and Global Environmental Governance," *Global Governance: A Review of Multilateralism and International Organization* 3, no. 1 (January–April 1997): 83–102. Copyright 1997, Lynne Rienner Publishers, reprinted with permission of the publisher; Ronnie D. Lipschutz, "Members Only? Citizenship and Civic Virtue in a Time of Globalization," *International Politics* 36, no. 2 (June 1999): 203–233. Copyright 1999, Kluwer Law International, reprinted by permission; and Ronnie D. Lipschutz, "Politics among People: Global Civil Society Reconsidered," in Heidi Hobbs, (ed.), *Pondering Postinternationalism* (Albany: State University of New York Press, 2000).

1❖
THEORY OF GLOBAL POLITICS

The nation-state is in trouble. It is under siege by contradictory forces of its own making and its leaders have no idea how to proceed. Paradoxically, these forces are grounded in the end of the Cold War as well as the broadly held goals of economic growth and the extension of democracy and open markets throughout the world, the very things that are supposed to foster peace and stability. Why should this be so?

As states open up to the world economy, they begin to lose one of the raison d'êtres for which they first came into being: defense of the sovereign nation. Political change and economic globalization enhance the position of some groups and classes and erode that of others. Liberalization and structural reform reduce the welfare role of the state and cast citizens out on their own. As the state loses interest in the well-being of its citizens, its citizens lose interest in the well-being of the state. They look elsewhere for sources of identity and focuses for their loyalty. Some build new linkages within and across borders; others organize into groups determined to resist economic penetration or to eliminate political competitors. The state loses control in some realms and tries to exercise greater control in others. Military force is of little utility under such circumstances. While it remains the reserve currency of international relations, it is of limited use in changing the minds of people. Instead, police power and discipline, both domestic and foreign, are applied more and more. Even these don't really work, as any cop on the beat can attest. Order is under siege; disorder is on the rise; authority is crumbling.

These are hardly new arguments. The search for a unifying theory of international politics and world order has been underway for centuries, if not longer. Such ideas were offered by classical and premodern theorists of politics, such as Thucydides, Hobbes, Kant, List, and various geopoliticians, beginning with Admiral Mahan in the final decade of the 1800s, continuing with Halford Mackinder and Nicholas Spykman during the middle of the twentieth century, and ending with Colin Gray in the 1990s. After World War II, new theories were offered by Morgenthau, Aron, Waltz, and others. Most recently, in the wake of the Cold War's end, these theories have been restated, albeit in a different form, by Samuel Huntington (1996), Benjamin Barber (1995), and Robert Kaplan (1994, 1996). So why another book on the subject of war, peace, and global politics? One reason is that most of the others have it wrong. That the world is changing is doubted by only a few; how and why it is changing, and what is its trajectory, is hardly clear to anyone.

The approach of the millennium has further enflamed the collective imagination, both popular and scholarly, adding fuel to the fire. But most books and films—*The Coming Conflict with China* (Bernstein and Munro, 1997), *Independence Day* and *Armageddon*, and the "Y2K" furor come to mind here—offer the reader (and the policymaker) a biblical dichotomy: the choice between order and chaos, light and darkness, civilization and barbarity. Order draws for its inspiration on both the recent (and antedeluvian) pasts (Noble, 1997), suggesting that a world of well-defined nation-states, under American rule and discipline, still offers the best hope for reducing the risks of war and enhancing the possibilities for teleological human improvement. Chaos reaches even farther back, to the authors of the Bible, as well as the writings of Hobbes, Rousseau, and others, who warned that, in the absence of government, there is only a "State of Nature," the "war of every one against every one." The reality (and here, I wish to avoid debates over what is "real" and what "real" means; see Kubálková, Onuf, and Kowert, 1998) is more likely to be found somewhere in between these two poles or even elsewhere. It is always difficult to ascertain the trajectories of change when one stands in the midst of that change.

In a prescient 1991 inaugural lecture at the University College of Wales in Aberystwyth, site of the world's first department of International Relations, Ken Booth put his finger on the central point. He argued that

> sovereignty is disintegrating. States are less able to perform their traditional functions. Global factors increasingly impinge on all decisions made by governments. Identity patterns are becoming more complex, as people assert local loyalties but want to share in global values and lifestyles. The traditional distinction between "foreign" and "domestic" policy is less tenable than ever. And there is growing awareness that we are sharing a common world history. . . . The [metaphor for the] international system which is now developing . . . is of an egg-box containing the shells of sovereignty; but alongside it a global community omelette is cooking. (Booth, 1991:542)

What Booth did not pinpoint were the reasons for the "disintegration of sovereignty" or, for that matter, where it might lead. Indeed, although virtually everyone writing on the future of world politics takes as a starting point the decline in the sovereign prerogatives of the state, almost no one places the responsibility for this loss directly on the state itself. It is not that the governments of contemporary states have meant to lose sovereignty; they were searching for means to further enhance their power, control *and* sovereignty. Rather, it was that certain institutional practices set in train after World War II have, paradoxically, reduced the sovereign autonomy that was, after all, the ultimate objective of the Allied forces in that war.

Indeed, if there is a single central "unintended consequence" of the international politics and economics of the past fifty years, it is the replacement of the sovereign state by the sovereign individual as the subject of world politics. In saying this, I do not mean to suggest that states are bound to disappear, or that the "legitimate monopoly of violence" will, somehow, be reassigned to tribes, clans, or individuals (although some, such as Kaplan [1996] and Martin van Creveld [1991], argue that, in many places, this has already happened). Instead, it is to argue that the project of "globalization" (an ill-defined and all-encompassing term, discussed in chapter 2), its commitment to individualism in politics, markets, and civil society, and the decline in the likelihood of large-scale wars and threats around which national mobilization can occur, have made reification of the individual the highest value of many societies, both developed and developing. But because globalization has different effects on different people, and some find themselves better off while others are worse off, individual sovereignty is not accepted by all as a positive value; there is reason to question, moreover, whether it *should* be regarded positively (Hirsch, 1995). The heedless pursuit of individual self-interest can have corrosive impacts on long-standing institutions, cultures, and hierarchies, and can lead to a degree of social destabilization that may collapse into uncontrolled violence and destruction.

The implications of this process for sovereignty, authority, and security are manifold. Whereas it used to be taken for granted that the nation-state was the object to be secured by the power of the state, the disappearance of singular enemies has opened a fundamental ontological hole, an *insecurity dilemma*, if you will. Inasmuch as different threats or threatening scenarios promise to affect different individuals and groups differently, there is no overarching enemy that can be used for purposes of mass mobilization (a theme of one of Huntington's more recent articles; see Huntington, 1997). Those concerned about computer hackers penetrating their cyberspace are rarely the same as those concerned about whether they will still be welcome in their workplaces tomorrow. Whereas it used to be taken for granted that threats to security originated from without—from surprise attacks, invading armies, and agents who sometimes managed to turn citizens into traitors—globalization's erosion of national authority has managed to create movements of "patriotic" dissidence whose targets are traitorous governments in the seats of national power.[1]

The old threats were countries with bombs; the new threats are individuals with mail privileges. The old threat was the electromagnetic pulse from exo-atmospheric nuclear detonations; the new threat is information warfare by rogue states, terrorist groups (and corporations?). The old threat was communist subversion by spies, sympathizers, and socialist teachers; the new threat is juvenile subversion by pornography on the World Wide Web. The old threat was aggressive dictators; the new threat is abusive parents. In short, loyalty to the state has been replaced by loyalty to the self, and national authority has been shouldered aside by self-interest. The world of the future might not be one of 200 or 500 or even 1,000 (semi-) sovereign states coexisting uneasily; it could well be one in which every individual is a state of her own, a world of 10 billion statelets, living in a true State of Nature.

What This Book Is About

This book reflects on these matters, on the "end" of authority, sovereignty, and national security at the conclusion of the twentieth century, and on the implications of that end for war, peace, and individual *and* global politics in the twenty-first. I am not so foolish as to argue here that these phenomena will cease to exist in the near future or that the state is doomed to disappear. And I have no intention of brushing over the genealogies of these concepts or, for that matter, the state and state system in speculating on the global political environment of the twenty-first century. But I do propose here that, in the long view of history, the two hundred-odd years between 1789 and 1989 were exceptional in that the nation-state was unchallenged by any other form of political organization at the global level.[2] That exceptional period is now just about over.

What *will* emerge over the coming decades is by no means determined or even clear. As the extent of social change becomes more evident, strong states could reassert their primacy and drive the world back into a new period of geopolitical competition (as could happen in East Asia; see, e.g., Bernstein and Munro, 1997). It is entirely possible that global civil society and institutions of transnational governance will, to a significant degree, supplement or supplant national governments, without undermining the basis for the nation (as appears to be taking place in Europe; see Lipschutz, 1996). Or, the resulting social tensions might be so severe as to cause a collapse into violent chaos and nonstate forms of governance (as some suggest is occurring in various parts of Africa and some urban agglomerations; see Jackson, 1990). Perhaps these, and other, forms of political community and action will coexist, as the medieval and the modern were forced to do during the transition from one to the other. I make few predictions, and no promises.

I begin, in chapter 2, with "The Worries of Nations." One of the much-noted paradoxes of the 1990s is the coexistence of processes of integration and fragmentation, of globalism and particularism, of simultaneous centralization and decentralization often in the very same place. James Rosenau (1990) has coined the rather unwieldy term "fragmegration" to describe this phenomenon, which he ascribes largely to the emergence of a "sovereignty-free" world in the midst of a "sovereignty-bound" one. Rosenau frames this "bifurcation" of world politics as a series of conceptual and practical "jailbreaks," as people acquire the knowledge and capabilities to break out of the political and social structures that have kept them imprisoned for some centuries. Rosenau's theory—if it can be called that—is an essentially liberal one and, while he acknowledges the importance of economic factors in the split between the two worlds, he shies away from recognizing the central role of material and economic change and the ancillary processes of social innovation and reorganization in this phenomenon.

Without falling into a deterministic historical materialism, it is critical to recognize just how central "production," as Robert Cox (1987) and Stephen Gill (1993) put it, is to the changes to which we are witness. Production is more than just the making of things (by which I mean material goods as well as knowledge); it is the making of *particular* things under particular *forms* of social organization to fufill particular societal *purposes* (Latour, 1986). These purposes are not autonomous of the material basis of a society but neither are they superstructure to that base. The two constitute each other and, through practice, do so on a continuous and dynamically changing basis. Social organization then becomes the means by which things are produced and used to fulfill those purposes. Lest this all seem too tautological, or functionalist, there is more at work here than just reproduction, as we shall see. Rosenau's "fragmegration" is, thus, a consequence of more than just the acquisition of knowledge and skills in a postsovereign political space; it is a direct result of the particular ways in which production and purpose have been pursued and the forms of social organization established to facilitate that pursuit.

The simultaneous conditions of integration and fragmentation are, then, part of the process of social innovation and reorganization that go hand-in-hand with changes in production and purpose. Why, after two hundred or more years of state consolidation and centralization, this should happen now, is not immediately apparent although the consequences are all too clear. Whether, on balance, this is to be regarded as a positive or negative development remains to be seen. What is clear is that there is no teleology invoked or involved here. I do, however, attribute recent changes to forces similar to those described by Karl Polanyi (1944/1957) in explaining the causes of the two World Wars, and to the ways in which knowledge and social innovation have transformed our relationship to the nation-state and to each other.

In chapter 3, I turn to the "Insecurity Dilemma" and its relationship to globalization. What does it mean to be threatened? What does it mean to be secure? As in the myth of the Golden Fleece, the slaying of the Great Soviet Dragon seems to have given rise to a proliferation of smaller, poisonous lizards, most of which are merely annoying, but some of which might be deadly. The difficulty comes in telling the two apart. Integration and interdependence, it has long been supposed, foster communication, understanding, and peace, especially among democracies, but if fragmentation is taking place at the same time, in which direction does the arrow of safety point?

Forty years ago, John Herz (1959) pointed out how the efforts of some states to make themselves more secure often made other states feel less secure (see also Jervis, 1978). Inasmuch as intentions could not be known with certainty, while capabilities could be observed with surety, it was better to assume the worst of one's neighbor. Today, with the proliferation of imagined threats—imagined in the sense that virtually none have, as yet, come to pass—even capabilities can no longer be fully scrutinized. Terrorists might have acquired weapons of mass destruction—but we do not know for sure.[3] Illegal immigrants are subverting our cultures—but they are also supporting them. Mysterious diseases lurk in uncharted forests—but they can escape at a day's notice, without warning. And even the state cannot protect everyone against these myriads of threats if it does not know whether or not they are real (Lipschutz, 1999b).

The result is a wholesale transformation in the security apparatus of the state. Not only is it now directed against external enemies, whomever and wherever they might be, but also against domestic ones—

and these just might be the boy or girl next door. Soldiers become cops. Cops acquire armored cars and tanks. Citizens are scrutinized for criminal proclivities. Criminals adopt military armaments and practices. Even the paranoid have enemies and, in a paranoid society, can anyone trust anyone except her/himself? (There may be good reason to be paranoid, as we shall see in chapter 7; the chances are that someone *is* watching *you*).

Historically, the purpose of "security" was to protect state and society against war. In chapter 4, "Arms and Affluence," I ask "Whatever happened to World War III?" War has long been a staple topic of film, fiction, and philosophy, if only because it is so uncommon. For those in the midst of battle, there is hardly a big picture: One's focus is on survival from one moment to the next. For those who are observers, it is the infrequency and extremities of war that is so fascinating. Yet, in virtually all discussions by international relations specialists, war is taken not as a social institution that can, somehow, be eliminated through deliberate political action, but as a "natural" outgrowth of human nature and relations between human collectives (see, e.g., Waltz, 1959). Where the interests of such collectives come into conflict, it is assumed, war will result; conversely, if collectives can negotiate over their interests, peace is possible. Experience suggests we be more cautious in making such unqualified claims.

Paradoxically, while the war of all against all develops apace, the wars of state against state become ever more uncommon. The United States prepares itself for future regional wars, such as the one undertaken against Iraq, in the face of compelling evidence that such wars erupt no more than once every decade or two. In place of really existing war, we now confront virtual warfare, or what I call here "disciplinary deterrence." This is war by other means: by example, by punishment, by public relations. It rests upon the United States not as world policeperson but as dominatrix, or global vice-principal strolling down the high school hallway, checking miscreants for hall passes. Violators, such as Iraq, get spanked (giving new meanings to bondage and domination), and serve as warning to others who might think about causing trouble. I return to the implications of this metaphor in chapter 7.

Hobbes and Locke argued that Leviathan and the social contract were necessary to counter the State of Nature, a condition in which the sole moral stricture was to survive. Only through the state could men (and women) begin to build societies and civilizations. In chapter 5, "Markets, the State, and War," I examine wars over nature, so-called resource wars that some think could take place over scarce water. In these cases, the limits of nature are presumed to lead to conflict and war among those who require scarce natural goods (Lipschutz, 1989). This amounts to a political redistribution of access meant to redress the arbitrary boundaries of state and geography.

The solution offered to impasses of this sort is exchange in the market, a practice and institution that, left to operate on it own under orderly conditions, can impose peace through the price mechanism. But markets are no less political than any other human institution; they require rules to operate properly, and someone must formulate such rules (Attali, 1997). Moreover, relying on markets to defuse conflicts over resources and environment could have the perverse effect of returning us to something much closer to the State of Nature through the naturalization of market relations. Naturalizing the market removes it from the domain of everyday politics by representing it as immutable and subject neither to change nor to external authority. This, as I point out, is an act of power and domination whose outcomes are quite unlikely to be equitable or legitimate. Indeed, letting the market work its magic may result in no more than a transitory "neoliberal" peace that ultimately leads to vast distributive inequities and a new round of violence (Lipschutz, 1999a).

Most contemporary wars are neither between states nor about resources. Chapter 6, "The Social Contraction" explores the causes and consequences of wars *within* nation-states, especially as manifested through what we have come to call "ethnic" or "sectarian" conflict. Conventional wisdom attributes these cultural wars to sociobiology, ancient animosities, and the need for human beings to differentiate themselves from one another. Yet, there is a fundamental problem with such explanations: They fail to tell us in convincing fashion why such violence did not develop earlier or why earlier periods of violence were followed by times of relative peace and stability. Even such arguments as authoritarian governments "keeping the lid on the kettle" are no more than inaccurate metaphors; politics is neither classical mechanics nor thermodynamics nor even chaos theory.

Rather than being understood as some sort of atavistic or premodern phenomenon, cultural conflict should be seen as a modern (or even postmodern) response to fundamental social change. The unachievable dream of political theorists and practitioners is stability, now and forever; the undeniable truth is change, always and everywhere. During periods of "normality," change is slower and more predictable; it can be managed, up to a point. Over the past few decades, we have been witness to more rapid and less predictable changes, brought about by globalization and social innovation. These changes have destabilized the political hierarchies that rule over social orders—even democratic ones—and provided opportunities for those who might seek greater power and wealth to do so. The conflicts and clashes that result can tear societies apart.

The tools for popular mobilization are both contextual and contingent; the phenomenon of social warfare, as Jim Seaton (1994) calls it, has changed only in form, but not in content. During the Cold War, political elites mobilized polities and gained power using the discourse of East versus West, Marxist versus Capitalist. Today, culture has become the language under which political action takes place, and elites operate accordingly. In all cases, it is the contractual basis of social order that is under challenge and being destroyed. When people find their prospects uncertain and dismal, they tend to go with those who can promise a better, more promising future. Cultural solidarity draws on such teleological scenarios and pie in the sky, by and by.

In Chapter 7, "The Princ(ipal)," I explore how the state—especially the American state—is engaged in both international and domestic discipline in the effort to maintain political order amidst the disorder generated by globalization. While conventional wisdom sees the nation-state as a functional provider of security, identity, and welfare, it is better understood as an actor that seeks to project its own, unique, *national* morality into world politics. Each nation-state, as guardian of its own civil religion and inheritor of a moral authority bequeathed to it by Church and Prince (yes, even the United States!), is seen by its members as the total embodiment of good. In this ethnocentric ontology, therefore, all other nation-states come to be representatives of evil. Those states with power try to impose their moralities onto world politics, in the view that the triumph of good can follow only from total domination. If this is not possible, the next best thing is obedience.

The globalization of markets, however, poses an unprecedented challenge to statist moralities. In market society, consumption is a *good* (and *is* good), and it is the individual's responsibility to consume according to his or her needs and desires. Authority thus comes to rest within each individual, whose self-interested behavior becomes, ipso facto, a moral good (although some might call it nihilism). The state, seeking to reimpose order, is forced to demonstrate its authority by acting as a moral agent able to impose its wishes both abroad and at home. Culture wars are one result, for material girls and boys are not so easily lured back inside the old moral borders.

Are politics in the twenty-first century destined to be so grim? Not necessarily. Trends are never destiny. We are constrained, but we can make choices. In chapter 8, "Politics among People," I suggest a more optimistic possibility. For better or worse, the end of the twentieth century has seen a gradual shift of political power away from the nation-state to the local and the global. Downward decentralization and upward concentration could be disempowering, or they might provide the means for global diversity and democratization. Some governance functions are becoming globalized; others are being devolved to the local level. If we are not to let the global capture the critical functions and leave the irrelevant ones to the local, it is necessary to find ways to have global rules and local diversity, a transnational politics that is both democratic and action-oriented. I suspect that "global civil society" might be one means of accomplishing this end, but there are other possibilities to offer, as we shall see.

If we leave politics to the market, we will be able to choose among cereals, toilet paper, automobiles. If we bring politics back in, opportunities for choices will be broader, more appealing and more just. Political action is, therefore, an absolute necessity; if we fail to act, we may be fat but we will not be happy. The world, "after authority," can be ours to fashion, if we so decide.

2❖
THE WORRIES OF NATIONS

*Our thesis is that the idea of a self-adjusting market implied
a stark utopia. Such an institution could not exist for any
length of time without annihilating the human and natural
substance of society; it would have physically destroyed man
and transformed his surroundings into a wilderness.*

—Karl Polanyi, *The Great Transformation*

More than half a century has passed since Karl Polanyi penned those
words. He wrote *The Great Transformation* in the midst of the greatest
conflagration human civilization has yet known, and, ever since, his
book been regarded as one of the classics of modern political economy.
Polanyi sought to explain why the twentieth century, then not yet half
over, had already been rent by two great wars. Where most blamed
"accidents" for World War I, and Germany, Japan and the Great Depression for World War II, Polanyi found an explanation in the dreams
and failures of nineteenth-century laissez-faire capitalists and the market
processes originally set in train during the early years of the first
Industrial Revolution, between 1800 and 1850. The nineteenth century
was a time of social and technological innovation and reorganization
at a scale theretofore unexperienced by anyone. It left an indelible

mark on the world and its impacts are still being felt today. The "Great Transformation" led to the emergence of the modern nation-state as an active political and economic player in people's everyday lives and turned it into an aggressive agent in international relations. It also resulted, in the twentieth century, in the two world wars.

It would seem unlikely that a fifty-year-old book about events taking place almost two hundred years ago would have anything to say to us about either today or the future. Nonetheless, many of the same phenomena examined by Polanyi are, once again, at work today. In this chapter, I argue that we have entered a period of social change for which the history of the Industrial Revolution, and the events that followed, merit close scrutiny for contemporary parallels. To be sure, things are not the same, but there *are* a number of important similarities between then and now. In particular, as the twenty-first century begins, we find ourselves living through a period of social and technological innovation and reorganization, taking place not only within countries but also globally—a phenomenon that is often called "globalization." We might expect that, as happened in the past, unanticipated social and political consequences will follow (on globalization, see, e.g., Gill and Mittleman, 1997; Sakamoto, 1994; Castells, 1996, 1997, 1998). In the later chapters of this book, we shall see that these consequences may be violent or peaceful, integrative or fragmenting, bringing prosperity to some and poverty to others. For now, these are mostly only possibilities. At some point during the coming century, however, it is likely that new patterns of global politics will become clear. We may then be able to look back, as Polanyi did, and describe how events, processes of change, and human actions during the second half of the twentieth century led to the new patterns of the twenty-first. At this point, the future remains cloudy and we can only speculate.

I begin this chapter with a general discussion of industrial revolutions and their impacts within nation-states and on relations between them. The key element here is social innovation and reorganization at scales running from the household to the global. I then turn to an analysis of the "Cold War Compromise," the concerted attempt following World War II to avoid the reemergence of those conditions that were thought to have led to the two world wars, and especially World War II. The "compromise" represented the United States' attempt to steer the global political and economic system toward stability and prosperity by reproducing, as much as possible, domestic American conditions abroad. As we shall see, the Compromise was largely a success, but it has had quite unforeseen results. I then describe the origins of the Third Industrial Revolution (a.k.a. the "information revolution") in the great applied science projects of World War II (the Manhattan Project, in particular), which became the model for technological research and innovation during the decades that followed. More specifically, it was the mobilization of knowledge in the pursuit of a better world that, paradoxically, has served to undermine the very welfare state that gave birth to the teleological, self-interested, Web-centered global crusade on which we have embarked.

What Are Industrial Revolutions?

The causes and consequences of the social, political, and economic changes, and the seemingly continuous disorder and violence, both interstate and intrastate, that wracked Europe between 1750 and 1850 remain the subject of vociferous controversy (see, e.g., Mann, 1993). For some, it was the mechanization of industry—industrialization— that was central; for others, it was the transition from merchant capitalism to manufacturing and finance capitalism. Still others have argued that it was the destruction of the old post-Reformation hierarchical order by the Enlightenment and the French Revolution that was directly responsible for domestic and international disorder. In many ways, the central contradiction facing the societies of the time was the collapse of authority, as sovereign ruler gave way to sovereign people.

Polanyi's argument was, however, somewhat more subtle than this. He claimed that there was, in effect, a structural mismatch between the emerging system of liberal capitalism and then-existing social values and social relations of production. The enormous investments made in the new factory system by the holders of capital required workers—primarily male, as women were expected to remain at home— willing to work for wages. The workers were not willing to do so. At the beginning of the nineteenth century, society was not organized so as to facilitate the operation of an capitalist industrial system; labor, land, and money were hedged about with all kinds of customary and legal restrictions on use and sale. Indeed, the social organization of people's lives was such that they had few incentives to leave the land or enter unregulated labor markets. To be sure, the first stages of capitalist production had already been in existence for some time, especially where woven goods were concerned, but these were mostly made through the cottage industry's "putting-out" system, based in weavers' homes.

The marriage of water and steam power with such industry, dating from the eighteenth century, made putting out and its social relations of production obsolete. Now it was possible to run multiple looms at one time in one place, with laborers working for a daily wage under the direction of a few on-site managers. But factory owners faced a problem: How could they get male weavers out of their homes and into the factories? The answer was, in effect, to undermine the social support systems that made it possible for them to stay at home, an objective accomplished through the introduction of a self-regulating market economy—that is, *liberalization.* In such an economy, labor, land, and money would be treated as what Polanyi called "fictitious commodities," to be bought and sold without any kind of obvious political manipulation (although, to be implemented and made to work, such liberalization required major intervention into society and regulation of social relations; see Gill, 1995:9). Deregulation would ensure availability of the three commodities at least cost to capital and would, in turn, maximize capitalists' return on investment. It would also generate the funds needed for further national economic expansion (for an exploration of this phenomenon in a contemporary context, see Edmunds, 1996).

These were the circumstances under which the first stage of the Great Transformation took place. England, which had operated under principles of mercantilism for some 150 years, made the transition to a self-regulating market system, free trade, and the gold standard (Gilpin, 1977, 1987). Lands held as village commons or bound to particular uses by customary rules were transformed into alienable private property. (This process had begun in England some 150 years earlier, and continues today. Enclosure was recently written into the Mexican constitution with privatization of the *ejidos*; it is being effected through privatization of intellectual property rights; it is even being applied in implementation of the UN Framework Convention on Climate Change.) The Poor Laws, which had functioned to depress wages and pauperize the common people, were repealed and replaced by the "workhouse" and competitive labor markets that undermined residual social solidarity.[1] And free trade made it possible to import cheap grains, which made food less costly and small-scale agriculture unremunerative. Polanyi dated "industrial capitalism as a social system" from 1834, the date of the Poor Law Reform. As he put it (1944/ 1957:83), "[N]ow man was detached from home and kind, torn from his roots and all meaningful environment." What ensued was massive social change. Karl Marx put it more poetically in 1856 (1978:577–78), observing that "all that is solid melts into air" (the phrase also appears in chapter 1 of *The Communist Manifesto*).

By mid-century, what had begun in England was being repeated throughout much of Western and Central Europe and the Americas, with attendant consequences (see, e.g., Berend and Ránki, 1979, esp. 9–120). Technological innovation in the wake of industrialization exposed the inefficiencies of the old order and led to the political legislation that reorganized social relations. But such reorganization was not cost free to ruling elites; it threatened the social stability that had been laboriously reestablished through repressive means and the balance of power after the Napoleonic Wars. The Concert of Europe was able to keep interstate peace, more or less, but it was hard pressed to address the domestic turmoil and disruption that followed social restructuring. The newly emerging middle classes, heretofore largely excluded from political participation, saw their prospects under threat and began to agitate for political and economic reform that would give them both a say and a stake in the state. The Revolutions of 1848 were, in part, a result of this agitation; the repression that followed, a response (Gerö, 1995).

Nationalism, and what later came to be called the welfare state, emerged from this crisis as deliberate political interventions designed to address both domestic political instability and challenges from without. Together, the two could be seen as a form of "social contract," nationalism representing the commitment by the citizen to the well-being of the state, welfarism the commitment by the state to the well-being of the citizen (a point developed in chapter 6). To a considerable degree, such mutual obligations helped to temper the social disruption caused by the self-regulating market system.

But this contract also, according to Polanyi, set the scene for the outbreak of World War I. The reason was that nationalism set states against one another, as emerging doctrines of geopolitics combined with forms of Social Darwinism, rooted in Charles Darwin's theories of natural selection (but not advocated by Darwin himself), were extended from individual organisms as members of species to nations as representations of superior races (Agnew and Corbridge, 1995:57). As we shall see in chapter 5, according to German philosophers, who elaborated the biological and evolutionary metaphor, states could be seen as "natural" organisms that passed through specific stages of life. Thus, younger, more energetic states inevitably succeeded older, geriatric ones on the world stage. States must therefore continually seek individual advantage in order not to succumb prematurely to this cycle of Nature (Dalby, 1990:35).

The point here is not that the first Industrial Revolution led, ultimately, to the world wars of the twentieth century, although that is one important aspect of Polanyi's argument. Rather, it is that modern capitalism was made feasible only through massive, social innovation and reorganization (which are sometimes described as "strategies of accumulation") affecting Europe, North America, and much of the rest of the world. When the first industrial entrepreneurs discovered that they could not entice labor out of their homes and into the factories in exchange for a full day's pay, they found ways of rendering unviable the family and social structures that, in the towns and villages, had provided some degree of social support even in the midst of privation. Then, workers had no choice but to go into the factories.

When later in the nineteenth century, agitation by workers over low wages and undesirable working conditions led to the formation of the first labor unions, which elites saw as a threat to their control of state and economy (the "spectre haunting Europe"), new regulations and incentives were put in place to, once again, foster a restructuring of social units even while buffering labor and society against some of the worst features of industrial capitalism. Nevertheless, according to Polanyi, these were insufficient to maintain domestic stability. Governments found it necessary to further protect their citizens from the excesses of the system transmitted through the ups and downs of the business cycle, increasingly competitive national policies, and the surplus production capacity that in both the 1870s and 1930s led to major world depressions. Governments responded with growing degrees of protectionism, imperialism, and neomercantilism. Competition and suspicion led to arms races and mutual hostility. Eventually, wars broke out.

The Cold War Compromise

Polyani's book was published in 1944, the year that Allied policymakers gathered at Bretton Woods, New Hampshire, to put together their plan for a postwar economic system (Block, 1977; Kapstein, 1996:20). These men—and they were virtually all men, among whom were John Maynard Keynes and Harry Dexter White—were well aware of the history described by Polanyi. They recognized the inherent tension between states trying to reconcile their participation in an international economy with the need to maintain political satisfaction and stability at home; this, after all, had been the dilemma faced by both Allied and Axis powers during the 1930s. Hence, the economic system proposed by Keynes, White, and others was designed to allow countries to maintain full domestic employment and growth while simultaneously avoiding the consequences for domestic stability of trade imbalances and unregulated capital flows, along with semiliberalized trade to reduce the problem of surplus capacity (Gilpin, 1987). These goals were to be accomplished through free and stable exchange rates maintained by borrowing from and lending to an International Monetary Fund (IMF), provision of longer-term liquidity through reconstruction and development loans from the World Bank, free trade regulated by an International Trade Organization (ITO), and dollar-gold convertibility to provide an international medium of exchange (for discussions of the Bretton Woods institutions and how they were meant to work, see Block, 1977; Ruggie, 1983a, 1991, 1995).

The Bretton Woods arrangements failed almost from the start. Efforts to restore convertibility of the pound sterling collapsed in the face of Britain's enormous wartime debts, insufficient global liquidity, and the international preference for dollars. Convertibility was postponed. Both the IMF and World Bank were undercapitalized, too, and the United States soon found it necessary to inject money into the international economy through grants, loans, and military assistance, which had its own negative consequences during the 1960s and 1970s in the "Triffin Dilemma."[2] The ITO never came into existence, although the

GATT provided something of a substitute until the establishment of the World Trade Organization in 1995.

The compromise of "embedded liberalism," as John Ruggie (1983a) has called it, nonetheless remained on the books. Embedded liberalism was based on a commitment by national governments to the principles of nineteenth-century economic liberalism, with adequate safeguards *and* the recognition that a rapid return to such a system might well recreate the conditions of the 1930s. Inasmuch as full-blown liberalization was politically impossible in 1944, the Western allies agreed to move over time in the direction of a fully liberal system. There would be a gradual transition from a more protectionist and neomercantilist world to a more liberal one, in which "self-regulating markets" would be phased in through negotiations among states.[3]

As the dollar liquidity shortage began to bite toward the end of the 1940s, this more-or-less implicit agreement was greased by financial transfers through the Truman Doctrine, the Marshall Plan, the Korean War, and the Mutual Defense Act (see Pollard, 1985; the Mutual Defense Agency subsequently became the U.S. Agency for International Development, which, in 1998, was transformed into a wholly owned subsidiary of the U.S. Department of State). Full convertibility of Western currencies finally arrived in 1958, and successive GATT rounds served to dismantle many of the protectionist barriers that had been put up in the aftermath of World War II. Still, full-blown international liberalism was not yet in sight.

Although it is generally argued that the purpose of the Cold War liberalization project was both defensive and economic (as the conventional and revisionist accounts would have it), this is not quite correct.[4] Rather, the intention of U.S. policy was to reproduce domestic American society (or, at least, its underlying structural conditions), as much as possible, the world over. The implicit reasoning behind this goal, although specious and faulty, was that stability and prosperity in the United States were made possible by capitalism, democracy, growth, freedom, and social integration. If such conditions could be replicated in other countries, everyone would become like the happy Americans (Packenham, 1973; see also Lederer and Burdick, 1958). They would not threaten each other, they would not fight each other, and the number of twentieth-century world wars would be limited to two.[5] Whether or not the USSR, the Warsaw Pact, and miscellaneous radical regimes throughout the developing world posed a mortal threat to this project is largely irrelevant. The very existence of the Soviet bloc provided an external enemy that motivated fractious allies to compromise on liberalization (and defense), even when it was not to everyone's taste or benefit.

This ambitious project of liberalization from above came to an end in the late 1960s. Throughout the 1940s and 1950s, the economy of the free world was greased mostly by the dollars that the United States was able to spend abroad or transfer to its allies. The export of dollars helped to maintain high levels of international liquidity and growth, which was to America's benefit. Already in the late 1950s, as noted earlier, Robert Triffin had warned that this state of affairs could not continue indefinitely. Other countries' need for additional dollars would eventually reach a limit. They might then demand gold in exchange, more gold than the United States had squirreled away in Fort Knox.[6] The expenditures associated with the Vietnam War only hastened the day when the dollar-gold exchange standard would have to end. That day arrived in 1971 (Gowa, 1983).

Not altogether coincidentally, it was during this same period that President Nixon enunciated his eponymous doctrine, which promised to place greater reliance on U.S. allies to maintain regional stability and security. Nixon and Kissinger meant to get the United States out of Vietnam but the Nixon Doctrine had wider implications, too. In the future, countries would be expected to provide for their own defense rather than relying on the United States, although the latter would gladly sell to the former the armaments needed for this purpose. It was also during these years that the oil-producing countries finally began to demand higher prices for their product, so that they could purchase the weapons and technology needed to implement the doctrine. The oil embargoes, price hikes, gas lines, and inflation that followed were all of a piece (Schurmann, 1974, 1987; Saul, 1992).

The Third Industrial Revolution

These events, and those that followed later, might not have been the most important happenings during the 1960s and 1970s. There was another, much more subtle process underway whose significance had not yet been noticed fully, but whose origins could be traced back to the 1940s: the Third Industrial Revolution, or what is often called today the "information" or "electronics revolution." This latest great transformation is usually ascribed to the invention of the transistor and the enormous increases in computing speed and capability that followed as more and more semiconductor devices could be crammed into smaller and smaller spaces. But the information revolution is better understood not as a *cause* of that innovation but rather as a consequence of fundamental innovation in the *social organization* of scientific research and development and higher education that began during World War II.

Prior to 1945, the economic systems of the industrialized countries were organized around consumer-oriented mass production, or "Fordism" (Rupert, 1995). Fordist production, characteristic of the Second Industrial Revolution, was especially widespread in the United States during the first half of the twentieth century, and well into the second half. It came to be emulated throughout the world, although it faltered during the Great Depression as the supply of manufactured goods and raw materials outstripped the demand of domestic and foreign consumers. The Allied victory in World War II was based on Fordist mass production, which only reinforced the virtues of this type of economy (Milward, 1977; Rochlin, 1985; for an argument that military Fordism is over, see Cohen, 1996). Subsequently, at the end of World War II, factories converted back to civilian production and, after a few ups and downs of the business cycle, Keynesian military spending helped to ensure that consumers would be able to purchase the products turned out by the factories with the wages they earned making the goods.

What changed? In 1945, Bernard Brodie made the observation that, with the advent of nuclear weapons, everything had changed. The only function of the military, he said, would now be to prevent future wars (quoted in Freedman, 1983:44). Brodie was only half right; the bomb changed much more than he thought. Neither he nor anyone else recognized then that the development of the atomic bomb also signaled the beginning of the end for Fordism, marked by a subtle shift from production based on *material* capabilities to a system driven by *intellectual* ones. The advent of the information revolution coincided with the origins of the "nuclear revolution" and, indeed, was inherent in it. The change did not come suddenly; just as the First Industrial Revolution had its roots in steam technology that was developed decades before 1800 and coexisted for some time with the putting-out system, and the Second in electricity and electrification of factories, so did Fordism continue to thrive even as it was becoming obsolete.

For example, thinking that numbers would make the difference in World War III as they had in World War II, the initial American approach to defense and deterrence was to mass-produce enormous numbers of atomic and hydrogen bombs (some twenty-five thousand by the end of the 1950s) so as to bomb Russia to rubble. As time passed, however, it became obvious that total war with nuclear weapons might not be such a good idea. Most of the nuclear deterrence and arms-control debates of the following forty years pitted those advocating mass use of force (mutually assured destruction, or MAD) against those arguing for niche-targeted "finesse" (MIRVing and counterforce targeting; see Freedman, 1983).

The mass production approach to war was obsolete almost as soon as the dust cleared over Hiroshima, but it had yet to be fully applied to science (although it was already being applied in some sectors; see, e.g., Burnham, 1941). In the aftermath of the successes of the Manhattan Project and other state-funded wartime projects, this new model of scientific research *and* production emerged, organized around "human capital." Technological change and social innovation once again came into play in the service of the state.[7] Science became highly institutionalized. Directed research and development became critical to maintaining the United States' technological and military edge over its competitors. Education of the workforce in the intellectual tools and skills of this new world became essential. Education itself was transformed, as it became clear that traditional rote learning—reading, writing, and 'rithmetic—was appropriate to creating a "cannon-fodder" citizenry for the mass armies of world wars I and II, but would not produce the critically and scientifically trained cadres needed in this new era of U.S.-directed global management.

In response, over the following decades, the American system of higher education expanded manyfold. In the 1960s, University of California President Clark Kerr called the new model the "multiversity"; others ridiculed it as the "educational cafeteria." No matter; specializations proliferated. A college degree became a prerequisite to advancement and mobility out of the working class and into the "middle" class (aided and abetted in this by the GI Bill, Pell Grants, and other forms of educational "credit"). And, because intellectual ability and competence were not distributed by class, race, or gender, it also became necessary to provide access to these opportunities to women as well as minorities.[8]

Finally, just as had been the case in earlier times, the programs of the leading country were adopted by others (Gerschenkron, 1962; Crawford, 1995). The growth in numbers of educated cadres was not limited to the United States, because the American university model was universalized. Foreigners were encouraged to come to the United States to acquire the skills and training necessary to rationalize their own societies and make them more like America.[9] Their way and tuition were often paid by the U.S. government as, for instance, in the "Atoms for Peace" program. Other countries recognized the prestige and political benefits inherent in systems of higher education, as well as *their* need for trained individuals so that *they* could compete in this new global system. They built national university systems, too.

The Revolution at Home

Left to its own devices, the information revolution might have gone nowhere. Just as in the absence of the impetus of markets and profits, the steam engine would have remained a curiosity with limited application, so were the dynamic of capitalism combined with political and economic instability required to really get this latest industrial revolution off the ground. That these elements were necessary to the new regime of accumulation (if not essential) is best seen in the trajectory and fate of the Soviet Union. The USSR was able to engineer the first steps of the transformation and acquire advanced military means comparable in most respects to the West's,[10] but eventually it was unable to engage in the social innovation necessary to reorganize the productive process and maintain growth rates (Crawford, 1995).

In the United States, the education of cadres of citizens during the Cold War, the erosion of the political legitimacy of the state, and public protests during the 1960s were key parts of the process of social reorganization. The slow decline of American economic dominance was another. The political upheavals of the 1960s had their origins in the extension of American national interest to all parts of the globe during the 1940s and 1950s, as well as the growth of higher education. The expansion of interests meant that specialized knowledge about foreign societies, and their cultures, politics, and economics, were essential if the "free world" were to be managed for the benefit of the United States. The "old boy" banker-lawyer network that had supplied diplomats and specialist throughout much of the twentieth century (Barnet, 1973) could no longer meet the demand. The result was a system dedicated to production of specially trained individuals, who could deal with foreign affairs and comparative politics, to staff embassies, the State Department, and other agencies, at home and abroad. And, as I noted above, the emergence of a scientific problem–solving paradigm as the dominant model for managing of the new global system also generated the need for large numbers of individuals trained in a variety of scientific disciplines. Growing numbers of highly skilled individuals were thus trained, with the expectation that they would participate in projects addressing social as well as scientific matters.[11]

But what would happen to these educated elites after college? In many countries, including the United States, new college graduates expected to find employment with their own national and state governments, state-owned and defense-related private industries, or systems of secondary or higher education. For some decades, there was a balance between graduates and jobs, supported by relatively steady economic growth rates. At some point, however, the supply of competent individuals began to exceed the official demand for their skills (Arenson, 1998). Moreover, as the failure in Vietnam demonstrated during the 1960s and 1970s, even the government's mobilization of expertise in the pursuit of national security objectives did not always turn out successfully.

One result of the Vietnam fiasco was a serious challenge to the legitimacy of Cold War politics; another was the breaking open of the culture of expertise, with all of its hegemonic restrictions on opposition to the "dominant paradigm" (Barnet, 1973). Competing centers of expertise, skills, and knowledge began to surface, epitomized in the global proliferation of "think tanks" and nongovernmental organizations of the right and left. These centers came to represent a system of analytical capabilities, knowledge, and practice parallel to that of the state's, providing gainful employment to many "symbolic analysts," as Robert Reich (1992) has called them, at all levels of society, and a series of way stations to those who might wish to move in and out of government positions. Indeed, it is somewhat paradoxical that, even as Lyndon Johnson's Great Society was increasingly excoriated for its domestic policy failures, conservative and liberal think tanks were only too happy to rush in with new, usually untested policy advice.

Into the Breach

Thus, the international political and economic turmoil of the 1970s—the collapse of the Bretton Woods currency exchange system, oil embargo and price hikes, recession, inflation, and implementation of the Nixon Doctrine (Schurmann, 1987)—provided the initial impetus to innovation and reorganization in industry and production. Among the effects were the shift from large, gas-guzzling cars to smaller, more fuel-efficient foreign ones—a trend now being reversed with the shift to SUVs as a result of extremely low oil prices—a greater reliance on market mechanisms to generate supplies of raw materials, and the emergence of what came to be called the "new international division of labor." Of comparable importance in this transition were the growing social costs of the welfare state, which capital saw as a drag on profits, and an emerging attack on the "liberal" American government by Cold War conservatives. The fact that some of America's allies and client states had successfully followed, and in some cases surpassed, the leader in terms of technological and social innovation was also crucial. This last change should not have come as a surprise, but it did. (Indeed, it is important to recognize that the postwar reorganization and economic development of Japan and Germany represented major successes of U.S. foreign policy!)

Reestablishing growth rates and profits, suppressing inflation, and restoring economic management required a reorganization of social relations and relations of production, although this was not so evident in the 1970s and 1980s; moreover, what followed was certainly not carefully planned. Nonetheless, one result of this change was that growing numbers of women and minorities began to enter the U.S. workforce. Not only did they need the money—incomes were subject to high rates of inflation during the 1970s, came under growing pressure as the 1981–82 recession began to bite, and grew more slowly between the mid-1970s and mid-1990s than during the 1950s and 1960s—they also commanded lower wages relative to white men. Moreover, as they acquired heretofore unheard-of purchasing power women and minorities turned out to be good marketing tools and consumers for corporations seeking new markets (Elliott, 1997). Alternative lifestyles and new family structures became necessary and acceptable, in part because of social innovation, in part for economic reasons. As a result, gays and lesbians came out in growing numbers and they, too, offered an attractive niche market toward which capital could target new products and services.

By the beginning of the 1980s, this transformation was in full swing, and so was the reaction against it. The conservatism of Ronald Reagan and his supporters is best understood as a backlash against the cultural and social change fostered by social innovation and reorganization, but it is difficult to argue that the Reaganauts did anything to slow it down. To the contrary: Reagan's economic policies were designed to shrink the welfare state and squeeze inflation out of the economy but they had a quite unintended effect on American society and the rest of the world. The 1982–83 recession reduced inflation but was devastating for Rust Belt "metal-bashing" industries—the core of Fordist production—in the United States and abroad.

Liberalization, deindustrialization, privatization of the state, and the rise of finance capital actually worked to undermine families. Self-interest became the sure path to success, and parents and children were inculcated with a "what's in it for me?" sensibility. The road to profit was clearly marked, and did not involve the fostering of any sense of social or even familial solidarity. Spatial mobility was the key to upward mobility and, for some, the traditional nuclear family became an albatross. Adam Smith believed in the power of the "invisible hand," but he had also expected that religious and social values would restrain people from uncontrollable self-interest (Coats, 1971, cited in Hirsch, 1995:137). Smith never reckoned with mass secularization, rampant consumerism, and the social indifference the morality of the market might foster.

Pat Buchanan's "culture war," declared from the podium of the Republican National Convention in 1992, should have come as no surprise to anyone; the conflict had been brewing for years (Lind, 1991; see also Lipschutz, 1998b; Rupert, 1997). What was ironic, perhaps, was that Buchanan and his colleagues blamed political "liberals," rather than hyperliberal capitalism, for the problems they saw destroying American society.[12] To have put the blame on the real cause would have been to reveal to the listening public that the new economic system is not—indeed, cannot be—fair to everyone, and that those who begin with advantages will virtually always retain them (Hirsch, 1995).[13] Admitting such a contradiction would be to repeat the fatal mistake of Mikhail Gorbachev, when he announced that the Communist Party of the Soviet Union was no longer the vanguard of socialist truth: Attack the legitimacy of your social system's ideology, and there is no end to the destruction that might follow (Lipschutz, 1998b). It might happen, anyway, if the parallels between today and Polanyi's Great Transformation are germane.

There are three notable similarities between the two "transformations." First, although it can hardly be said that there was a welfare state in England in 1800, there did exist various forms of social support for the poor. These, as Polanyi and others pointed out, served to depress wages to the benefit of capital and also, it was argued, made it more attractive for people to go on relief than to work (Himmelfarb, 1995)—arguments that sound eerily familiar today.

Second, the privatization of various forms of public property and commons, which had also provided a resource buffer for the rural poor, was deemed necessary to foster wider markets and provide the labor pool necessary for industrialism to develop. There are not many peasants left in the United States, but the downsizing and the dismantling of the state, and the drive to make corporations meaner, leaner, and more profitable, have eliminated large parts of the social safety net and job security, both of which could be thought of as a form of common-pool property right guaranteed to workers. The result has been to inject large numbers of college-educated but no longer appropriately skilled mid-level, middle-aged managers and civil servants into what is already a highly competitive labor market. This is a market in which much job creation is either in the lower-wage service sector or in areas, such as writing software code, requiring knowledge the newly unemployed do not possess and could acquire only with great difficulty and considerable expense.

Third, "opportunity only knocks once." As people find it necessary to move to where the jobs and money are, other considerations come second. High spatial mobility weakens families, ties to communities, and such other social-support systems as still exist in this country. Like the fabled elders left behind on ice flows by the Inuit, those who cannot move may be left behind or thrown into public shelters or out on the streets.

Another interesting, but possibly more significant, parallel to the Great Transformation is the creation of new fictitious commodities akin to Polanyi's labor, land, and money. The first is embodied in the concept of *human capital* (or "human resources," as it is more prosaically known). During the First Industrial Revolution, people found it necessary to sell their physical strength to capital and, during the second, their manual skills. Now, a premium is placed on intellectual strengths and capabilities and an individual's ability to process and package information in ways that can be commodified and sold for premium prices.

The second fictitious commodity is information, which has been transformed from a common-pool resource into "intellectual property" whose ownership is hedged all about with legal restrictions. While information and knowledge have long been bought, exchanged, and stolen, these activities have usually occurred in concert with the production and consumption of material goods. Today, however, even raw data on individual habits and behavior can be turned into proprietary information and sold. Sometimes, the very methods by which people accomplish their everyday objectives are gathered, processed, and resold to them (Have you used your supermarket club card lately?).[14]

Finally, the third fictitious commodity is the vast expansion in consumer credit, or what we might call "virtual money," available primarily to those who are most likely to use it. Whereas the monetization of the English economy was a necessary prerequisite to undermining barter and direct exchange of goods, the creation of virtual money eliminates even the need for face-to-face transactions, inherent value in coinage, or the guarantee of legal tender by governments. Such funds appear virtually *ex nihilo* as physical and intellectual properties are securitized, as stocks rise on the strength of no apparent material causes, and as individual credit lines are magically increased through the daily mail.[15]

Of course, not everybody is automatically eligible to participate in this new system of fictitious commodities. Many lack the required property or income qualifications to gain access. But as Stephen Gill (1995:22) has pointed out, such access is a prerequisite for citizenship in contemporary liberal democracy:

> [T]he substantive conception of citizenship involves not only a political-legal conception, but also an economic idea. Full citizenship requires not only a claim of political rights and obligations, but access to and participation in a system of production and consumption.

Beginning in adolescence, he argues, this acts to discipline and socialize consumers. Failure to meet the terms of economic citizenship, through late payments or bankruptcy, means social marginalization. The threat of exclusion keeps consumers in line. The result, says Gill, is the replacement of "traditional forms of discipline associated with the family and the school" with "market discipline" (1995:26; see also Drainville, 1995). In this way, the workers of the world of the future are bound into domination by the new global economy (points that are further elaborated in chapters 7 and 8).

Whether this Third Industrial Revolution has yet reached its apogee is anybody's guess (Paul Krugman has suggested that it will take at least fifty years to mature fully; 1994a:28–29). Two points, however, are clear. First, the social innovation and reorganization that has undermined the older material basis of American society—and much of the rest of the world, as well—cannot be halted on command. Contemporary change is a global phenomenon that some societies are carrying out more efficiently and equitably than others, but to quit the race would be to return to some form of neomercantilism and severe economic contraction at home and abroad, and this would play well neither in Peoria nor on Wall Street.

Second, this Great Transformation is likely to be as severe as, if not worse than, the one that wracked Britain in the first part of the nineteenth century. Not everyone will suffer equally, of course, or suffer at all, for that matter. Just as some did extremely well by the First and Second Industrial Revolutions, so will many benefit from this one. A global class of the better-off (numbering perhaps 1 billion, if that many) and a global class of the poor (as many as 8 to 10 billion) will emerge. Many members of the better-off class will reside in what today we call "developing countries"; a not considerable number of the poor will live in the "industrialized ones." If things work out, by the middle of the twenty-first century we might even see a global middle class that will provide bourgeois support for this new global order and, perhaps, demand some form of representative global democratization (see chapter 8). Then, again, we might not.

[handwritten margin notes: Elite in poor countries & poor in elite countries]

Spare Change in World Politics

What are the implications of these changes for state, society, citizen and security? The answers to this question are treated in the following chapters. In one sense, the realist mantra—"The world is a dangerous place"—is correct. Life is full of risks, and it always ends in death. There may well be an asteroid somewhere out in space with Earth's name written on it. But we should always ask *Dangerous for whom?* Perhaps the world is dangerous, especially for those who would manipulate people and politics in pursuit of individual self-interest. We see an example of this in another literary classic, a work of fiction (even though it was not quite meant as a fiction when published in 1962). Toward the end of Eugene Burdick and Harvey Wheeler's Cold War novel *Fail Safe*, the president's advisor on nuclear strategy, Harvard professor Walter Groteschele (modeled on Henry Kissinger, among others), contemplates his prospects *after* the thermonuclear annihilation of Moscow and New York City (a catastrophe due, in no small part, to *his* notions of danger in the world). Foreseeing the likelihood of an end to the arms race between the two superpowers (whose danger has made *him* so prominent and well-off),

> Groteschele swung his attention to what his future work would be. If there were drastic cutbacks in military expenditures many businesses would be seriously affected; some of them would even be ruined. A man who understood government and big political movements could make a comfortable living advising the threatened industries. It was a sound idea, and Groteschele tucked it away in his mind with a sense of reassurance. (Burdick and Wheeler, 1962:272)

The postwar project of economic globalization has, perhaps unintentionally, shifted the discursive locus of sovereignty, security, and peace from the state to the individual. The state retains a dominant position in terms of military force, economic management, and so on, but for capitalism to grow successfully beyond the bounds of national markets and become truly global, social innovation must be allowed to take place across all kinds of borders. This can happen *only* if individuals (and the corporations and organizations they represent and populate) are allowed untrammeled access to all parts of the world and can be assured that they will not be expelled, thrown into jail, or killed if they wander across both figurative and literal borders. Not all governments follow this line, but global innovation is likely to bypass those that don't. Places that, for one reason or another, find themselves excluded from this process of globalization are also strong candidates for recidivism, revanchism, and reaction. The former Yugoslavia and Myannmar are good examples (Lipschutz and Crawford, 1996; Gagnon, 1995).

Even those in the thick of globalization, and reaping extensive benefits from it, are not very comfortable with its implications. The movement of peoples across borders in the interest of social innovation provides entry not only to those seeking work, but some who might have other agendas, too. As we saw in the reactions to the Oklahoma City bombing in 1995 and the crash of TWA Flight 800 in July 1996, the initial impulse was to blame bombs and missiles in the hands of "foreign terrorists," although subsequent evidence indicates this not to have been the case in either (Lipschutz, 1999b). Nevertheless, as countries lose sovereign control over their borders and the possibility of managing the movement of people, goods, and ideas, they seem to be focusing more closely on the new subjects of transnational sovereignty, the individuals, in the hope that keeping a watchful eye on such free subjects will serve also to discipline them (Gill, 1995; see also chapter 7). This is, most probably, a vain hope: people are very clever, and only the inept—who are not very dangerous—usually get caught.

If (Cold) War made the state, and the state made (Cold) War, to paraphrase sociologist Charles Tilly, what is the state to do now? Some ultracompetitive entrepreneurs suggest that "business is war" and, so, we might have to rethink Tilly's dictum. Wars are a messy business, and it might be prudent to clean them up. That effort is well under way.

3❖
THE INSECURITY DILEMMA

What is "security?" What does it mean to be "secure?" Who or what secures us? And why do we feel so insecure? Security demands certainty; to be uncertain about the present and future is to be insecure about them, as well. We try to reduce or eliminate uncertainties in order to become more secure. But risk analysts often tell us that the cost of eliminating a risk is infinite, which suggests that we can never be fully secure. Security is, therefore, something of a chimera, inasmuch as only the dead can be absolutely sure that nothing about their condition will change (and even then, the promises of Christian millennialism auger some uncertainty about *that* future).

For many, particularly in the United States, the absence of a coherent, concentrated threat or enemy seems to have become especially troubling (Huntington, 1997). The president and Pentagon warn darkly of surrounding dangers (Clinton, 1997). Some describe coming conflicts with non-Western civilizations (Huntington, 1996); others fear the collapse of pivotal states (Chase, Hill, and Kennedy, 1996); a growing number see in China a challenger to U.S. dominance (Bernstein and Munro, 1997). Environmental degradation and economic change are deemed to be security "threats," while hackers and pornographers lurk in cyberspace, ready to steal information and poison young minds.

The boy or girl next door could cut our throats, as we are told in films and articles "based on true stories." Diseases are poised to escape from disappearing tropical forests, flying out on the next 757, to be deposited in the midst of urban insurrections. Drugs, illegal immigrants, and terrorists are everywhere. And a few far-sighted individuals (and film producers) even tell us that, somewhere out in distance space, there is a comet or asteroid with Earth's name on it. The universe of threats seems infinite; the only limit is our imagination (Foster 1994; Kugler, 1995).

Why so many threats? Although a decade has passed since the "end" of the Cold War, the basic premises of U.S. national security policy remain uncertain, ill-defined, and contested. Despite the precise language of President Clinton's *National Security Strategy* (1997; see chapter 4), no consensual agreement on the nature or source of present or future threats has developed; no comprehensive strategy akin to containment has emerged; no stable policies regarding force structures and deployments have been formulated (Levin, 1994). The U.S. defense budget continues to grow, albeit more slowly than in the 1980s, but who is the target? NATO expands, but who is the enemy? The world of 170 states on the march against each other is a nostalgic memory; who or what now threatens to stalk us? And why, even though we are, in many ways, more secure than we have been for fifty years—especially with a decline in the probability of large-scale nuclear war—does the search for security continue, more frantically and, some might argue, more fruitlessly, than ever? Is it a failure of policy, or a flaw in reasoning?

We face, in short, an *insecurity dilemma*. Forty years ago, John Herz (1959) formulated the idea of the "security dilemma," a concept later picked up and further developed by Robert Jervis (1978). Both argued that many of the ostensibly defensive actions taken by states to make themselves *more* secure—development of new military technologies, accumulation of weapons, mobilization of troops—had the effect of making neighboring states *less* secure. There was no way of knowing whether the intentions behind military deployments were defensive or offensive; hence, it was better to be safe and assume the worst. The result was, in many instances, an arms spiral, as each side tried to match the acquisitions of its neighbor.[1] While there were continual arguments over whether security policy should be based on observable capabilities—what the other side *could* do—or on intent—what the other side *meant* to do—there was, minimally, a material basis for arriving at assessments, whether correct or not.

Today, the basis for assessing threats and potential consequences is of a quite different character, for three fundamental reasons. First, those structural features of international politics that constrained and directed security policies and practices between 1947 and 1991 have vanished, even as most of the institutions and many of the capabilities associated with the Cold War remain in place. Institutions can find new ontologies, from which will follow policies, but these must have some fit to new political configurations or they will lose their legitimacy. Thus, we have NATO trying on a variety of new missions without being quite sure of their purpose. Is NATO to remain a security "blanket" for an expanded Western Europe, on standby against the possibility of a newly aggressive and imperial Russia (as many think was the purpose of inclusion of Poland, Hungary, and the Czech Republic)? Is it to become a security "regime," encompassing all of Europe, as well as North America and the former Soviet republics, intended to provide psychotherapy for aggrieved countries and nations? Can it best function as a security "maker," uniting its forces, as over Kosovo, to intervene in ethnic and other conflicts that, many fear, could undermine European stability? Or, should it concentrate on deterring the proliferation of weapons of mass destruction in the hands of "rogues" and "terrorists" (Erlanger, 1998)? In the end, the absence of what seems to be clear and definable threats leads to the "hammer-nail" conundrum: you fit the task to the tools rather than first defining the task and then choosing the tools.[2]

Second, the disappearance of nuclear bipolarity and the "Great Transformation" set in train by the Cold War have led individuals and groups to recover and re-articulate various frameworks of belief and practice, or "historical structures" (to use Robert Cox's term; Cox, 1987), that create enemies where they did not exist before. The result is the institutionalization of uncertainty, even in parts of the world that, for decades, seemed quite fixed and stable. Thus, speculate some analysts, civil conflict in Iraq, Yugoslavia, Somalia, Rwanda, and others would not have broken out had the Cold War not come to an end (leading some, such as John J. Mearsheimer, to predict that "we will soon miss the Cold War"; Mearsheimer, 1990a). As we shall see in chapter 6, the working assumption of such analyses is that these wars are, somehow, premodern or primordial, afflicting only places not fully socialized into twentieth-century modernity, and that such violence was prevented prior to 1989 by the pressures imposed on those countries by the United States and the Soviet Union. But it is also quite possible that such bloodlettings are very postmodern (see, e.g., Beck, 1992:9–16). Consequently, we might behold the futures of global politics in both the European Union as well as in the world's chaotic places. As globalization works its way on self, state, and society, we may see the emergence of the "insecurity dilemma" at the social level, rather than between the black-box states of classical realist politics.

Finally, the anchors that once permitted self-reflective collectivities to fortify themselves and their friends from foes and threats are decomposing, making it ever more difficult to specify *which* self is to be made secure from *what* threat. A proliferation of new identities—as states, as cultures, as *ethnies*, as individuals—indicate that fundamental units of global political interaction have been destabilized, thereby rendering problematic the finding of new anchorages on which to base stable political relations. What is the political structure of a confrontation between Microsoft or Boeing and the European Union (Strange, 1996)? Can computer hackers wage war against the Pentagon? Could every (wo)man be a country, if not an island?[3] Such questions are not meant to lead to dictums such as "the state is obsolete," or "interdependence confounds sovereignty." Rather, it is to suggest that the boundaries that, for forty-odd years, disciplined states and polities no longer do so. To rephrase Yeats' oft-cited line, it is not that the center cannot hold; rather, it is that the margins cannot be contained. And make no mistake, new margins are emerging everywhere, even in the center (Luke, 1995; Enzenberger, 1994).

The disintegration of conceptual containers gets only at the ideational core of the insecurity dilemma. Material processes have their consequences, too, and in today's world, the struggle over security also arises from another phenomenon: changes in the material constitution of the state itself. Under the pressures of globalization and other systemic forces discussed in chapter 2, the state is being transformed into something different from what it was, even in the recent past. To make this new object "secure" implies different constructions of both threat and security than those with which we are familiar from the past fifty years. Under fluid conditions such as this, the very act of defining security becomes the subject of struggle, providing not only access to material resources and authority but also the opportunity to establish new boundaries of discourse and research (Thompson, 1979; Lipschutz, 1999a). Those who win the debate win more than just the prize, for they also get to mark those boundaries. Those who find themselves left outside have not only lost the game, they have been banished from politics, made outsiders. They may even become the new enemy. Ultimately, it would seem, the only boundary that is truly secure is the one drawn around the self—and even this is open to doubt—which suggests that security is more than just a material condition, and that insecurity might just be a fact of life. Such insecurity is not to be confused with Hobbes' State of Nature, however; rather, it is a condition associated with uncertainty, difference, and individuation, as we shall see.

In this chapter, I address the twin problems of security and insecurity. I begin with a discussion of the end of the national security state, pointing out how U.S. Cold War policy undermined the very security system meant to protect the West during that period. I then turn to what I call the "insecurity dilemma" and ask why, if the level of global threats has diminished, do societies feel so insecure? Pace Herz, Jervis, and others, the insecurity dilemma arises not from threats but from difference. In the third section of this chapter, I discuss how threats are constructed, and by whom. Finally, I conclude by arguing that we would do better to come to grips with insecurity and difference than to try to eliminate all those things we believe might threaten us because they are different and make us feel insecure.

The End of the National Security State?

It has become fashionable (once again!) to say that "states no longer matter" (Ohmae, 1991; 1995). Borders are porous—if they are there at all—and people, capital, goods, and information flow across them with both alacrity and disdain for political authorities.[4] The result, some argue, must be productive of peace and harmonious relations among people, as they become comfortable with and trusting of one another through growing familiarity and similarity (an idea first proposed by

Norman Angell in 1910; see Angell, 1910). There is a contrary school of thought that insists that states still do matter, more than ever, and that they will be with us for decades, if not centuries and longer, to come. Flows across borders do not foster peace and understanding; if anything, they illustrate just how different societies really are and how few interests they have in common. The result, argue such contrarians, is likely to be increased friction, and even war.[5]

As is often the case, neither side in the debate has asked or answered the correct question. Moreover, advocates of both versions tend to reify the state, either in terms of its growing weakness or growing power. Consequently, there are only two "states" of the state, as it were: here or gone, on or off. But the state of the state is hardly a binary condition. Political comparativists never tire of pointing out that what international relations scholars and diplomats call "states" represent, in fact, a wide variety of political forms with an incredible diversity of domestic structures and actors (Jackson, 1990; Inayatullah, 1996). And as sociologists and others often suggest, states are, after all, made up of people acting alone and together in the pursuit of many different goals. Frequently, these goals are contradictory, and the group that "wins" is the one better able to bring to bear its power and capabilities in relevant fora (Smithson, 1996). To the extent that such efforts succeed in narrowing down the range of critical issues facing state and society, it may be possible to say that the state still "matters" in one realm or another (as we shall see, below).[6]

National security is often taken to be a matter where the state *does* matter: The survival of the state—and, by extension, society—is paramount. Consequently, where security is concerned the state must take the lead because no other institution, whether domestic or international, can provide comparable amounts of this "public good" to a specific polity. Therefore, the state continues to be important in at least this one realm—or so it is said. The flaw in this argument is that the need or demand for security is not fixed over time or across issue areas or, indeed, the same for all of the individuals and collectives that constitute a state's society.

During periods of high international tension, whether real or imagined, the state can force the priority of security policy; the argument that state and society might vanish under external onslaught carries considerable weight. Under other conditions, making such an argument is much more difficult. Some scholars of foreign policy, such as Graham

Allison (1971) and John Steinbruner (1974), argued this point more than twenty-five years ago, articulating theories of "bureaucratic politics," "high politics" versus "low politics," and "cybernetic decision-making," in order to explain the resolution of national security crises. A constant in all of these offerings was, however, that the state was central to the conceptualization of threats, formulation of responses, and implementation of security policy. It was also the primary object of that policy.[7] In keeping with the search for universal laws and theories, as proposed by Hans Morgenthau and others in the discipline, the basic principles were broadly assumed to be true over both space and time.

Yet, if we look at the state as an institution that has changed over time, and continues to change, we discover that such formulations obscure more than they reveal. Today's "Great Powers" often have the same names as those of a century ago, and they are located in more-or-less the same places (although a few have shifted eastward or westward). We would nonetheless be hard put to argue that, in spite of historical and geographic continuity, they are the *same*. Changes have taken place not only in domestic politics and the external environment, but also in the relationship between citizen and state and in the very constitution and identity of the citizen herself (Drainville, 1995; Gill, 1995). Such changes fundamentally alter both the national and international political environments in which state, society, and self exist, thereby rendering most discussions of "redefining security" almost beside the point.[8]

What is lacking in these old and new analytical frameworks? To repeat a point made earlier, conventional perspectives on national security ignore a critical existential factor: The state, as well as the threats it faces and the security policies that result, are mental as well as material constructs (Buzan, 1991; Lipschutz, 1989). That is to say, the *reproduction* of the intellectual and emotional logics of the state and its need for security against "enemies" is as important to national security as the *production* of the technology, soldiers, and military hardware that are meant to provide the physical infrastructure of protection (Huntington, 1997). As the collapse of the Soviet Union indicated, even a materially powerful and evidently secure state can be undermined if the mental constructs supporting it come under sustained pressure, both domestic and international (Crawford, 1995). Indeed, it might be that, of all types of states extant in the world, it is the national security state that is most likely to be affected by the erosion of these nonmaterial constructs.

What, then, is the national security state (NSS)? The NSS is best understood as a particular type of institution whose origins are found in the logics of the Industrial Revolution and the Social Darwinist geopolitics of the late nineteenth century. Through these two epistemological frameworks, the consolidation of geographically contiguous territories and the integration of societies within those territories became the sine qua non of national power and survival. The founders of national security states were animated by two overriding motivations. First, they directly correlated national power with the domination of resources, territory, people, and violence; second, they directly correlated national power with a state-directed project of industrialization, nationalism, and social welfare. The NSS was premised further on a world of external threats—almost always state-centered in origin—directed against national autonomy and territory, from which the nation must be defended. The interests of state and citizen (and corporate actors, as well) were thereby seen to coincide, even in the economic and cultural spheres (Lipschutz, 1989: ch. 5).

This process of national consolidation was neither quick nor simple. National states emerged only very slowly out of the monarchies and empires of the eighteenth and early nineteenth centuries, and they were constantly opposed and suppressed, as evidenced in the Congress of Vienna in 1815 and the counterrevolutions of 1848 and 1872. But the idea of the *nation-state*—an autonomous entity that contained within itself all those who met specified (and largely constructed) ascriptive requirements and excluded or assimilated those who did not (Brown, 1992)—proved more powerful in the longer run. To protect against revanchism and reaction, however, it was also necessary for states to develop military capabilities.

By the end of the nineteenth century, moreover, it was clearly in the strategic interest of some nation-states that other territorial entities become nation-states, too. This would reduce the dominance of the European empires as well as the economic potential inherent, if not realized, in control of extensive territories. It would also transfer power to the more capital-intensive and concentrated nation-state (capital intensive in terms of both "human capital" and finance). It can be said fairly that the NSS reached its apogee during World War II, with total social and industrial mobilization by both Allied and Axis coalitions; even during the first decades of the Cold War, the two superpowers failed to achieve this level in either scale or scope (Friedberg, 1991; Davis, 1991). World War II nevertheless fatally weakened those empires that had survived World War I and, under an American logic of "divide and conquer," the remaining empires slowly decomposed into smaller, militarily and economically weaker nation-states during the twenty years following 1945.

The coincidence of interests between the NSS and its citizens has not always been either obvious or stable. This can be seen, for example, in the relationship between Nazi Germany and its Jewish residents. In that instance, Jews were claimed to be a threat to the "German people," and anti-Semitism helped to recreate shared interests among non-Jewish Germans that had been dissolved by the spread of capitalism and the crises of the Weimar Republic. Historically, such antagonisms have developed, or have been cultivated, for political and strategic reasons. This is not what is happening today.

With the trend toward individualism and the growing reliance on markets, what is good for General Motors is not always good for the United States (or vice versa). Today, the policies that generate national military power may very well create individual insecurity, and the actions of individuals in the market may very well weaken the state. While this trend began as long ago as the 1970s, the extent of the divergence between state and citizen only became really evident during the 1990s, as the supposed global threat posed by Communism receded and was replaced by more localized and inchoate ones.

Why has this happened? To understand the causes of the decomposition of the NSS, we need to look more closely at the intersection of security strategy and economic policy during the Cold War (Pollard, 1985; McCormick, 1996). For the NSS, this connection was manifest in neomercantilism, and during and after World War II, the neomercantilist geopolitical discourses of Mackinder (1919/1962, 1943), Spykman (1942, 1944) and others were transmuted into the containment policy attributed to George Kennan (Gaddis, 1982) and formalized in documents such as NSC-68 (Dalby, 1990; Agnew & Corbridge, 1995). There was, however, a contradiction inherent in containment. The neomercantilistic geopolitical framework of the late nineteenth and early twentieth centuries was unsuited for the postwar period, especially as envisioned by the founders of the Bretton Woods system. Such a geopolitics treated the nation-state—or empire—as the natural unit of analysis and policy. The liberalization project of American postwar planners posited a non-imperial, open economic realm much larger than the national territorial space. As Fred Block (1977) has pointed out, such a system could not exist if limited to national capitalist markets.

Consequently, a new unit of analysis and action emerged: the Free World. Inside the borders of the Free World, all states would be united in pursuit of common goals based on individualism and the human propensity to "truck and barter." Outside would be those states whose mode of behavior was "unnatural," spoken of in terms of "rotten apples" threatening the Free World's future (a point further developed in chapter 7). The survival and success of the Free World thus depended on creating and extending boundaries around a "natural community" (Stone, 1988) that had not, heretofore, existed. The survival and prosperity of the Free World on one side of the boundaries of containment came to rest upon keeping out the influences of the Soviet bloc on the other side of those boundaries. Indeed, the Free World could not have existed without the "Unfree World."

Within the Free World, however, the maintenance of community was more problematic, for it relied on broad acceptance of a hierarchy that often rankled lower-ranked members. Economic liberalism would make the Free World stronger, but it required a globalized version of neomercantilism in which those inside were restricted in dealing with those outside. Inasmuch as there was only so much that could be done to prevent such exchange from taking place, making the Free World work also required a shift of sovereignty from the state to the individual, the "natural" unit of interaction in the market. This, in turn would prevent Free World states from asserting too strongly *their* national autonomy as against the economic rights of their citizens.

To fully carry through this shift meant that the state would have to yield up its sovereign prerogatives to the market and loosen its control over the domestic economy, a move with security implications (Moravcsik, 1991). Free trade and comparative advantage apply not only to wool and wine, but also to guns and gyroscopes, goods with military potential. For this reason, COCOM, the Coordinating Committee, was established to prevent such goods from falling into Communist hands. Rather than regulating what could be *produced* domestically, the state was now allowed only to limit what could be *exported* (Pollard, 1985; Crawford, 1993; Mastanduno, 1991). The borders of Free World nations would be breached by flows of raw materials, manufactures, technology, capital, and even labor—in theory if not practice—in the name of growing and spreading markets (but see Ruggie, 1983a). And the idea that the state was the "natural" unit of self-defense would gradually wither. The United States, as the core of this global system, was expected to remain technologically dominant, thereby retaining its edge and autonomy (although this is not what has actually come to pass, much to the dismay of numerous analysts and policymakers; see Sandholtz, et. al., 1992). In theory, all barriers to economic intercourse would have to fall to fully realize the potential of liberalization; in practice, there was (and continues to be) strong resistance to this on the part of some countries, although to little avail.

The Soviet Union's approach to economic control was not entirely dissimilar. Stalin sought to establish an economic sphere dominated by the USSR, while hewing more closely to the mercantilistic prescriptions of Friedrich List (1856; see also Davis, 1991; Crawford 1993). Within what came to be called the "Soviet bloc," a division of labor emerged too, but one directed by central planning rather than the "invisible hand" (Bunce, 1985). This unit was never as economically integrated as the Free World and, more to the point, actively sought to restrict the kind of exchange that, in its opposite number, fostered rapid technological innovation (Crawford, 1995). Ultimately, that strategy failed. But note: in a world of states and blocs organized around "national capitalism" rather than Free World liberalism, the Soviet bloc might well have measured up to anything the West could have offered.[9] There is no way to verify such a counter-factual but, throughout the 1950s and 1960s, Soviet bloc growth rates and technological achievements were impressive and were seen to be quite threatening (Davis, 1991).

Such area-based economic arrangements also played important *domestic* roles in the security strategies of both the United States and the Soviet Union. The NSS sought to maintain discipline within its borders in order to keep enemies out and citizens loyal. I use the term "discipline" here not to denote militarization or regimentation but, rather, to describe a social regimen whereby those who questioned or challenged the premises of the NSS were either chastised or ostracized (see chapter 7). While such discipline was, quite clearly, much harsher on the Soviet side of the East-West divide, it was not wholly unknown in the West. By opting for autarky and authoritarianism, and an economy whose main customer was the state rather than the consumer, the Soviet approach made the task of social control that much easier (although more visible and generative of resistance).

The United States, pursuing liberal economic and political organization, focused on individual well-being at home and state power abroad. This made social discipline more difficult, because it was premised on a particular type of mental and material conformity that penalized aberrant thoughts and practices through social ridicule and rejection, rather than on an outright totalitarianism that rewarded dissidence with prison or exile. People whose behavior went beyond accepted limits were tagged as Communists or social deviants, and offered the opportunity to rejoin the community only if they would recant their heretical beliefs. Many did. Those who didn't were labeled "un-American" and blacklisted. This system of social discipline began to break down in the 1960s, but it has only been seriously undermined during the past two decades as hyperliberal tendencies have begun to bite deeply into American society (Hirsch, 1995; Barber, 1995).

The result of hyperliberalism has been a squeeze on labor and the privileging of capital.[10] Gradually, the squeeze has been extended from the blue-collar to the white-collar workforce, as well as the military and defense sectors, with successive "downsizings" and mergers among corporations, as they struggle to reduce costs, improve balance sheets and maintain share value (Nasar, 1994; Edmunds, 1996; Uchitelle, 1998). By now, whether or not it is statistically correct, there is a widespread perception within major segments of the American labor force that no forms of employment are secure (Uchitelle, 1994; Marshall, 1995a; *New York Times*, 1996). Policymakers and academics such as Robert Reich (1992: part II) argue that "symbolic analysts," the production workers of the information age, are secure for the future; the reality is that new information technologies may make many of them redundant, too.[11] Even as the U.S. economy continues to grow, so do the conditions for alienation, atomization, and social disintegration.

The impacts of this change are visible in efforts to rediscipline society. Thus, policymakers struggle to find new threats and define new visions, strategies, and policies for making the world "more secure." People, losing faith in their leaders and the state, take things into their own hands. Gated communities proliferate in order to keep out the chaos. The privitization of security continues apace and becomes another realm of commodification. Conservative disciplining of liberals and gays mounts. And the most popular television and film "true-life" stories and newscasts inform us just how insecure each of us should really feel. In a perverse inversion of Herz and Jervis, the national security state is brought down to the level of the household, and each one arms itself against the security dilemma posed by its neighbor across the hedge or fence.

Confronting the Insecurity Dilemma

The difficulties associated with "redefining security policy" (Krause and Williams, 1996, 1997) to meet these changing circumstances suggests the appearance of a fundamental ontological hole within national identities, especially that of the United States. In the absence of threats or enemies that affect equally all citizens of a country, there can be no overarching ontology of security, no shared identity differentiating the national self from threatening others, no consensus on what—if anything—should be done.[12] No single real or constructed problem—short of the alien invasions and cometary impacts depicted in recent films— offers the comprehensive threat of total destruction once promised by East-West nuclear war. What are national security planners to do when, in succeeding beyond their wildest visions in making the country safe, they have also set the stage for domestic anarchy? The simple answer: find new sources of threat and insecurity, both internal and external.

Security has been defined conventionally in terms of the state as a nonarticulated or non-internally-differentiated unit. The "black box" state of realism has always been understood to be a heuristic simplification. Nonetheless, that model does suggest that external threats affect all members of the polity living inside the box to a more-or-less equal degree. In the case of war, everyone's future would be challenged; in the case of nuclear war, anyone (if not everyone) might die. Even Communist subversion could strike at any place, at any time. Whether this was ever "true" or not, it is no longer the case. This loss of total coverage is problematic: In place of comprehensive threats, the "new" ones discussed or imagined by policymakers, academics and strategists affect only selected groups and classes within states, with differential impacts that depend, to a significant degree, on an individual's economic, cultural, and social backgrounds.

The social consequences of poverty are not deemed to be a broadband threat; the social consequences of Internet pornography are. The impacts of generally poor health are of concern, but are not a national priority; the impacts of biological weapons in one or two cities are. A U.S. congressman can argue that "We can no longer define our national security in military terms alone. Our ignorance of world cultures and world languages represents a threat to our ability to remain a world leader" (*San Francisco Chronicle*, 1991a). A newspaper editorial can warn that "the major threats to security today are probably found in such disparate sources as the world's overcrowded classrooms, understaffed health facilities, shrinking oil fields, diverted rivers, and holes in the ozone layer" (*San Francisco Chronicle*, 1991b). A conservative commentator can suggest that threats arise from "the explicit assault on Western culture by 'politically correct' radicals," manifested in 'multiculturalism'" (Lind, 1991:40). And President Clinton (1997) can propose that "[T]he dangers we face are unprecedented in their complexity."

The segmentation of threats is especially manifest in different areas of American public and private life. For instance, in June 1996, then-CIA director John Deutch (U.S. Senate, 1996) told the Senate Governmental Affairs Committee of

> [e]vidence that a number of countries around the world are developing the doctrine, strategies and tools to conduct information attacks. . . . International terrorist groups clearly have the capability to attack the information infrastructure of the United States, even if they use relatively simple means. . . . [A] large-scale attack on U.S. computer networks could cripple the nation's energy, transportation, communications, banking, business and military systems, which are all dependent on computers that could be vulnerable to sabotage ranging from break-ins by unauthorized "hackers" to attacks with explosives.

Asked whether the threat of such attacks was comparable to those associated with nuclear, chemical, and biological weapons, Deutch replied, "I would say it was very, very close to the top." Another witness warned that failure to prepare for such attacks could result in "an electronic Pearl Harbor" (U.S. Senate, 1996). None of the witnesses noted that most computer network breakdowns have, so far, been directly attributable to snafus in hardware and software.[13]

Of particular interest here are the content and implications of the language used to frame the dangers of information warfare. Deutch and his colleagues compare an incident with a fairly selective *class* impact, which would affect those tied into long-distance cyberspace systems, with two of the best-known images of war from the past fifty years, suggesting a quite improbable degree of disruption and destruction. While neither Pearl Harbor nor Hiroshima led to national destruction, the image of a "bolt from the blue," drawn from nuclear war discourses, certainly suggests such a possibility.

Deutch's testimony raises a further set of questions: If so-called international terrorists can use simple means to attack the information infrastructure, why have they not done so? Where are the nuclear suitcase bombs? Who has spread radiation and bacteria over American cities? When has anyone put drugs and poisons in urban water supplies? And, against whom would the United State retaliate should such incidents occur? There is a not-so-subtle implication in Deutch's statement that the United States—perhaps through the National Security Agency—is itself capable of conducting information attacks, and has practiced them. This, in turn, suggests self-induced fears generated by projecting U.S. national capabilities onto imagined others (see below). Ironically, Deutch's warnings of "hackers" remind us that villians might also be the boy or girl upstairs or next door or down the road!

Such rhetorical tactics are hardly new or innovative; Deutch's objective is to mobilize legislators into action "by scaring the hell out of them," as Senator Arthur Vandenburg counseled President Truman to do in 1947. As well, the broadening of national security language to encompass a wide range of social issues and problems has a long history. In the 1950s, education, health, and highways were brought under the "National Defense" blanket. During the 1980s, all manner of commercial research and development were deemed essential to national security. But what is missing from pronouncements such as Deutch's is a conviction that all Americans are exposed equally to information warfare. The truth is that, although the American economy is heavily dependent on electronic software, hardware, and networks, warnings about information warfare are a lot like those about prospective climate change. Both might happen, but there is also a lot of handwaving going on. Still, why do we seem so eager to engage deeply with the former and not the latter? Is it because we already have the hammer?

The contemporary search for threats to which we can match our capabilities has a rather frantic quality about it, as though even those who warn about them are not wholly convinced that they are imminent or "real." This suggests, in turn, that the process whereby contemporary national security policy is made is not so simple as discovering and specifying foreign "threats" to which we can then rationally respond.

New Threats or No Threats?

It is in this context that the insecurity dilemma emerges full-blown to challenge the ontology of the national security state: If there are no plausible threats, what is the purpose of the NSS? If imagined threats are selective and domestic, why continue to expand military capabilities? And if individuals are more concerned about themselves than their society, how can support for security policy be mobilized? It is in this context, too, that the struggle to redefine security has been and is taking place. To understand both the insecurity dilemma and the struggle over "redefining security," we must consider how security is constituted as both concept and practice. Conceptualizations of security—from which follow policy and practice—are to be found in *discourses of security*. Such discourses of security are neither strictly objective assessments nor purely analytical constructs of threat. They are, rather, the products of historical structures and processes, of struggles for power within the state, of conflicts between the societal groupings that inhabit states and the interests that beseige them.

Hence, not only are there struggles over security among *nations*, there are also struggles over security among *notions*. Winning the right to define security provides not just access to resources but also the *authority* to articulate new definitions and discourses of security, thereby directing the policy that leads to real, material outcomes. As Karen Litfin (1994:13) points out,

> As determinants of what can and cannot be thought, discourses delimit the range of policy options, thereby functioning as precursors to policy outcomes. . . . The supreme power is the power to delineate the boundaries of thought—an attribute not so much of specific agents as it is of discursive practices.

Discourses of security, however clearly articulated, thus remain fraught with contradictions that are ignored or minimized but that nonetheless provide important insights into them.[14]

How and where do discourses of threat and security originate? Barry Buzan (1991:37) has pointed out that "There is a cruel irony in [one] meaning of secure which is 'unable to escape'." To secure oneself is, therefore, a sort of trap, for one can never leave a secure place without incurring risks. Moreover, security appears to be meaningless either as concept or practice without an "Other" to help specify the conditions of insecurity that must be guarded against. James Der Derian (1995), citing Nietzsche, points out that this "Other" is made manifest through differences that create terror and collective resentment of difference—leading to a state of fear—rather than a coming to terms with the positive potentials of difference. As these differences become less than convincing, or fail to be made manifest, however, their power to create fear and terror diminish, and so it becomes necessary to discover ever more menacing threats to reestablish difference.

For this purpose, reality may no longer suffice.[15] What is substituted, instead, is a dangerous world of imagined threats. Not *imaginary* threats, but threats conjured up as things that *could* happen. Paradoxically, then, it becomes the imagined, unnamed party, with the clandestinely assembled and crude atomic device, and not the thousands of reliable, high-yield warheads mounted on missiles poised to launch at a moment's notice, that is used to create fear, terror, and calls for action. It is the speculation about mysterious actors behind blown-up buildings and fallen jetliners, and not rather banal defects in wiring and fuel tanks, that creates the atmosphere for greater surveillance and control. It is suspicion of neighbors, thought to be engaged in subversive or surreptitious behaviors, listening to lewd lyrics or logged-on to lascivious Web pages, and not concerns about inner-city health and welfare, that brings calls for state intervention.

None of this means that threats do not exist, or that these particular matters could not do substantial damage to U.S. society, *if realized as imagined*. Rather, it is to point out that *imagination sets no limits to the threats we might conjure up*. As David Campbell (1992:2) argues,

> [I]nfectious diseases, accidents, and political violence (among other factors) have consequences that can literally be understood in terms of life and death. But not all risks are equal, and not all risks are interpreted as dangers. Modern society contains within it a veritable cornucopia of danger; indeed, there is such an abundance of risk that it is impossible to objectively know all that threatens us. Those events or factors that we identify as dangerous therefore come to be ascribed as such only through an interpretation of their various dimensions of dangerousness.

Finally, although they might only be imagined, even threats that never come to pass can still have real, material consequences if they are treated as though they were real and imminent. And such treatments can be only too deadly. The weapons sent to the Siad Barre regime in Somalia during the late 1970s and 1980s were intended to counter an imagined Soviet "resource war" in the Horn of Africa (Lipschutz, 1989), but they proved quite enough to kill Americans and Somalis alike during the 1990s.

Two consequences follow from the production of a world of imagined threats. The first is that particular social issues may be recast in militarized terms. Thus, although the consumption of drugs within American society has domestic social and economic roots, the "war on drugs" is conducted largely within a military mind-set that turns parents and teachers into soldiers, children into threatened civilians, and inner-city residents into enemies (Campbell, 1992: chap. 7; see also Massing, 1998).

The second consequence is that the long arm of the state's security apparatus is extended into those realms of everyday life that otherwise might be considered to be insulated from it (Gill, 1995). Consider U.S. laws that permit the government to examine the personal and professional lives of air travelers as a means of finding individuals whose personality profiles match those of putative "terrorists" (Broeder, 1996), or the militarization of urban police departments as part of a "war on crime" (Gaura and Wallace, 1997). All individuals, whether citizen or permanent resident, whether legal or illegal, become potential threats to state security, even though the absolute numbers of terrorists, criminals and chronic drug users is quite small (I return to this point in chapter 7; see also Lipschutz, 1999b).

That security might be, therefore, socially constructed does not mean that there are not to be found real, material conditions that help to create particular interpretations of threats, or that such conditions are irrelevant to either the creation or undermining of the assumptions underlying security policy. But enemies often imagine their Others into being, via the projections of their worst fears onto the Other (as the United States did with Japan in the late 1980s and with China in the 1990s). In this respect, their relationship is intersubjective. To the extent that each acts on these projections, threats to each other acquire a material character. In other words, nuclear-tipped ICBMs are not mere figments of our imagination, but their targeting is a function of what we imagine their possessors might do to us (I return to this point in chapter 4).

Present at the Creation?

As I noted earlier, the ways in which social matters come under the security umbrella is only too familiar to those in the United States who grew up in the 1950s and 1960s, when interstate highways, mathematics, and social science all were subsumed under "national defense." Today, however, a different logic is at work. Social welfare issues and matters of culture are cast as *threats* to the body politic, not as things to be brought within the security sphere. How such threats and dangers can affect national security is not made clear. What such examples do suggest, however, is that threats are not necessarily the product of verifiable, objective material conditions outside of a state's borders (or inside, for that matter). Rather, conceptions of threats arise, as argued above, out of discursive practices *within* states and, only secondarily, *among* states (Banerjee, 1991; Kull, 1985, 1988).

As data flow in and information accumulates, someone must make sense of it. There is an excess of data that must be interpreted. Information that is not easily understood because of its uniqueness or complexity is likely to be interpreted in terms of existing frames of reference (as George Kennan did in the Long Telegram of 1946). The most available frames are those already widely accepted. QED. If this is so, then we must also ask: "Who defines security?" Who proposes how the elements of national power should be mobilized, and to what end? Who has the legitimacy and power to make such proposals? Who is engaged in the social construction of threats and security policy? And how are those ideas disseminated and, finally, realized?[16]

The fundamental assumption underlying many discussions of "security" is that the creation and propogation of security discourses falls within the purview of certain authorized individuals and groups within a state's institutions. They possess not only the legitimate right to define *what* constitutes a threat to security, but also to specify *which* definitions of threat and security will be legitimate. Generally speaking, such individuals and groups are assumed to be aware of:

1. A *consensual definition* of what constitutes security—there is, in other words, an empirical reality to which the definition applies and on which all can agree;

2. *Objective* conditions of threat that stand regardless of any individual's subjective position;

3. *Special knowledge* of conditions that allows for the formulation and conduct of policies required by this single definition of security—that is, an understanding of causal relations that will point to determinate outcomes.[17]

Possession of what is presented as an unambiguous understanding of cause and effect enables these individuals and groups to define threats to security and, in response to specific conditions, formulate policy that will, in their judgement, best secure the state. To be sure, policymakers define security on the basis of a set of assumptions regarding vital interests, plausible enemies, and possible scenarios, all of which grow, to a not-insignificant extent, out of the specific historical and social context of a particular country and some understanding of what is "out there."[18] But while these interests, enemies, and scenarios have a material existence and, presumably, a real import for state security, they cannot be regarded simply as having some sort of "objective" reality independent of these constructions.[19]

Borrowing from the work of Ole Wæver (1995), I want to suggest that what actually happens in the formulation and implementation of security policy is quite different from the standard model. Wæver argues that elites securitize issues by engaging in "speech acts" that frame and freeze discourses. The very *act* of designating an issue or matter as having to do with security helps to establish and reproduce the conditions that bring that issue or matter into the security realm.[20] As Wæver (1995:55) puts it,

> By uttering "security," a state-representative moves a particular development into a specific area, and thereby claims a special right to use whatever means are necessary to block it.

In intervening in this way, the tools applied by the state look very much like those used during the wars the state might launch if it chose to do so.[21] Definitions and practices of security consequently emerge and change as a result of discourses and discursive actions intended to reproduce historical structures and subjects within states and among them (Banerjee, 1991).

Who are these security elites? That is, who "constructs" threats and makes security policy? As far as the process of making security is concerned, there are three potentially different answers. First, we can point to those individuals (or groups, interests, or classes; it doesn't really matter which) responsible for overseeing the *power* of the state (e.g., the military, defense analysts in and out of government, etc.). Second, there are those responsible for overseeing the *institutions* of the state (policymakers, legislative representatives, bureaucrats). Finally, there are those responsible for overseeing the *idea* of the state (heads of state, leaders, national heroes or symbols, teachers, religious figures, etc.; see Buzan, 1991). Each of these groups may conceive of security somewhat differently, and they may intrude on each other's turf, but under "normal" conditions, there is little or no basic disagreement among them about the amount of security required.

In a cohesive, conceptually robust state, a broadly accepted definition of both national identity *and* the security speech acts needed to freeze that identity is developed and reinforced by each of these three groups as a form of Gramscian hegemony. Each group, in turn, contributes to the discourses that maintain that conventional wisdom.

The authority and power of these groups, acting for and within the state, is marshaled against putative threats, both internal and external. The institutions of the state oversee policies directed against these threats, and the specific "idea" of the state—and identity of its citizens—comes to be reinforced in terms of, first, how the state stands and acts in relation to those threats and, second, the way those responsible for maintenance of the idea (through socialization) communicate this relationship. The outcome is a generally accepted authorized (by authorities) consensus on what is to be protected, the means through which this is to be accomplished, and the consequences if such actions are not taken.

Such a consensus is by no means immutable. Things change. A catastrophe can undermine a consensual national epistemology, as in the case of Germany and Japan after World War II. But it is also possible that what might appear to others to be a disaster, for example, Iraq's defeat in 1991, can also provide an opportunity for reinforcement of that epistemology, as has been apparent in Iraq since 1991. The systemic changes discussed earlier can also undermine consensus, although much more slowly. Domestic and external forces can act so as to chip away or splinter hegemonic discourses by undermining the ideational and material bases essential to their maintenance and the authority of those who profess them. If there is some question about the legitimacy of the state and its institutions, or the validity of its authority, those in positions of discursive power may decide to rearticulate the relationship between citizen identity and state idea. Russian president Yeltsin's (unsuccessful) search for a new "national idea" is an example of this. Another involves the restoration or refurbishment of old epistemologies (as in "despite the end of the Cold War, the world remains a dangerous place; therefore rely on our judgement which so often before has proved valid").

To put my point another way, a consensual conception of security is stable only so long as people have a vested interest in the maintenance of that particular conception of security. If social change undermines the basis for this conception—for example, by diminishing the individual welfare of many people, by making the conception seem so remote as to be irrelevant, by forgetting the civic behaviors that once reminded everyone about that conception—consensus can and will break down. This may happen, as well, if a particular concept or construction is increasingly at odds with material evidence, or if state institutions are unable to "deliver the goods." Particular discourses can also shift back and forth, as enemies become friends (Russia) and friends threaten to become enemies again (China). But contradictions between older definitions and changing material conditions can also lead to contestation between competing discourses of security (as in "computer hackers' ability to engage in information warfare is paramount," so we need new tools and organizations to catch them).[22]

The failure of any particular discourse to establish its hegemony means that there can result discursive confusion and contestation over the meaning(s) of security among those who, for one reason or another, have a vested interest in a consensual construction. This interest, or the expected benefits, may well be material and not just a matter of patriotic loyalty to nation; by defining security in a particular way, one serves to legitimate a particular set of policy responses. Associated with these are very real armaments, force structures, diplomatic strategies, domestic economic policies, jobs, titles, and incomes (Smithson, 1996). Wall Street has a particular stake in maintaining good relations with China; cultural conservatives and defense corporations have a stake in imagining a Chinese threat against which we must "be prepared." The risk in the former is that such relations have an impact on domestic industry and employment, and could delegitimate that policy; the risk in the latter is that the People's Republic of China (PRC) might take the conservatives seriously (especially if they can affect security policy) and respond in commensurate fashion.

A discursive remodeling of security may also reinforce the identification of citizens with their state, or it can further divide them. If threats to security can be framed in a particular fashion as, for example, arising from a particular enemy, the differentiation between "us" and "them" becomes clearer; states tend to be defined, at least in part, in terms of "negative organizing principles" (Buzan, 1991:79; see also Huntington, 1996, 1997). The security framework is also buttressed intellectually through reinforcement or establishment of individual roles in a variety of structures and institutions—government, industry, academia. These are linked to a negative organizing principle and its substantiation, in the form of national security advisors and analysts, pundits and professors. Individuals, as well as states, can thus come to define themselves in relation to national security. But, as we are reminded by conspiracy theories about the New World Order, black helicopters, and UN forces in Canada, some discursive frames can decompose the formerly linked security of state and people (Lipschutz, 1998b).

To return to an earlier question: Who constructs and articulates contesting discourses of national security? Among such people are mainstream "defense intellectuals" and strategic analysts, those individuals who, sharing a certain political culture, can agree on a common framework for defining security threats and policy responses (what might be called a security "episteme"). While their discourse is constructed around the interpretation of "real" incoming data, their analysis is framed in such a way as to, first, define the threat as they see it and, second, legitimate those responses that validate their construction of the threat (see, e.g., Schlesinger, 1991). To repeat: this does not mean that threats are imaginary. Rather, they are imagined and constructed in such a way as to *reinforce* existing predispositions and thereby legitimate them. This legitimation, in turn, helps to *reproduce* existing policy or some variant of it as well as the material basis for that policy.

Finally, we might ask why "redefine security?" Who advocates such an idea? During the 1980s, at the time this argument was first made (Ullman, 1983; Mathews, 1989), the individuals comprising this group were an amorphous lot, lacking an integrated institutional base or intellectual framework (a situation that has slowly changed during the 1990s). Most tended to see consensual definitions and dominant discourses of security as failing to properly *perceive* or *understand* the objective threat environment, but they did not question the logic whereby threats and security were defined. In other words, the redefiners proposed that the "real" threats to security were different from those that policymakers and defense authorities were generally concerned about, but that the threats were "really out there."

The redefiners argued further that the failure to recognize real threats could have two serious consequences: First, it might underminine state legitimacy, inasmuch as a national defense that did not serve to protect or enhance the general welfare (which is what "security" often comes to mean) would lose public support. Second, it would reproduce a response system whose costs would increasingly outweigh benefits. At the same time, however, the redefiners did not propose a shift away from state-based conceptions of security; rather, their arguments sought to buttress eroding state authority by delineating new realms for state action. Thus, for example, discussions of "environmental security" focused on the need for governments to establish themselves as meaningful actors in environmental protection *as it related to state maintenance.* This would mean establishing a sovereignty claim in a realm heretofore unoccupied, and defining that realm as critical in security terms.[23]

Interestingly (and, perhaps, predictably), since the concept of environmental security was first offered, it has gradually acquired acceptance among Western military and political institutions, not because the threats are necessarily evident or can be addressed through military means but because it provides them with a new mission, both conceptual and material. Many of the arguments for redefining security can be seen in retrospect, therefore, as part of an effort to shore up crumbling rationales for state sovereignty, a goal not so far from that desired by security authorities themselves.

The success of the redefiners has been considerable, especially in terms of the "new threats" being integrated into the existing machinery of national security (see chapter 4). A few analysts have argued that the purity of the security field must be maintained if it is to have any disciplinary rigor or meaning (Walt, 1991; Deudney, 1990). Others have written that traditional security concerns will soon reemerge, in one form or another, and that it is premature to turn our attention to new problems (Kugler, 1995). Certainly, the lexicon of "new threats" has been picked up and disseminated relentlessly, as seen in the 1997 *Quadrennial Defense Review* issued by the Pentagon (and addressed in chapter 4). It is less clear whether the U.S. military has a clearly conceived strategy for responding to these problems or whether they have simply offered new rationales for old policies.

Perhaps security is an outmoded practice—as slavery, colonialism, and the use of land mines have all come to be—both normatively and materially bankrupt. Or perhaps the more traditional functions of the state are being undermined by processes of interactive (and intersubjective) change: States and governments can no longer manage what they once did, and cannot yet manage what is new. Under these circumstances, it begins to make less and less sense to see the state as the referent object of security. Hence, we not only have to unwrap the ways in which changing material conditions affect the state materially, we also have to understand how these changes alter the very *idea* of the state—as well as the idea of security—thereby creating new referents of political activity and, perhaps, security.

(B)orders and (Dis)orders

To ask, then, the logical question: What *is* security? In a book published in 1988, the authors could still argue that national borders remained authoritative and determining of security:

> In the most basic sense, what the American people have to deal with when they adjust to the world outside U.S. frontiers is 170 [sic] assorted nation-states, each in control of a certain amount of the earth's territory. These 170 nations, being sovereign, are able to reach decisions on the use of armed forces under their government's control. They can decide to attack other nations. (Hartmann and Wendzel, 1988:3–4)

By 1989, it appeared that the roster of states had been fixed, the books closed for good. Only Antarctica remained an unresolved puzzle, where international agreements put overlapping national claims into indefinite abeyance. There were many "international" borders, to be sure, but these were understood to be fixed in number and location, inscribed in stone and on paper. States might draw imaginary lines, or "bordoids," as Bruce Larkin (forthcoming) has stylized them, defining and encompassing "national interests" beyond their borders. They might extend their borders in a somewhat hypothetical fashion in order to bring allies into the sphere of blessedness, as in practice of extended deterrence in Europe. They might effectively take over the machinery of other states, as in Central America and Central Asia, even as they paid obeisance to the sacred lines on the ground, claiming to be protecting the sovereignty of the fortunate victim. Enemies and threats were, however, always across the line.

Is it the lines themselves that are the problem? If so, this suggests that security discourse irreducibly invokes the *authority* of borders and boundaries, rather than their physical or imagined presence, for its power. Borders and boundaries presume categories of things, be they people, states, or "civilizations," and categories presume differences between subjects on either side of the boundary. The practical difficulty is always how authority is to be linked to these borders and boundaries in order to maintain difference and constrain change. What authority is capable of authorizing such lines?

James Der Derian (1995: 34) has pointed out that establishing borders involves the drawing of lines between the collective self and what is, in Nietzsche's words, "alien and weaker." In this way, the boundary between known and unknown is reified and secured. But such distinctions are not so easily made. Before 1989, Croat, Serb, and Muslim had lived together in relative peace as "Yugoslavs" for forty-five years. After 1991, the borders between them were, somehow, authorized so as to magnify small differences and turn them into an authorization for "ethnic cleansing." These borders, moreover, were drawn both on the ground *and* in the mind, so that the "alien" could be identified, wherever his or her physical location (chapter 6).

Thus, conventionally and historically, borders have been drawn not only by dint of geography but also between the self and the enemy, between the realm of safety and the realm of danger, between tame zones and wild ones, between the supposedly known and the presumably unverifiable and unknown. Traditionally, it was practitioners of diplomacy and security who marked such borders between states, or between groups of states, and they did so as the authorities who drew the lines, maintained their integrity, and validated those characteristics, whether cultural or political, that distinguished insider from outsider, one side from the other.[24]

But such boundaries can be very fluid. Because they are as much conceptual as physical, the insider must be disciplined (or self-disciplined) to remain within them. Hence, when the authority of borders and boundaries weakens or disappears, the old (b)orders become disordered. In retrospect, the revolutions of 1989 actualized what had already been underway for some time but was not recognized: the fluidization, diminution, and dissolution of borders and intrastate boundaries. This was represented by a phenomenon that some observers had, in the past, called "interdependence." But interdependence assumes the continuity of borders and boundaries, not their dissolution or the intermingling of previously separated groups (see chapter 5).

Paradoxically, as old borders disappeared, new ones emerged, first in the mind and only then on the ground (Dawson, 1996). Former comrades and compatriots now found themselves on the opposite sides of borders, sometimes on the "wrong" side, as was the case with the 25 million Russians in the "near abroad." New boundaries were drawn through what had once been states or titular republics, creating multiple identities where before there had been (nominally) only one. Even industrialized countries were not immune to this phenomenon, as new lines were drawn between "true" nationals and the children of immigrants who had never traveled to the old country. The post-1989 borders had much the same effect, with newly imagined nations militarizing their identities in order to establish their imagined autonomy from old ones. In doing so, these new nations rejected the old ones, rendering them both illegitimate and undesirable.

But new borders did not, and cannot, put an end to the old questions: Who are you? Who am I? Why am I here? Boundaries are always under challenge and they must always be reestablished, not only on the ground but also in the mind. Here is where security is, ultimately, to be found; here is where insecurity is, ultimately, generated. The marking of borders and boundaries is never truly finalized, never finally set in stone. Borders are meant to discipline, but they also offer the opportunity of being crossed or transgressed. Borders are lines on maps and markers on the ground, but border regions are rarely so neat. Borderlands are places where mixing occurs, or has occurred, or might occur. They are, in themselves, a contradiction to, a rejection of, the neatly drawn limits of the nation-state. Borderlands are thus a threat to the security supposedly established by the authorized borders precisely because they offer the possibility of people freely moving back and forth across lines without ever actually crossing borders. It is for this reason, as much as anything else, that border zones are sometimes cleansed of people in the name of security.

How did this insecurity dilemma—the loss of firm boundaries—come to pass? As is so often the case in human affairs, the causal mechanism is overdetermined. Liberalization and globalization have been major factors, but the "nuclear wars" that were "fought" between 1950 and 1989 also played a central role. Those wars were never fought on the plains of Germany, as the planners of Flexible Response and the AirLand Battle thought they would be, but they *were* fought in the minds of the military, the policymakers, and a fearful public. What became clear during the 1980s was that no amount of drawing of lines or borders between friend and foe could limit the destruction that would follow if missiles should be launched and opposing armies thrown into battle. In the end, both sides would suffer immeasurable consequences.[25]

Nuclear deterrence, in other words, came to depend not on physical destructiveness, but rather on the maintenance of borders on the ground *and* in the mind: To be secure, one had to believe that, were the Other to cross the line, both the self and the Other would cease to exist; to maintain the line and be secure meant living with the risk that it might be crossed. Although neither side would dare to physically cross the line, it was still possible that mental crossings—what was called "Finlandization" (a slur)—could occur. The threat of nothingness secured the ontology of being, but at great political cost to those who pursued the formula. Authority deemed the fiction necessary to survival.

Since 1991, the nuclear threat has ceased to wield its old cognitive force, and the borders in the mind and on the ground have vanished, in spite of repeated efforts to draw them anew, perhaps farther East, perhaps elsewhere. To be sure, the United States and Russia still do not launch missiles against each other because both know the result would be annihilation. But the same is true for France and Britain, or China and Israel. It was the existence of the Other across the border that gave national security its power and authority; it is the disappearance of the border that has vanquished that power. Where Russia is now concerned, we are, paradoxically, not secure, because we see no need to be secured.[26] France is fully capable of doing great damage to the United States, but that capability has no meaning in terms of U.S. security. In other words, if safety cannot be distinguished from danger, there is no border and, hence, no security problem.

The debates over the expansion of NATO, and the decision to bring Poland, Hungary, and the Czech Republic in from the cold, have revived these very same questions. Who is inside? Who is outside? And why does it matter? As a multilateral security alliance aimed at the enemy to the East, NATO's long-term mission had been to guard the border, to keep the Elbe the line separating the Free World from its unfree doppelgänger. Defining a new "mission" for NATO, or taking in new members, does not eliminate the conceptual insecurity arising from the new boundaries or lack thereof. A new line is drawn, but every one is careful not to authorize a new meaning for it. Yet, lines are fraught with meanings and so, inevitably, a meaning is sought for this one. Expansion is not directed against Russia, but it might be. NATO will not use its military power to suppress ethnic groups within Europe, but it has (and will, apparently). A Rapid Reaction Force would not intervene in civil wars, but who knows for sure? What else is NATO good for? Applying its military might against terrorists, computer hackers, pornographers and pederasts, drug smugglers, and illegal immigrants would be akin to killing a fly with a Peacekeeper (whether missile or Colt .45).[27]

Conclusion

The insecurity dilemma is a permanent condition of life. This is not, however, the same as the insecurity of a Hobbesian State of Nature, or the fear that arises when neighbors, whether in the house or the state next door, begin to arm. In today's world, the insecurity dilemma arises out of uncertainty, out of a changing and never fully predictable world. Securing the self and the state against change works both ways: it seeks to freeze lines on the ground and in the mind, and it keeps baleful influences out, but also imprisons those protected within the iron cage. I can do no better in ending this chapter than to quote James Der Derian (1995:34), who argues that "A safe life requires safe truths. The strange and the alien remain unexamined, the unknown becomes identified as evil, and evil provokes hostility—recycling the desire for security." Surely we can do better than this.

4❖
ARMS AND AFFLUENCE

If you would have wealth, prepare for war.

—Unattributed

Whatever happened to World War III? For almost forty years, two great military alliances faced off across a line drawn through the center of a middling-sized peninsula, ready to destroy the world at a moment's notice in order to save it. John Lewis Gaddis (1987) called this time the "Long Peace," Mary Kaldor (1990), "the imaginary war."[1] When it was over, a few sentimentalists warned that we would soon miss it, and tried to tell us why (Mearsheimer, 1990a, 1990b). For many—especially the 20 or 30 million who died in Third World wars— the violence was only too real. For other billions, there was a peace of sorts, purchased only at great cost (Schwartz, 1998) and perpetual terror. For the United States and its allies, it was a time of great opportunity and prosperity. The 10 trillion or more dollars expended on the Long Peace brought a period of unprecedented economic growth and wealth. Affluence, it often seemed, was possible only with arms.

But even imagined wars must end (Iklé, 1971). Those that exist in the fevered fantasies of war gamers and war-game writers can continue on computer monitors everywhere but, after a time, those played out by nuclear strategists within the Beltway, or by Special Forces in far-off countries begin to lose their raison d'être as well as their authority and ability to discipline when the "big one" does not come to pass as threatened. If threats are to retain their power to terrorize, therefore, they must be reimagined and fought, over and over, through words, through symbols and images, through languages and rhetorics.

World War III was such a war. Although it never took place, it was always about to break out. Peace became a fragile interregnum of not-war. Preparations for the imaginary war were extensive and, in the end, the war that never happened was extravagantly expensive. A poorer world could not have afforded the peace of World War III, but it was that peace that made the West so rich that it could afford to imagine fighting World War III in Europe (and to actually fight it at a much lower level in other parts of the world).

These days, there is no shortage of wars, despite the end of the Cold War. But these are minor wars, relatively speaking. Big wars are too expensive to wage in human terms, although they have also become too costly not to imagine. No U.S. president, present or future, could afford the political costs of even a fraction of the fifty thousand American deaths suffered in Vietnam (apparently, the millions of Vietnamese who died carried no such costs for American presidents). At the same time, neither could a U.S. president, present or future, afford the political costs of abandoning preparations for the "big one."[2] The Gulf War cost more than $50 billion, but at a loss of less than two hundred American lives (more died in accidents before and after the fighting than in actual combat). The immediate costs of the war were paid for largely through grants from allies; the strategy, underlying technology, and resulting weaponry, however, were the products of the imagined World War III. In the short term, the Gulf War gave no great boost to the U.S. economy; in the longer term, the enduring "problem" of Iraq has provided a justification for not abandoning imagined wars. Pace Clausewitz, imagined war is the continuation of economics by other means.

So, what does this mean for the future of war? The literature is vast and growing. For some, the next enemy has been chosen, and the coming war already imagined (Bernstein and Munro, 1997). But most theorists and journalists of war are like the fabled drunk, looking for opponents in the well-lit places, rather than in the shadows. For them, prevention of major wars through reliance on nukes, cruise missiles, and the electronic battlefield remain paramount (Cohen, 1996). Yet, such wars are the least likely. Moreover, most commentators seem to remain fascinated by the kill rather than the whip, by missile defense rather than mental offense. Few analysts of war bother to ask *why* a war might begin or, for that matter, whether the kinds of wet-dream weapons that excite soldier and civilian alike even have a role in the wars of the future. After all, real war costs money—remember Bob Dole complaining about wasting those expensive cruise missiles? Preparations for war are good for business; deaths, however, are bad for politics.

Most contemporary discussions of strategy and battle are, therefore, not about "real" war. They are better understood as "discourses of war" meant, in the absence of an omnipotent and omnicompetent enemy, to terrorize and discipline both friend and foe, citizen and immigrant, alike. A discourse, as noted in Chapter 3, is best understood as an authoritative framework that purports to explain cause and effect and, through practice and repetition, rules out and quashes alternative explanations (Litfin, 1994). Discourses are rooted in the real world, but their power comes from their narrative authority, and not their assumed descriptive or analytical "objectivity" (for an excellent discussion of discourses, see Hajer, 1993).

There are, to be sure, many discourses of war that could be discussed here. With variations, however, the three that dominate American thinking are: the last/next war, wars in small countries far away, and imagined wars. In this chapter, I compare and contrast discourses of wars with really existing war, and argue that the two bear little relation to each other. I then discuss how several competing discourses of war have been framed, and assess their political and disciplinary character. Finally, I offer some speculative thoughts on the future of war, especially in a global system in transition: Ten years after, do we face perpetual peace or perpetual war?

Imagined Wars

In May 1997, the Clinton administration issued "A National Security Strategy for a New Century" (Clinton, 1997). In it, the president waxed enthusiastic about the future:

As we enter the twenty-first century, we have an unprecedented opportunity to make our nation safer and more prosperous. Our military might is unparalleled; a dynamic global economy offers increasing opportunities for American jobs and American investment; and the community of democratic nations is growing, enhancing the prospects for political stability, peaceful conflict resolution and greater hope for the people of the world.

But, do not get too excited; Clinton also warned darkly that

ethnic conflict and outlaw states threaten regional stability; terrorism, drugs, organized crime and proliferation of weapons of mass destruction are global concerns that transcend national borders; and environmental damage and rapid population growth undermine economic prosperity and political stability in many countries. (Clinton, 1997)

Needless to say, these are difficult problems to address. Moreover, they raise a host of additional questions: Whom do these phenomena threaten, and how? Do they affect everyone to an equal degree? How should we respond? Will our allies help? How much would it cost? Who will pay? Is there reason to think we can solve such problems?

The detailed responses offered in this and other similar government documents focus on the availability and utility of military power. No surprises there: Deployment of military force remains the apotheosis of state sovereignty, an arena in which the state exercises its greatest discretion and control. Yet precisely how such capabilities are to be used to control or eliminate these "new" threats remains problematic, and this poses real epistemological difficulties for strategic planners. According to the *Quadrennial Defense Review* (*QDR*, 1997), issued by the Pentagon in April 1997,

The security environment between now and 2015 will . . . likely be marked by the absence of a "global peer competitor" able to challenge the United states militarily around the world as the Soviet Union did during the Cold War. Furthermore, it is likely that no regional power or coalition will amass sufficient conventional military strength in the next 10 to 15 years to defeat our armed forces, once the full military potential of the United States is mobilized and deployed to the region of conflict (*QDR*, 1997: sec. 2, pp. 2–3).

Why, then, have a Pentagon? Searching for contingencies that demand maintenance of the military, the authors of the *QDR* focus on "regional dangers," and conclude that

> foremost among these [contingencies] is the threat of coercion and large-scale, cross-border aggression against U.S. allies and friends in key regions by hostile states with significant military power . . . [i]n Southwest Asia . . . [i]n the Middle East . . . [and i]n East Asia [on] the Korean peninsula . . . (*QDR*, 1997: section 2).

But if strength brings peace, it seems also to be debilitating. Despite expressions of confidence regarding the future security environment, U.S. military power and dominance are, rather paradoxically, also portrayed as potential *weaknesses*. Enemies too cowardly to fight on the field of battle will find other ways to strike back. Thus, the *QDR* (1997: section 2, p. 2) warns that

> U.S. dominance in the conventional military arena may encourage adversaries to use such asymmetric means [e.g., terrorism and information warfare] to attack our forces and interests overseas and Americans at home. That is, they are likely to seek advantage over the United States by using unconventional approaches to *circumvent* or *undermine* our strengths while *exploiting* our vulnerabilities. (Emphasis added)

In this analysis, capabilities become impediments, and the ability to act is transformed into a formula for paralysis. The apparent contradiction is not explicable, however, in conventional strategic terms. It arises because, on the one hand, nuclear deterrence has no effect at the substate level. On the other hand, both the costs of reallocating defense resources to respond appropriately *and* the costs of losing young men and women in conventional ground combat, whether interstate or intrastate, are too high in domestic political terms. Moreover, such major changes might also be interpreted by some as "lack of resolve" and a sign of "weakness."

A nuclear World War III would have avoided such ontological difficulties. Tens of millions might die on the home front, but their deaths would make the loss of tens or hundreds of thousands on the front seem minor by comparison. Today's conventional warriors suffer losses only on the battlefield, and each one is carefully counted by politicians (if not voters). Yet, as we were warned when NATO began to bomb Yugoslavia, if we do not prepare for such wars, or shift our attention to "not-wars," aggressors (recalling Munich) will act aggressively against us.

Virtual Nukes

Is there an answer to this dilemma? Apparently there is: the electronic battlefield, whose ultimate application emerges through what is called the "Revolution in Military Affairs" (RMA). The RMA envisions technicians safely ensconced in bunkers thousands of miles from the fighting, using remote-control weapons to kill the enemy's human soldiers, destroy its material infrastructure, and encircle its territory (Cohen, 1996). In practice, such technology is neither infallible nor cheap; to paraphrase Senator Everett Dirksen, when B-2 bombers cost a billion dollars each, the loss of even one or two means that pretty soon you are talking real money. Hence, the *imagining* of such wars becomes the means of avoiding them (that the recipients of such visions might not emerge unscathed is, it would seem, of no concern to policymakers and strategists). And, the communication of such imagined futures to the global audience becomes central to the RMA and its task of deterrence.

This is not really new, of course; deterrence—especially of the nuclear variety—fulfills a similar communicative function. Nuclear deterrence threatens to turn the world into a blackened cinder—to bring a decidedly non-Hegelian end to history—if a putative enemy chooses to transgress what the issuer of the threat considers the boundaries of acceptable behavior. The nuclear threat posits an imagined future if certain actions are taken, but there is no intention to turn the imaginary into the real; that would defeat the entire purpose of the exercise. Our experience with such scenario building suggests, however, that the credibility of such an imagined threat remains problematic, and this points to a structural flaw inherent in such deterrence.

Whereas conventional deterrence consists of threats to punish the offender and can be tested, nuclear deterrence, according to most conventional wisdom, cannot. Who, after all, *would* sacrifice New York for Paris, or Los Angeles for an island in the South China Sea? The use of a single nuclear weapon, as in the "firing of a warning shot across the bow," would prevent the enemy's use of a second, according to some (see, e.g., Scheer, 1982), but implicit in that first step is the imagined escalation of a single nuclear explosion to thousands (Iklé, 1996). If such a calculus exists only in the imagination, however, it can hardly be said to constitute a material threat or one whose veracity can be demonstrated by example. Again, it is not action in response to a provocation that halts an offender, but imagination that disciplines prior to the initial offensive act.

In his famous "ladder of escalation," Herman Kahn (1965) sought to illlustrate through imagined scenario-building that there were many nonnuclear way stations before Gehenna. Inasmuch as his was a theory that could not be fully tested, much less tolerated, the scientific method could not be vindicated for nuclear war. Consequently, World War III, the Imaginary War, had to be conducted by other means, and enemies had to be disciplined not by really existing wars but by wholly imagined ones. The result was the war of things said and displayed, and the curious way in which nuclear weapons were used. By not being used in a *literal* sense, but only as a *medium* of exchange in an *imagined* exchange, nukes disciplined Americans, Europeans, and Soviets alike.[3] The notion of use thus began to acquire a peculiar function. The threat to "use" nuclear weapons, as Thomas Schelling and others pointed out, was credible only to the degree that those in a position of power could convince not only others, but also themselves, that the weapons would be used under appropriate circumstances (Schelling, 1966: chap. 2). But such circumstances could never be too well-defined, for to specify actual conditions of attack might someday require an unwanted launch for the sake of maintaining credibility. The "use" of nuclear weapons consequently took the form of speech acts (Wæver, 1995), backed up by doctrine and deployment, but hedged all about with hypotheticals and conditionals.

The plausibility of an imagined action poses a further epistemological problem, however, not only for the threatened but also for the threatener. To transform an imagined threat into one that might credibly be fulfilled, the issuer must behave in such a way that s/he actually believes that s/he would execute the imagined action. This will to act must be conveyed fully to the recipient of the threat, or it may be regarded as empty. Such intentionality requires a certain insouciance of speech that reduces the apocalyptic act to a mundane one (as documented by Robert Scheer (1982) in *With Enough Shovels* and Steven Kull (1988) in *Minds at War*; the original effort in this direction is Kahn, 1965). How else is one to explain pronouncements such as that made by then-secretary of defense Caspar Weinberger (1982), who argued in 1982 testimony before the Senate Foreign Relations Committee that

> to deter successfully, we must be able—*and must be seen to be able*—to retaliate against any potential aggressor in such a manner that the costs we will exact will substantially exceed any gains he might hope to achieve through aggression. We, for our part, are under no illusions about the consequences of a nuclear war: we believe there would be no winners in such a war. But this recognition on *our* part is not sufficient to ensure effective deterrence or to prevent the outbreak of war: it is essential that the Soviet leadership understands this as well. (First emphasis added)

In place of a thermonuclear holocaust, then, the nuclear establishment conducted a war of the imagination, of possible futures, of horrors best avoided. Aided and abetted by science-fiction films and novels, studies by the RAND Corporation and numberless institutes of strategic studies, and offhand remarks by policymakers and military officers, nuclear deterrence was raised to a perverse form of art(iculation), in which a convoluted but safe rhetoric came to substitute for risky and explicit action. Deterrence thus became a practice akin to telling ghost stories around the campfire: if one could scare oneself silly, perhaps others would be scared, as well (as Tom Leher put it, "If Brezhnev is scared, I'm scared"). But one would never want to become too scared, for to do so might be to lose self-control. . . .

A graphic example of nuclear discipline—one of many—took place with the deployment of the intermediate-range nuclear "Euromissiles," the Pershing-II and Ground Launched Cruise Missiles in Europe during the early 1980s. These missiles were intended to fulfill an imagined lacuna in deterrence created by Soviet SS-20s intermediate-range nuclear missiles discovered in Eastern Europe during the mid-1970s. The SS-20s, it was claimed by then-West German chancellor Helmut Schmidt, imperiled the West by taking advantage of a "gap" in the hypothetical ladder of crisis escalation that might be climbed during a future confrontation over Berlin or some other point on the East-West borderline. In such a crisis, the gap could be used by the Soviets, according to Schmidt and others, to *menace* and *discipline* Western Europe simply through the motions of preparing to launch the SS-20s. Inasmuch as to actually let loose the SS-20s would have unpredictable, not to mention undesirable, consequences, the result of their presence in the East was to create a Western vision of an imagined future in which such threats might be issued or even executed. In the face of such an eventuality, the failure to respond appropriately could lead to the "Finlandization" of Western Europe, which would be forced to submit to demands made by the Soviet Union out of fear of the imagined future.[4]

Such demands, of course, had not been made, and never were. Indeed, it would have been considered exceptionally bad manners to actually make such a demand. Rather, they were demands that some in the West *imagined* might be forthcoming at some future date, and they were demands that, if met, would change Western Europe into something with a different identity and loyalty (a Greater Finland, perhaps?). Imagined threats could not be left alone; they had to generate material responses. To remedy the hole in the whole of nuclear deterrence, policymakers determined that NATO must deploy its own equivalent missiles, thereby countering one imagined war-fighting scenario with another.

Again, the Euromissiles were never intended to be *launched*; they were only put into Europe to fill an imagined gap that had not existed prior to the West's awareness that the SS-20s had been deployed and pronouncements that they were, indeed, a threat (see Smith, 1984a, 1984b, 1984c, 1984d). To underline the imaginary quality of the threatened futures invoked by both East and West, in 1987, after some six years of off-again on-again negotiations, the gap disappeared, along with both sides' missiles.[5] As is true with most magical thinking, the "gap" had never been real in any objective sense; it was created through discourses of deterrence and the projection of imagined intentions onto the "Other." A whole world of the future was created out of dreams, casting its unreal shadow on the present.[6] Through virtual exchange of nuclear weapons was mutual deterrence assured. As we shall see, the Revolution in Military Affairs (RMA) and its electronic battlefield have problems of their own.

Fighting the Next War

It is a well-known cliché that, in planning for the next war, generals always fight the last one. One of the lessons of Vietnam seems to have been that nuclear deterrence and discipline have little, if any, impact on nonnuclear adversaries. The president of the United States could hardly contemplate nuking a regional adversary—even one in putative possession of a few atomic weapons—in response to a conventional provocation. How, then, could s/he respond to an "unconventional attack" with a small nuclear bomb in the mythical suitcase? On whom could a retaliatory device be dropped? Who could be punished?[7] Fortunately for generals and strategists, the Gulf War intervened to suggest some answers.

The classical image of war is one of a tightly controlled, well-executed *pas de deux* between two enemies, using the most advanced of weaponry, fighting along a well-defined front, each exerting maximum will. This is the idealized war, the AirLand Battle of NATO (whose imagined clarity, Clausewitz warned us, would prove wholly illusory if it came to pass), the conflict reimagined by Tom Clancy (1987) in his mind-numbing *Red Storm Rising*. In that novel, Clancy pits the brains of NATO against the brawn of the Warsaw Pact, and NATO wins. The war turns out, however, to have been triggered by a misunderstanding. The war games fought by General Norman Schwartzkopf's "Jedi Knights" and their counterparts in Iraq (Der Derian, 1992) in preparation for an imagined conflict in the Gulf—one that did take place—relied on a similar paradigm and, according to some, was also the result of a "misunderstanding" arising from Ambassador April Glaspie's replies to Saddam Hussein's inquiries.

The wars to come, according to the conventional wisdom about the RMA, will look a lot like these two, although they are unlikely to be launched as a result of miscommunication. Fought out on electronic battlefields, prosecuted by means of real-time intelligence and weapons controlled through satellite uplinks, won by dint of superior technology, future wars will be something quite different but also much the same (Cohen, 1996; Libicki, 1996). There will be a front line, but our s/he-bots will face the enemy's flesh-and-blood boys and girls. Technological capital will protect political capital, but the basic choreography will remain the same.

Or will it? Most of today's *discourses* of war are, somewhat paradoxically, characterized by conservatism in imagination even as they are prosecuted with the as-yet uninvented weapons and strategies of the future. These fantasies belie the form, moreover, of most contemporary wars, which follow Hobbesian lines more closely than Cartesian ones (Kaplan, 1996). Planning for future wars requires some idea of what they might look like, but where are we to look? Inasmuch as both *fortuna* and fog play central roles in any battle, no two wars can be alike, much less resemble one another. But because the "last war" almost always comes as a surprise, in the absence of accurate prognostication it usually stands in as the model for the next.

For better or worse, therefore, the Gulf War of 1991 has become the current model for the future, as well as the standard against which all debates are conducted (Libicki, 1996). This is *not*, it should be noted, the type of conflict that is either most often imagined—if fantasies are to be believed—or the most common—if newspaper column inches are measured. As an *interstate* war for which a detailed account is available, and with a clearly-defined enemy and set of front lines, however, it is the most straightforward in terms of preparations and buildup (see the first quote from the *QDR* above). That, too, is reason enough that the Gulf War is unlikely to be repeated.

Even determining under what circumstances war might erupt or be justified is itself problematic. Violation of fundamental material and social norms among states, such as triggered the Gulf War, are exceedingly rare. When one state invades another, the violation of borders is clear.[8] A moral outrage has taken place. More than this, such an infraction can be understood as a threat to *all* states, even those with no immediate interest in the violation. If a border can be crossed with impunity in one place, there is no reason that it cannot happen elsewhere. Consequently, not only do states react to border violations, alone and collectively, they also have reason to fortify their defenses against potential violations by their neighbors (for this is where it is presumed such attacks will come—but, because the United States has no overtly threatening neighbors, it is also why U.S. strategy is so problematic). Given this reasoning, even though Gulf-type wars might be quite uncommon, the safest bet is that the Gulf War will occur again, somewhere, sometime.

This was the path pursued by the Bush and Clinton administrations. In the early 1990s, a full review of U.S. strategy and forces was undertaken—the "Bottom-up Review"—with an eye toward rationalizing the military while cutting the defense budget. Out of this exercise came the authoritative war-fighting strategy of the Clinton administration—and the official successor to containment—organized around "major regional conflicts," or MRCs (a concept recently rechristened by Defense Secretary William Cohen as "major theater wars," or MTWs). An MRC/MTW is modeled roughly on the Gulf War experience, multiplied by two. More to the point, the MRC strategy assumes the simultaneous outbreak of two such conflicts, for example, a reprise of the Gulf War and the Korean War at the same time.

Although most strategic analysts agree that the probability of such a scenario is rather low, others have argued that the beginning of one regional war offers an opportune time for a regional "rogue," such as North Korea, to launch an attack. The United States therefore requires a range of airlift, manpower, and light equipment capabilities that would allow it to respond expeditiously to provocations with rapid troop deployments, followed by the emplacement of large numbers of troops and heavy battlefield weapons—but in less time than the six-month buildup to the Gulf War. Whether American capabilities would permit response to two MRCs at the same time remains unclear, with the result that some propose a "block and hold" approach, whereby regional wars would be fought and won sequentially.

The MRC/MTW strategy—and its essential restatement in the 1997 *QDR* and the 1998 secretary of defense's *Annual Report to the President and the Congress*—is best understood not so much as a war-fighting plan as an effort to buttress the presumption of rationality in order to avoid the supposed miscommunication that preceded the Gulf War. It is also a (pre)cautionary tale for both friend and foe. Foes are meant to be cowed by these capabilities and threats of retribution should they try to change things—or so U.S. policymakers hope. The loudly articulated American ability to wage the MRC/MTW strategy is meant to incite in others imagined consequences and thereby prevent them from ever launching a war. The outcome of the Gulf War, and the repeated attacks on Iraq, serve as a morality tale for those who might choose not to believe. This, in turn, relieves the United States of having to fight such a war and, once again, conserves political capital at home. For FOUS (Friends of the United States), the strategy presents the world as a dangerous place, full of unseen although very real enemies but, nonetheless, in good hands under American management and tutelage. Meddle with this arrangement at the risk of loosing chaos upon the land (as France found out when it demanded a larger role in NATO by attempting to take over the European Southern Command).

What is absent from these discussions and plans is the "why?" Why would so-called rogues—and these are the only countries that, according to Washington, threaten U.S. forces, allies, or interests— choose to do so? No rational reason can be given, and so irrational ones are offered instead.[9] They hate us, but for no reason, since we have no designs on them. They desire vengeance, but for no reason, since we have never offended them. They wish to injure us, but for no reason, since they have only been injured through *their* interference with *our* pursuit of order (a lesson more recently taught to Slobodan Milosevic and Yugoslavia).

It is here that the MRC/MTW discourse of war, and the general U.S. strategy, begin to collapse or, at least, run into conceptual trouble. The MRC strategy assumes that all parties to a conflict operate on the basis of the same rational calculus to which the United States adheres, and that each side understands any given situation in similar terms. A failure by the other party to respond appropriately is then attributed to irrationality, insanity, or miscalculation—a "sane, rational" leader would not risk such injuries to society or self—rather than a logic or rationality that we might not understand or to which we might not subscribe.[10] In seems safe to say that the number of wars begun by the insane and irrational is probably quite small, and that so-called misunderstandings (i.e., "human error") are more frequently to blame. More to the point, if insanity or irrationality are to blame for wars, deterrence cannot work to prevent them.

But there is a much deeper flaw in the assumptions underlying this discourse, as noted earlier. The failure to deter Iraq in 1990 and 1991 has been attributed to Ambassador April Glaspie and a lack of clarity in the messages sent by the United States. The remedy was and is to develop, deploy, and advertise capabilities so as to communicate clearly, without question, the costs to enemies that would follow from a violation of the status quo. To a determined government, however, the prospective cost in money and lives of a Gulf-scale war might not seem so great as to constrain it from launching an attack on U.S. interests or allies or failing to respond with alacrity when the bombs start to fall. That much is clear from Iraqi behavior prior to, during and after the Gulf War (and, more recently, by Yugoslavia's), although it is a lesson yet to be learned by U.S. policymakers. Furthermore, rationality and irrationality, sanity and insanity might not even be the appropriate concepts to apply to this case. Assuming *either* rationality *or* irrationality (and nothing else) disregards questions of deep causality in explaining the onset of wars, ignores what is clearly a result of problematic histories of relations among and within states, and attributes events as they inexplicably occur to factors beyond anyone's control (e.g, faulty genes, chemical imbalances, or Comet Hale-Bopp). Other causal processes simply drop out.

This assumption of rationality—that a commitment of force (and the threat of escalation) deters a rational opponent—was, nevertheless, central to the Carter administration's original "Rapid Deployment Force" (RDF) later configured into the "Central Command" (CC) under General Norman Schwarzkopf. It was, as well, the theory behind the military buildup prior to the four-day war of January 1991. It remains the logic behind U.S. disciplining of Iraq and others. Here, however, the conflation of nuclear and conventional discipline becomes truly problematic.

The original purpose of the RDF/CC was to deter the Soviet Union from launching an attack through Iran toward the Gulf. In that imagined future, the RDF/CC was to have functioned as a tripwire (the same function filled by the 300,000 U.S. troops then in Western Europe) whose triggering would lead to the use of nuclear weapons. Working backward, then, it was the threat of imagined nuclear war that would secure American interests in the Gulf and serve to prevent the Soviets from initiating such an attack (but see Clancy, 1987). According to this logic, therefore, the threat to send military forces to oust Iraq from Kuwait should have been sufficient to accomplish that end. This latter theory was tested and found wanting because it relied on nuclear threats backed up by virtual forces, and not conventional threats backed up by material ones. That the Gulf tripwire was never intended to be a "real" threat was originally indicated by the fact that the Central Command existed only on paper and could never have made it to the Gulf in time to become a nuclear sacrifice to Soviet aggression.

Here, then, was the flaw that is to be studiously avoided by the MRC/MTW strategy. To make credible a threat to deploy and defeat an opponent, not only must the United States *have* the capability to deploy, it must also make *manifest* that capability without having actually to deploy. This might be accomplished through war games, rhetoric, and showing the flag, although such exercises suffer from several potential costs. First, it is extremely expensive to maintain such a capability, especially if it requires that troops and equipment be stationed at some distance from potential arenas of conflict (as is the case with the Central Command). Second, there is the very real chance that one's bluff might be called. One might then be forced to fight and suffer casualties, on the battlefield and in the political wars at home. These are the very things the MRC strategy with its capital-intensive weaponry is meant to avoid. We might conclude, therefore, that the strategy wants some rethinking.

Disciplinary Warfare

This leaves us with one remaining question: *Is* the Gulf War *the* archetype of future wars? Are the electronic battlefields of the MRC/MTWs plausible? Or do they simply provide a distraction from lower-intensity, higher-probability conflicts that are so much more difficult to prevent or resolve? From this latter perspective, the wars in Chechnya, the Balkans, Central Africa, and elsewhere might be more appropriate as models, especially if predictions of continuing national fragmentation are borne out (see chapter 6). From a techno-warrior's point of view, however, Chechnya-like wars are of little interest and no consequence. Combatants engaged in block-by-block urban combat, using assault rifles, bazookas, and artillery of ancient provenance (relatively speaking) are at high risk of injury or death. Such wars are messy, difficult to orchestrate, and notoriously hard on weapons engineered with high-precision mechanics and fancy electronics. Moreover, the possibility of American involvement in such postmodern struggles—even in a peace-keeping capacity—always appears to be an occasion IRAQ for policymakers to run for cover.

Postmodern warfare is, consequently, regarded by industrialized country foreign ministries and militaries mostly as a nuisance; it is the high-tech stuff that is sexy and porky. But, because "real" war is costly and messy, it has become necessary to find a means of managing wayward parties who fall out of line and violate the principles of a world order whose form and rules are not always so clear. So, even as neighbors in far-away countries slaughter each other with clubs and machetes, the tools of future wars between the United States and unpredictable aggressors are on display in *Time*, *Newsweek*, *The Economist*, and on CNN. I call this *disciplinary deterrence*.

Disciplinary deterrence is executed through demonstration, through publicity, through punishment. It is a means of engaging in war without the discomforts or dangers of battle. It relies on imagined rather than actual warfare, on the dissemination of detailed information about military capabilities rather than on their actual exercise in combat, on the proliferation of the image rather than the application of capabilities. It is a child of the media age, taking advantage of rapid communication and virtual simulations that look all too real. It communicates a none-too-subtle message to potential miscreants. Finally, in its application to Iraq and more recently, Yugoslavia, disciplinary deterrence warns others to stay in line (see chapter 7). There are other benefits to be had from disciplinary deterrence, too. Expenditures on high-tech equipment and strategies bolster local economies in important congressional districts while reducing the demand for combat forces (see Rochlin, 1997: chaps. 8–10; Kotz, 1988).

For the United States, the costs of disciplinary deterrence are relatively low. The military equipment is in hand, because the defense sector cannot be downsized any further without serious political costs. Those in charge of the communications infrastructure, both military and civilian, are only too happy to report on the amazing feats of which the technology is capable (even if the information offered is not always correct). And the elites of all countries—even "rogue states"—pay close attention to CNN and other media outlets in order to keep up with cultural and political attitudes and activities in the United States.

The required publicity about the technology (although not about tactics or intelligence) illustrates an emerging paradox associated with disciplinary deterrence and warfare: Whereas countries once tried to keep their military capabilities a secret, so as not to alert or alarm real or potential enemies, it has now become common practice to reveal such capabilities, in order to spread fear and foster caution. A typical example of this can be found in advertisements that regularly appear in *The Economist*. These are, presumably, read by elites and militaries the world over. Northrop Grumman tells the reader about "information warfare . . . *the ability to exploit, deceive and disrupt adversary information systems while simultaneously protecting our own.* Example: EA-6B Prowler" (emphasis in original).

Continues the advertisement

> In the future, conflicts will be resolved with information as well as hardware. Northrop Grumman has the capability to create and integrate advanced Information Warfare technologies, such as electronic countermeasures and sensors. Northrop Grumann. Systems integration, defense electronics, military aircraft, precision weapons, commercial and military aerostructures. The right technologies. Right now.

Accompanying the text is a shadow of an "EA-6B Prowler" superimposed over an unidentfied landscape of land and water. The message? "(Y)our bomb here." With sophisticated computer graphics lending verisimilitude to the scene, the weapons are once again used without ever being fired.

The epistemological flaw in disciplinary warfare is that there is no here there. For the most part, disciplinary warfare is conducted against imagined enemies, with imaginary capabilities and the assumed worst of intentions. As pointed out earlier, where these enemies might choose to issue a challenge, or why, is not at all evident (while their failure to issue a challenge is likely to be interpreted as "disciplinary deterrence works!"). The only apparent reasoning is that we have what they want and they are going to try to get it. Projection is a weak reed on which to base policy or procurement. ⟶ *And eventual cause to modern day war.*

In retrospect, the Central Command can be seen as the United States' first effort at conventional disciplinary deterrence. As I suggested above, disciplinary deterrence is a fairly recent innovation; prior to the 1950s, wars between countries were fought to retake lost territory or acquire new land. The advent of nuclear weapons, and their potential to destroy that which they were meant to protect, made large-scale mass warfare highly risky, if not obsolete (Mueller, 1989). But, even smaller-scale wars, such as that in Vietnam or Afghanistan, came to be less about territory or restoration of a status quo ante than about the imposition of a particular moral order on the local parties. ⟶ *US today*

Disciplinary Deterrence not effective against current enemies in postmodern warfare.

The apotheosis of the disciplinary approach to war may have taken place in 1991 therefore, when the American military machine, in concert with the other members of the "coalition," ousted the Iraqi army from Kuwait without eliminating the regime that had violated the rules (a feat repeated in the Balkans in 1999). The Bush administration argued that the risk of Iraq's fragmenting was too great to engage in social engineering within that country, and that a collapse of the regional "balance" could set off a land rush by predatory neighbors. Perhaps.

More to the point, ever since that time, Iraq has existed in a state of limited sovereignty, as a zone of discipline and domination that the United States holds in semilegal bondage. The creation of "no-fly zones" in Iraq's northern and southern regions, the constant surveillance of the country by satellites and spy planes, the regular (attempted) inspections of its industrial facilities by UN representatives, the repeated vetoes on the restoration of even limited trade privileges, and the periodic bombings have all reduced Iraq to a region over which the United States exercises a suzerainty that extends even to domestic affairs. But Iraq also fulfills a demonstration function, illustrating to other rogues and adventurers their fate should they get out of line. Even Iraq's resistance plays into this game. Each time UN inspectors are prevented from going about their work, the United States begins, once again, to threaten punishment and war.[11]

This helps to explain, for example, the odd events of September 1996, when fighting took place in the Kurdish region in the north, while the United States loosed its cruise missiles on Iraqi radar stations in the south (it also explains the largely ineffective four-day bombing of December 1998). The U.S. response is best understood not as retaliation for the Iraqi "invasion" of the Kurdish zone, but rather as a punishment inflicted by the international equivalent of a high-school vice principal, intended not just merely to hurt Saddam Hussein but also to issue a warning to others who might think of stepping out of line. "We can do this with impunity," the White House might have been saying, "You can run, but you cannot hide." The demonstration has become more important than the effect. The loss of such opportunities would constitute a severe blow to U.S. policy (such as it is).

W(h)ither War?

World War III has come and gone. Some of us didn't even notice. Yet its implements are still with us. Indeed, inasmuch as their production is essential to the economies of many countries, they continue to proliferate at an accelerating rate. What is the purpose of such weapons, if not to wage shooting wars? War is costly in terms of lives lost and capital destroyed, but peace has its own costs in terms of politics and power. Interstate wars will come and go, no doubt, but not nearly as often as some might believe. Still, the true believers can argue that the absence of such conflicts after the Gulf War of 1991 is proof positive that deterrence "works" and that the electronic battlefield, even when restricted to computer and TV screens, will help to "keep the peace."

But postmodern war is not about the borders between states or even imaginary civilizations; as I proposed in chapter 3, it is about those difficult-to-see boundaries between and among individuals and groups. Who draws these lines? Who makes them significant? If they cannot be mapped, how can they be controlled? And what about the wars wracking so many far-away places? As we shall see in subsequent chapters, war as a disciplinary exercise is not limited to the international realm or those living in "failed states"; it includes in its application those at home, too.

5❖
MARKETS, THE STATE, AND WAR

According to a study published in 1995 by the World Bank, the "Wars of the next century will be over water" (*The Economist* 1995b).[1] Perhaps. Such warnings are not new. By now, the invocation of "water wars" is a commonplace, as a search of any bibliographic database will attest.[2] The Bank, however, conveys special authority with its pronouncements, both because of its international standing as well as its long involvement in the planning and development of "water resources management." Not only does the Bank rely on "experts" who are presumed to know everything there is to know about water and its use, as a central icon of the global economic system *and* a major funder of large-scale water supply systems, it must also be listened to, especially by those who may feel themselves short of water. But the Bank's analysis leaves a number of questions unanswered or, at least, unsatisfactorily addressed.

For instance, *who* will fight over water? According to *The Economist* (1995b), wherein appeared an article on the study, the Bank's experts, and most other water scholars, believe that

> the Middle East is the likeliest crucible for future water wars. A
> long-term settlement between Israel and its neighbors will depend

at least as much on fair allocation of water as of land. Egypt fears
appropriation of the Nile's waters . . . by upstream Sudan and
Ethiopia. Iraq and Syria watch and wait as Turkey builds dams in
the headwaters of the Euphrates.

It is clear that the combatants will be states.

But *why* would states fight over water? On this point, the Bank's
reasoning is less clear. On the one hand, it is taken for granted that
water is scarce in absolute terms, and that *people* and *states* (according
to conventional economic and political analysis) naturally come into
conflict over scarce resources.[3] On the other hand, geography (or, to
be more precise, Nature) has not seen fit to have rivers, drainages, and
mountains remain constrained within the confines of national boundaries. Indeed, rivers act as excellent borders between countries because
they are such prominent geographic features and are difficult to cross—
although it is true that they have a tendency to wander back and forth,
now and again. Nonetheless, the combination of geopolitical and neoclassical logics leads to the conclusion that, if resources are essential,
scarce, and "in the wrong place," states that *lack* them will go to war
with states that *have* them.[4] QED.

What, then, is the solution offered by the Bank? *Markets in
water.* But here emerges a paradox. First, we are warned of potential
struggles over Nature's scarcity and the possibility of war between
sovereign entities. Then, quite suddenly, we are transported from the
"State of Nature" to the nature of markets. In Nature, people fight and
often come out losers; in markets, they bargain according to self-
interest and come out winners. Thus, according to the Bank's Vice-
President for the Environment, the avoidance of water wars is to be
found in what he calls "rational water management"—that is, in the
transmogrification of economics from a doctrine of absolute scarcity
and consequent conflict arising from the maldistribution of state *sovereignty* over resources to one of relative scarcity and *exchange* of
resources—in this instance, money and water—between sovereign
consumers in peaceful markets.

How is this amazing transformation of interstate relations to be
accomplished? Quite simply: through the "appropriate pricing" of water
at its "true" marginal cost—although it is seldom noted that the "true"
marginal cost of water to people defending the national patrimony

may be incalculable. This move, argues the Bank, will lead to the assumption of water's "proper place as an economically valued and traded commodity" which, in turn, will result in efficient and sustainable use through technologies of conservation. As the author of the *Economist* article puts it (with no sense of irony whatsoever), "the time is coming when water must be treated as a valuable resource, like oil, not a free one like air." Not, perhaps, an ideal parallel—especially insofar as the Persian Gulf War was more about the political impacts of oil prices than absolute supply (Lipschutz, 1992a, 1992b)—but the point is well taken: it is probably better to truck and barter in natural resources than it is to fight for them—*if* these are the only choices available.

The Bank's program for peace is based, of course, on a neoliberal economic framework; indeed, recalling the injunction of Franklin Roosevelt's secretary of state, Cordell Hull, one might say "if water does not cross borders, soldiers will." Trade is offered here as the solution to imagined wars, as a way to prevent conflicts that threaten but have not yet (and might never) occur.[5] Yet, is it not conceivable that prognostications that predict water wars could drive the contending parties to another form of market-based exchange—in weapons—thereby heightening tension among them and bringing the prophecy to fulfillment? Or is it true that discourses do not kill people; people kill people?

In this chapter, I examine the prospect of "resource wars," a topic often framed as "environment and security" or "conflict and the environment" (see, e.g., Gleditsch, 1997). I first present an exegesis of the "nature of sovereignty and the sovereignty of nature," with particular reference to geopolitical discourses of sovereignty, scarcity, and security offered from the late nineteenth to the late twentieth century. I begin with a brief examination of the ideas of the classical geopolitical scholars—Mahan, Mackinder, Spykman, Gray—and the ways in which they sought to *naturalize* the relationship between geography and state power in order to legitimate efforts to redress scarcity through military means.

I then turn to a discussion of sovereignty and property. I argue that sovereignty is best understood as a mode of *exclusion*, as a way to draw boundaries and establish rights of property against those who would transgress against the sovereign state. Paradoxically, perhaps, although sovereignty is at the core of the state system, its exclusivity sets up the very dilemmas of control and scarcity that geopolitics finds so problematic and conducive to struggle.

The solution to this geopolitical dilemma was (and is) reliance on yet another naturalizing discourse, that of the *market*. Markets require the uneven distribution of resources and goods in order to function properly. Indeed, Malthus may have been "right," as one environmentalist bumpersticker claims, but scarcity, as we define it today, is a necessary condition for markets and property rights to function. For better or worse, however, neomercantilist power politics stands in the way of free exchange. What then to do?

Following World War II, the diffusion of "embedded liberalism" by the United States throughout the world helped to disseminate a new geopolitics that has, more recently, come to rely on the concept of *interdependence* in order to maintain the fiction, if not the fact, of political sovereignty. In recent years, as a result, we have seen the emergence of discussions of, on the one hand, "limits to growth" and "sustainability" and, on the other, "environment and security," both the direct descendants of earlier geopolitical discourses. As such, these discourses assume or attempt to reinstate sovereign boundaries where, perhaps, none should exist.

Geopolitics and "Natural Selection"

Scholars of the "science" of geopolitics believed that national autonomy and control were to be valued above all, and that to rely on the goodwill of others, or the "proper" functioning of international markets, was to court national disaster. Besides, territories could not be bought and sold; as parts of integral nation-states, they might be wrested or stolen in battle, but they were not for sale at any price.[6] Classical geopolitics was a product of its time, the Age of Imperialism and Social Darwinism, not the more-contemporary Ages of Liberalism and Ecology (which are, nevertheless, related ideologies). It is no coincidence that the best-known progenitors of geopolitics were citizens of those Great Powers—Britain, Germany, the United States— who sought to legitimate international expansion and control through naturalized ideological covers.

Classical geopolitics regarded the power, prosperity, and prospects of a state as fixed by geography and determined by inherent geographical features that could not be changed.[7] As Nicholas J. Spykman (1942:41) put it,

> Power is in the last instance the ability to wage successful war, and in geography lies the clues to the problems of military and political strategy. The territory of a state is the base from which it operates in time of war and the strategic position which it occupies during the temporary armistice called peace. . . . Ministers come and ministers go, even dictators die, but mountain ranges stand unperturbed.

To give some of these scholars their due, not all treated geography as so fully binding on state autonomy and action. Halford Mackinder (1919/1962), an Englishman, was initially less of a geopolitical determinist than the American Spykman (1942; 1944). But World War II hardened the views of both, inasmuch as Germany's efforts to expand appeared to vindicate Mackinder's dictum about "heartland" and "rimland" powers (a dialectic later picked up by Colin Gray).[8] Following World War II, a more vulgar geopolitical determinism came to dominate much realist theorizing as well as foreign policy analysis (Lipschutz, 1989; Dalby, 1990), rooted in no small degree in the sentiments of George Kennan's "Long Telegram" (Gaddis, 1982).

Such determinism became a routine part of every document to emerge from U.S. councils of strategy and counsels of war. A not untypical example can be found in NSC 94, "The Position of the United States with Respect to the Philippines":

> From the viewpoint of the USSR, the Philippine Islands could be the key to Soviet control of the Far East inasmuch as Soviet domination of these islands would, in all probability, be followed by the rapid disintegration of the entire structure of anti-Communist defenses in Southeast Asia and their offshore island chain, including Japan. Therefore, the situation in the Philippines cannot be viewed as a local problem, since Soviet domination over these islands would endanger the United States' military position in the Western Pacific and the Far East (cited in Lipschutz, 1989:103).

More recently, Colin Gray (1988:15), quite possibly the last of
the classical geopoliticians, argued that

> because it is rooted in geopolitical soil, the character of a country's
> national security policy—as contrasted with the strategy and means
> of implementation—tends to show great continuity over time,
> although there can be an *apparently* cyclical pattern of change.

If Gray's claim is correct, the facts of national fate are written in
Nature. At the risk of national (or natural) disaster, there cannot be,
and must not be, any struggle against such facts. Gray simply takes
boundaries—in this case, those between the United States and the
Soviet Union that, three years later, would cease to exist—as given
and as "natural" as the "geopolitical soil" in which they are drawn. (In
a subsequent book, Gray naturalizes *culture* as a product of geography
in order to warn that the United States, as a maritime power, must
remain on guard against Russia, a "heartland" power; see Gray, 1990.)[9]

The Age of Imperialism was also the age of Social Darwinism,
as noted earlier, rooted in Charles Darwin's ideas about natural selection, but extended from individual organisms as members of species to
states. John Agnew and Stuart Corbridge (1995:57) argue that

> naturalized geopolitics [from 1875 to 1945] had the following
> principal characteristics: a world divided into imperial and colo-
> nized peoples, states with "biological needs" for territory/resources
> and outlets for enterprise, a "closed" world in which one state's
> political-economic success was at another's expense . . . , and a
> world of fixed geographical attributes and environmental condi-
> tions that had predictable effects on a state's global status.

According to German philosophers, states could be seen as "natural"
organisms that passed through specific stages of life. As a result,
younger, more energetic states would succeed older, geriatric ones on
the world stage. In order not to succumb prematurely to this cycle of
Nature, therefore, states must continually seek advantage over others.[10]

As Simon Dalby (1990:35) puts it

> [S]tates were conceptualized in terms of organic entities with
> quasi-biological functioning. This was tied into Darwinian ideas

of struggle producing progress. Thus, expansion was likened to growth and territorial expansion was *ipso facto* a good thing.

British and American geopoliticians held a somewhat different perspective, seeing progress tied to "mastery of the physical world" through science and technological innovation (for more recent invocations of this idea, see Simon, 1981, 1996; Homer-Dixon, 1995). But Nature was still heavily determining:

> [B]efore the First World War, the current European geopolitical vision linked the success of European civilization to a combination of temperate climate and access to the sea. Temperate climate encouraged the inhabitants to struggle to overcome adversity without totally exhausting their energies, hence allowing progress and innovation to lead to social development. Access to the sea encouraged exploration, expansion and trade, and led ultimately to the conquest of the rest of the world. (Dalby, 1990:35)

Both perspectives—organic and innovative—helped to legitimate imperial expansion, colonialism, and conquest. The "life cycle" argument demanded adequate access to the material resources and space necessary to maintain national vitality—hence the German demand for colonies and, later, *Lebensraum*. The "struggle to survive" required both overseas outposts and physical position to command the vital geographic features that would provide natural advantage to those who held them—hence, British garrisons from Gibraltar to Hong Kong, the Canal Zone and Philippines under American suzerainty, French control of North Africa.

Geopolitics was a "science" well-suited to the neomercantilism and gold standard of the late nineteenth and early twentieth centuries. One hundred years of industrialization in Europe had provided the impetus to policies of state development as well as territorial unification under the rubric of "nation." Each nation was the autochthonous offspring of the land where it lived—which created problems for those nations, such as the Germans, who were scattered throughout Central and Eastern Europe. Thus the national territory was not only sacred but "natural." Only those within the natural borders of the nation-state could be mobilized to serve it and only those who were naturalized—that is loyal to the nation-state—could be relied on to support it. It is no accident that borders, so fluid during the age of sovereigns, became rigid, with passports required, during the age of sovereignty.

The ethnic cleansings and population transfers of the twentieth century illustrate this point. Woodrow Wilson's doctrine of national self-determination helped to further this process by extending the mythic principle of organic nation to all those who could establish a recognized claim to such status. Where competing claims arose within specific territories, the strong tried to assimilate, eliminate, or expel the weaker (see chapter 6). We continue to observe this process in many places around the world, even as markets have rendered borders porous and control over them problematic (see, e.g., Strange, 1996). Indeed, as I have suggested in earlier chapters, the "culture wars" that have spread through a number of industrialized countries over the past decade are as much about restoring the mental borders of the nation as it is about expelling those with alien ideas and identities (Lipschutz, 1998b). Passports can be falsified; "true" beliefs cannot.

The fundamental erosion of state sovereigny by markets is nowhere seen more clearly than in the realm of genetics, where the geopolitical discourse of states has been transformed into a "geopolitics of the body." The invocation of Nature to demonstrate the superiority of human groups is not a new phenomenon, and can be traced at least as far back as the ancient Greeks. During the past one hundred years, Darwin's theories of evolution were used to legitimate the genetic superiority of some races and nations over others. The latter form of naturalization was greatly delegitimated as a result of its application by the enthusiasts of eugenics, but it has reemerged in a somewhat different form over the past twenty years or so in efforts to link IQ to academic and financial success (e.g., Herrenstein and Murray, 1994). This new genre of naturalization—genetic determinism—has developed as both science and ideology, and its parallels to older geopolitical and organic theories of nation and nationalism are worth noting.

The contemporary scientific basis for genetic determinism is found in the various research efforts that seek to understand the basis for various congenital diseases and inherited characteristics, culminating in the Human Genome Project (Wingerson, 1991). The ideological manifestation, however, reflects a virtually pure version of liberal methodological individualism in its framing, to wit, an individual's potential is almost wholly inherent in her/his genetic inheritance. Twin and sibling studies seem to suggest that society and environment are at best minor contributors to that potential, with the result that, in effect, one is already of the "elect" at birth (so one would do well to be careful in choosing one's parents; Dahlem Workshop, 1993; but see also Harris, 1998).

As is true with geography and the state, an individual's "natural" inheritance is critical to that person's development. But the ways in which this particular (and not terribly innovative) insight is being used politically are rather alarming.[11] In particular, genetic determinism is helping to reinstantiate a vulgar Hobbesian-genetic "war of all against all," in which the individual has no one to blame but herself for anything that might befall her in the marketplace of life. Inasmuch as the state has been banished from this realm (except as a declining source of research funds), there is no one to turn to for protection against predation by others with superior genetic endowments or sufficient cash (Hanley, 1996). Another version of this ideology extrapolates natural inheritance back to race and ethnicity, arguing that society has no responsibility to redress historical inequities inasmuch as these are largely genetic in origin. Again, it is sink or swim in the genetic marketplace.

In this world of hyperliberal Nature, as a result, a new form of sovereignty accrues to the individual. Here, control is exercised by those with good genes—which are scarce—or those who have the wealth to acquire them via the purchase of new medical techniques. Because in the marketplace, wealth is power, money is also the key to preventing oneself from being contaminated by "bad" genes carried by the poor, the ill, the defective, or the alien. Such quality is transmitted, of course, into one's offspring. As with classical geopolitics, the naturalized discourse of genetics follows the dominant ideology of the day and, in some of its more extreme expressions, involves an almost complete move of the "natural rights" associated with sovereignty *from* the state *to* the individual. The result is that sovereignty as an attribute of the state is disintegrating in both material and ideational terms.

Sovereignty, Property, Interdependence

What, exactly, is "sovereignty"? Although the term continues to be the focus of vociferous controversy (Biersteker and Weber, 1996; Litfin,

1998)—especially as it appears to many to be "eroding"—here I follow Nicholas Onuf's (1989) lead and conceptualize it as a property of *liberalism*. Onuf cites C. B. Mcpherson's description in this regard:

> The individual is free inasmuch as he is the proprietor of his person and capacities. The human essence is freedom from dependence on the will of others, and freedom is a function of possession. Society has a lot of free individuals related to each other as proprietors of their own capacities and of what they have acquired by their exercise. (Mcpherson, 1962:2, quoted in Onuf, 1989:165)

Onuf (1989:166) points out that "States are granted just those properties that liberalism grants to individuals," among which are real estate, or property (this is easier to understand if we recall that, for the original sovereigns of the seventeenth century, states *were* property; see Elias, 1994). In a liberal system, individuals holding property are entitled to use it in any fashion except that which is deemed harmful to the interests or welfare of the community (Libecap, 1989; Ruggie, 1993). Indeed, this is precisely the wording of Principle 21 of the Stockholm Declaration: States have the right to exploit their own resources so long as this does not impact on the sovereignty of other states by constituting an illegal intrusion into the jurisdictional space of other states.[12] What this implies, therefore, is not only that sovereignty over property is important, so also are the boundaries constituting property. Inside the boundaries of property, the state, like the individual landowner, is free from "dependence on the will of others"; outside the boundaries, it is not. That, at least, is the theory.

Practice is quite different. The individual property owner finds *her* sovereignty not only hedged about with restrictions but also subject to frequent intrusion due to others' wills. Indeed, the state has the prerogative of violating the sovereignty of individual private property in any number of settings and ways. These can range from investigations into the commission of crimes on, in, or through the use of specific personal or real property, to the creation of public rights-of-way for highways, pipelines, and communication cables, to the taking of property in the greater social "interest"—subject, of course, to just compensation (markets are involved only so far as setting the "value" of the property is concerned). In these situations, an owner of affected property has little recourse except to courts (or rebellion). Such is the power of law.

The state, by contrast, has freed itself from such legal niceties through the fictions of international "anarchy" and "self-help," which comprise the essential elements of the doctrine we call *realism*. This permits the state to physically resist violations of its property, on the one hand, while declaring a national "interest" in violating the property of (usually) weaker states, on the other. Realism and national interests legitimate a state's right to transgress boundaries, notwithstanding the Stockholm declaration and other international laws of a similar bent.

For reasons that are beyond the scope of this chapter, egregious physical violations of territorial property and sovereignty are increasingly frowned on (Jackson, 1990). This has not, however, led to a diminution in violations of sovereignty; it simply means that such violations are legitimated under other names or processes (Inayatullah, 1996). Recall, for example, that the distribution of resources among states is uneven, a condition often blamed on Nature and geography, with the result that one state finds itself needing to acquire such resources through interaction with another. This state of affairs is sometimes characterized as *ecological interdependence*, a situation whereby state borders, characterized as "natural" under sovereignty and anarchy, fail to correspond to those of physical and biological nature (Lipschutz and Conca, 1993). It is the tension between the sovereignty of Territory and the sovereignty of Nature that sets up the basis for problems such as "water wars" in the first place. Below, I will examine the concept of ecological interdependence more closely; here, I only point out that, while it is often taken to describe a physical phenomenon—the existence of ecological phenomena or ecosystems extending across national borders—the term may actually serve to obscure relations of domination and subordination between the states in question.[13]

As the Nazi finance minister, Count von Krosigk, put it in 1935,

> If we fail to obtain through larger exports the larger imports of foreign raw materials required for our greatly increased domestic employment, then two courses only are open to us, increased home production or the demand for a share in districts from which we can get our raw materials ourselves. (Quoted in Royal Institute of International Affairs, 1936)

Inasmuch as rights of property inherent in state sovereignty reify the possession or control of a resource, neighboring states who may find the resource "scarce" for lack of access to or control of it also find themselves in a condition of relative powerlessness with respect to it. Their only recourse in such a situation is to physically capture the resource or to purchase property rights to it and thereby "legally" come to control it.

Scarcity and the "Limits to Growth"

There is no need to recount in detail the geneology of "scarcity" as a concept (even Thucydides mentions it; see 1954:10; also Dalby, 1995); suffice it to say that it is central to the theory and practice of neoclassical liberal economics. Here, I want to consider the relationship between scarcity and *boundaries* or, rather, between the conditions that differentiate *absolute* from *relative* scarcity, and the politics associated with both. Historically, people responded to a lack of food and water in a specific location, due to drought or war, by moving. But, while such conditions might lead to localized conflict or social instability, it is less clear that such deficiencies were causal factors in organized violence or war. The starving are rarely strong enough to wage war, and soldiers and guerillas cannot fight if they are weak from hunger (as evidenced by reports concerning the distribution of scarce food supplies in famine-ridden North Korea). Revolutions and rebellions are led by those who are better off and, we can presume, lacking neither for food nor water in absolute terms.

    Continuing the argument made above, therefore, relative scarcity can be seen as a product of control, of ownership, of property, of sovereignty, of markets. Economists tell us that absolute scarcity does not—indeed, cannot—occur if and when markets are operating properly, and that all scarcity is relative. Thus, in an "efficient" market, free of political intervention, when the supply of some good runs low, its price will rise and people will seek less expensive substitutes.[14] Doomsayers, such as the Reverend Malthus and the Professors Meadows and Ehrlich, have thus been attacked for ignoring the rules of supply and demand (Simon, 1996). But if we insert boundaries into our equation, it turns out that the doomsayers do have something germane to say.

Malthus (1803) was a prophet of absolute scarcity. As is well known, he argued that geometric population growth would eventually outstrip the arithmetic growth of agricultural production. This would result in circumstances whereby food would run short in absolute terms, leading to widespread starvation and death. His analysis has been—and continues to be—criticized for not taking into account either basic economics or technological innovation, but these criticisms are not very fair. As a cleric, Malthus was undoubtedly more interested in distribution than in markets or capital and, from a strictly ecological perspective, he *was* right: when food runs short, populations crash.[15] But it is less than clear that, for human societies, such crashes can be described as "natural." Most animal populations have recourse neither to markets nor the means of moving food from one place to another. *They* can move or change foods, of course, but if all neighboring niches are occupied and alternative foods are being consumed by others, the game may well be up.[16]

A similar notion of absolute scarcity was promulgated several centuries later by Dennis and Donella Meadows and their colleagues (Meadows, et al., 1972; Meadows, Meadows, and Randers, 1992) at MIT. They concluded that, given then-current trends in nonrenewable resource production, reserves, and consumption, and barring unforeseen circumstances or discoveries, the world would run short of various critical materials sometime during the twenty-first century. Meadows and his colleagues were also harshly attacked for ignoring the same factors as did Malthus. To the satisfaction of many, they were soon "proved wrong" by events. Even today, economists still take pleasure in pointing this out but, again, there was a sense in which the Meadowsists were not really interested in ecology, economics, or innovation, either.

What both crude Malthusianism and more sophisticated Meadowsism disregarded was the matter of distribution of resources—that is, for *whom* would food and minerals be scarce? And why would such scarcity matter? Certainly, it is by no means clear that the depletion of global cobalt supplies would matter as much to Chinese peasants as Cambridge academics. For this error, in any event, Meadows and his colleagues should be forgiven; economists tend to dismiss the same point, too, regarding distribution as a problem outside of their realm of concern and one that, in any event, can be addressed by economic growth. Their supply and demand curves do no more than illustrate the premise that, if scarcity drives prices rise too high relative to demand, markets will be out of equilibrium and no one will buy. Eventually, sellers will have to lower their prices, and buyers will be able to eat again.

The reality is slightly more complicated, inasmuch as even properly functioning markets can foster maldistribution and relative scarcity. As Jean Dreze and Amartya Sen (1989; see also Sen 1994) have pointed out, not everyone starves during a famine—indeed, food is often quite plentiful. What crude market analyses don't take into account is that, even at market equilibrium, there may be those for whom prices are still too high. Those who have money can afford to buy, those who do not, starve. Scarcity is only relative in this instance, but some people (and countries) do go hungry.

In other words, relative scarcity is also a condition of *boundaries*, in this instance political, cultural or social ones. In some instances, these lines are found between the physical personas of individuals: I am of one caste (class, ethnie, religion); you are of another. My money and food are mine (or of my group), not yours (or your group's). In other cases, the lines are drawn between countries: this land (and water) is ours, not yours. At both extremes, the money, food, land, water, and whatever else must be kept *inside that boundary* in order to maintain individual and collective integrity, identity, and sovereignty—that is,

> if I give you my money, so that you can buy food, I will have less and will not be able to live the way to which I am accustomed. This will lessen me. In doing this, I will also acknowledge a relationship with you that infringes on me and even acknowledges my obligations to you. If I do this, then I will not be who I have been because I will have yielded some of my autonomy to you. Moreover, because you have no money, you cannot buy from me; and because I have as much as I need, I don't have to buy from you. Hence, I can remain sovereign and strong.

Or

> If we give you our water, so that you can grow food, we will have less and will not be able to live the way in which we have been

accustomed. Then we will not be who we have been because we will have yielded some of our sovereignty to you. This will make us weaker.

In other words, the resources must remain *sovereign property*. The transfer of *anything* across a boundary—whether physical, political, social, cultural, or economic—serves to acknowledge the existence of a legitimate Other and thereby lessens sovereignty—that is, control and autonomy, whether individual or collective—in an absolute sense. It also creates social relations between and among actors that have little or nothing to do with markets or anarchy (but, see Wendt, 1992).

This is to say that sovereignty, whether individual or national, is about exclusion, autonomy, and keeping the Other out, both physically and mentally. It is also why uneven distribution is so central to international politics: it helps to perpetuate the hierarchy of power that, notwithstanding the acrobatics of neorealists, are central to international politics. That was the purpose of the princes' agreement at Westphalia; that is the point of the reification of methodological individualism today. Inside my boundary, I/we can act as we wish; outside of it, I/we can't. By redrawing or, in some circumstances, abolishing lines, we could change this premise, but that would mean sharing what we have with others and having less for ourselves. *It would change us.*

This is why autarchy—the abolition of relative scarcity through a redrawing of lines of control—was long the dream of realists and policymakers. But autarchy is economically costly and markets are politically costly. *Interdependence*, whether economic, ecological, or military, is one way of finessing this problem without redrawing boundaries, yielding sovereignty, or changing identity.

Embedded Liberalism and Interdependence

As I noted in chapter 3, after 1945 the United States found it useful to create the "Free World" in order to propagate economic liberalism beyond national markets. But creating such an imagined community was a difficult proposition. To institutionalize liberalism throughout the American sphere of influence required that states yield some portion of their individual sovereignty in two ways, both in the name of democracy and prosperity: to the systemic level, in the name of defense and free markets, and to the individual level, in the name of human rights and exchange in the market. The first move constrained states from asserting too strongly their autonomy and defecting from the Free World by offering them increased wealth and the threat of helplessness if they tried to defect. The second strengthened the bonds of interest between the Free World, as an emergent natural community, and sovereign individuals by offering the same.

Conditions within this Free World economic area did not constitute "interdependence" as that concept was eventually articulated; rather, they were a manifestation of the Gramscian hegemony of the United States (Augelli and Murphy, 1988; Gill, 1993). The geopolitical discourse developed during the 1970s and 1980s to explain the conditions of the 1950s and 1960s invoked "hegemonic stability theory" to explain why this condition was good and right (Kindleberger, 1973; Gilpin, 1981; Keohane, 1984; Kennedy, 1988). It is helpful to jump ahead of our story for a moment to consider the "double hermeneutic" of hegemony.[17] Originally, the concept was formulated as a term of socialist opprobrium, and used primarily by the Peoples' Republic of China against both the United States and the USSR, but during the period between about 1975 and 1988, which corresponded to the period of generalized worries about American decline (Kennedy, 1988; Nye, 1990), hegemony was naturalized and given positive attributes.

A "hegemon" now became a state destined for power and dominance as a result of the "natural" cycles of history and global political economy, and that took on the burdens of global economic and political management under anarchy (a description that, quite logically, fit the United States; see, e.g., Goldstein, 1988). The hegemon did this through the establishment of international regimes (Krasner, 1983) and, in so doing, served not only its own interests, first and foremost, but also those of allied countries, who were nonetheless free-riding on the hegemon. Under the skillful hands of non-Marxist scholars of international political economy (Gilpin, 1981), domination was thereby transmuted into a kind of benevolent stewardship—although some of these same scholars worried about what might happen to this particular world order "After Hegemony" (Keohane, 1984). The free riders, however, failed to appreciate the benefits and their good fortune in acquiescing to U.S. "leadership" (Strange, 1983) and, Americans argued, their reluctance to share the burden played a major role in the political disorder of the 1970s and the renewed Soviet threat during of the 1980s. Ungrateful wretches! The United States—the champion and protector of naturally free men [sic] and markets—had only the best interests of its allies in mind when it manipulated, disciplined, or coerced them.

"Interdependence theory," most closely associated with Robert O. Keohane and Joseph S. Nye Jr., was an academic product of the times (the 1970s) and its politics (the energy crisis), rather than an "objective" description or model of "reality." On the one hand, interdependence theory tried to account for what seemed to be the end of American hegemony over the Free World, after the dollar devaluations, the end of dollar convertibility to gold, and the oil embargo of the early 1970s. On the other hand, it sought to justify certain policies and actions that might otherwise be politically unpopular at home and abroad. But, whereas hegemony theory derived in large part from realism, interdependence theory was liberal in origin (although, as Robert Keohane (1984) has demonstrated time and again, the two are perfectly compatible).

Indeed, in their 1977 book Keohane and Nye proposed that "Interdependence in world politics refers to situations characterized by reciprocal effects among countries or actors in different countries" (1978/1989:8) What did they mean by "reciprocal effects"? Writing toward the end of the 1970s, in the aftermath of the first runup in oil prices, they clearly had the distribution problem in mind. The United States no longer owned sufficient oil under its private sovereignty, within its national boundaries, at an acceptable price; others owned too much and were offering it at too high a price. No one paid attention to the reciprocal effects on others of *too much* oil at *too low* a price, a condition that led originally to the establishment of OPEC in the early 1960s, some decades later to the Gulf War of 1990-91 (Lipschutz, 1989:129),[18] and that has since resulted in the disappearance of several of the Seven Sisters (the major oil companies). For the United States, the "reciprocal effect" was primarily a problem of *domestic* politics, the threat of a disgruntled electorate forced to queue and pay twice or thrice the accustomed price for a gallon of gas. A few hot-headed analysts and policymakers proposed taking the oil back, inasmuch as it was "ours." Cooler heads prevailed, but the United States was no longer the same nation as it had been prior to 1973.

Keohane and Nye further distinguished between sensitivity and vulnerability. If you are *sensitive*, they said, you feel the pain of an action by another but you can recover—that is, through adaptation you can eliminate the temporary infringement on your autonomy, sovereignty, and identity imposed by others. Then it is back to business as usual. If you are *vulnerable*, however, you feel the pain but cannot recover—your autonomy and sovereignty have been breached for good and *you* have been changed. You are now constrained within a relationship with the Other that, as much as you might dislike it, has served to establish a new element of your identity in terms of the Other (Wendt, 1992; Mercer, 1995). To be sure, such a merging of identities can exacerbate the sense of those differences that remain, a phenomenon most evident in the clash between religious fundamentalisms and human secularisms. But the two identities have become mutually constitutive, not oppositional; as with an old married couple, neither can maintain her/his identity unbound from the other. By contrast, *interdependence* connotes transactions across boundaries and, consequently, some degree of separateness. To speak, then, of interdependence is to make an effort to eliminate the breaches in boundaries between oneself and others—through markets, if at all possible—rather than to adapt to this new condition of mutual constitution.[19]

Whatever the merits of the distinction made by Keohane and Nye, however, both sensitivity and vulnerability posit impacts across borders, infringements on autonomy, and reductions in sovereignty. To eliminate either type of intrusion, adjustments must occur *inside* the boundaries—in the realm of domestic politics—so that the boundaries can be restored. Hence the contradiction: interdependence is acceptable if it allows us to maintain the boundaries and our national sovereignty; unacceptable if it does not. At best, this is a word game, at worst, a form of false consciousness that serves to perpetuate domination. Or, as Edward Said has written,

> [T]his universal practice of designating in one's mind a familiar space which is "ours" and an unfamiliar space beyond "ours" which is theirs is a way of making geographical distinctions that can be entirely arbitrary. (Said, 1979:54, quoted in Dalby, 1990:20)

In this manner lines are drawn around "natural" communities—that is, ones united by characteristics or culture whose origins are, supposedly, lost in history—alienated from one another by virtues of these differences.

Keohane and Nye (1977/1989:7) acknowledged (but deplored) the ideological content of the concept of interdependence when they wrote:

> Political leaders often use interdependence rhetoric to portray interdependence as a natural necessity, as a fact to which policy (and domestic interest groups) must adjust, rather than as a situation partially created by policy itself. . . . For those who wish the United States to retain world leadership, interdependence has become part of the new rhetoric, *to be used against both economic nationalism at home and assertive challenges abroad.* (Emphasis added)

Paradoxically, perhaps, the rhetoric and theory of interdependence was also intended to reinforce boundaries without sealing them off as those at home and abroad might wish. The unit of analysis remained the sovereign state; the impacts posited by Keohane and Nye impinged on states rather than individuals, classes, or other groupings; the responses would be taken by policymakers in the "national interest."

Consequently, political policies in response to these effects took the form of state-led actions. Thus, for example, the oil embargo of 1973 and subsequent price hikes were presented as being directed against countries and their citizens, portrayed as homogenous entities, even though there were differential effects within and across the target states and on people (see chapter 3). Politicians fulminated about OPEC taking "our oil" and infringing on "our sovereignty," even though the oil was "owned" by multinational corporations and stockholders, based in the industrialized states, who profited handsomely as prices rose. And state-led policies to redress these conditions—President Nixon's ill-fated Project Independence; President Carter's Synfuels Corporation, both the subject of fierce domestic attack for their intervention into highly profitable oil markets—were presented as schemes to reduce Americans' reliance not on petroleum, per se, but on the petroleum that the United States did not control.

For other countries, the rhetoric of interdependence did not signal the equalization of power relations among allies so much as a U.S. effort to rationalize anew its "natural" leadership of the Free World.

This coincided—not by accident—with the first stirrings of renewed Cold War, marked by the rise of the second Committee on the Present Danger (Sanders, 1983), the collapse of détente, and the political and academic reification of hegemonic stability theory. The erosion of boundaries around the world led to the effort to reinforce them in Central Europe, through emplacement of Euromissiles (see chapter 4) and similar activities elsewhere. By the end of the 1970s, the discourse of economic interdependence had dissolved, to be replaced by reassertions of sovereignty and autonomy under Jimmy Carter and Ronald Reagan, and legitimation of their policies through the newly created discourse of hegemony. You cannot, however, fool Mother Nature.

Limits to Sustainability?

The Stockholm Declaration was quite explicit about the environmental rights and responsibilities of states. States were sovereign entities where resources and environment were concerned and they were expressly forbidden to engage in activities that negatively affected the sovereignty—the property rights—of other states. What, in practice, did this mean? First, states possessed the absolute right to do whatever they wished with the natural resources located *within* their boundaries. Second, states were absolutely enjoined from doing anything with their resources that would somehow affect the sovereignty of any other state. Third, because the environment was not subject to these imagined boundaries, states were admonished to protect it within the conditions implied by the first two principles. In other words, the Stockholm Declaration reiterated the absolute impermeability of the boundaries of states as a condition of protecting the environment.

While there were (and are) any number of contradictions embedded in these principles, three stand out. First, in spite of long-standing evidence that Nature "respects no borders," the agreements signed at Stockholm in 1972, at Rio in 1992, and elsewhere during the intervening twenty years and since continue to reify the state as the sole appropriate agent of control, management, and development where environment is concerned. Second, the Stockholm Declaration grants to the state or its international agents the absolute right to discipline nonstate actors when degradation of environment and natural resources is involved—rather than the other way around—even to the point of appropriation through coercion (Peluso, 1992, 1993). That this might lead to further degradation, rather than protection, as well as ever greater concentrations of power in the hands of those who encourage degradation, has never been immediately obvious and certainly has never been an argument that diplomats and policymakers have wanted to hear. And third, it has the effect of reinforcing the natural separation of political units rather than fostering the mutual and respectful relationships between them that might serve better the goal of environmental protection.[20]

The reification of borders and sovereignty as "natural" has thus had two difficult-to-reconcile consequences where environmental protection is concerned. On the one hand, as is often recognized, it fragments jurisdictions that might better be treated as single units. Therefore, sulfur dioxide emissions from power plants in the midwestern United States are a domestic regulatory problem when they rain out in the Northeast, but an international transboundary problem when they rain out a few miles further on, in Canada. On the other hand, in order to address such transboundary issues, this reification mandates "cooperation" among states, who prefer to protect their individual economic prerogatives. Under these conditions, cooperation is described as "difficult" and "unnatural," because it goes against the grain of so-called anarchy (which is the term used to naturalize antagonism) and requires that states yield up a measure of their domestic sovereignty in order to address the consequences of the infringements on sovereignty enjoined by the Stockholm Declaration and periodically reiterated since then.

Both the rhetorics of "ecological interdependence" and "sustainable development" can thus be interpreted as responses to the ontological difficulties posed by Stockholm. More to the point, they can both be understood as direct descendants of the geopolitical discourses of the nineteenth and twentieth centuries. In 1987, the Brundtland Commission (also known as the World Commission on Environment and Development, or WCED) proposed that "The Earth is one but the world is not," and argued that the "world in which human activities and their effects were neatly compartmentalized within nations" had begun to disappear (WCED, 1987:4).[21] The commission further suggested "that the distribution of power and influence within society [sic; which society is not made clear] lies at the heart of most environmental and development challenges" (1987:38) In other words, according to the commission, even though the sources of the problems of environment and development were to be found at both supra- and subnational levels, sustainability would nonetheless depend on states acting within and across boundaries, even when it was not evidently in their interest, ability, or willingness to do so. The continued resistance of the United States to actually controlling its emissions of greenhouse gases is testimony to the faintness of this particular hope.

A more fundamental difficulty, however, has to do with *who* decides what is sustainable? From a crude ecological perspective, sustainability is frequently defined as a rough equivalence between inputs and outputs. This, it is widely assumed, is equivalent to conditions in the state of Nature that are naturally "balanced."[22] To exceed this balanced condition for too long, or by too much, will run up against natural limits and lead to the outstripping of supply by demand. From an economic (and nineteenth-century organic) perspective, however, growth is "natural" and "good" (see chapter 7). Consequently, sustainability rests on the continued accumulation of capital—and technology—that can be used to substitute for depleted resources or to rise above such limits. In its famous definition of the "solution," the Brundtland Commission (WCED, 1987:8) finessed this problem by including both conceptions and ignoring the contradictions between them:

> Humanity has the ability to make development sustainable—to ensure that it meets the needs of the present without compromising the ability of future generations to meet their own needs. The concept of sustainable development does imply limits—not absolute limits but limitations imposed by the present state of technology and social organization on environmental resources and by the ability of the biosphere to absorb the effects of human activities.

The naturalization of biospheric limits, whatever they might be, are balanced in this definition by the naturalization of both technology and social organization that know no limits. These, in turn, are to be discovered by recourse to markets that will—how is never specified—find a balance between needs and growth (WCED, 1987:44).

The second response to the ontological problem of boundaries and sovereignty—the conflation of statist realism and methodological individualism—is no more helpful. States fight over natural resources such as water because, as Peter Gleick (1994:8) has put it, "of its scarcity, the extent to which the supply is shared by more than one region or state, the relative power of the basin states, and the ease of access to alternative freshwater sources." In other words, the "cause" of water wars is distribution, not supply, per se. The prevention of water war lies in "formal political agreements" that will address the distribution problem, through the allocation of property rights to water and the appropriate pricing of water in markets among the apparently "rational" users (Gleick, 1994).

Voila! Those naturalized factors that lead to interstate competition and war in the first place are subsumed by processes of economic competition and exchange in naturalized markets. These, it is presumed, will produce more efficient and, therefore, more peaceful outcomes. As I suggested earlier, however, the problem of unequal distribution will not go away; it will simply be shifted to those who lack the power to make trouble. Sustainability will thus come to be defined not by the justice of distribution but by the judgement of markets. Ecological interdependence will fall before wealth rather than force of arms, as the rich disempower the poor. The boundaries will be naturalized once again and sovereignty restored to its rightful place in the hierarchy of Nature.

What Does It Mean to Be "Natural" Where States Are Concerned?

In the search for the causes of social conflict, both peaceful and violent, there is often the temptation to look for the things that can be counted, rather than the things that really count.[23] It is easier to calculate per capita availability of water, or the welfare requirements of immigrants, than to change the social relations and hierarchies of power and domination that characterize states and societies. It is easier to invent rhetorics and discourses that, somehow, obfuscate and naturalize the inequities inherent in these relationships than to point out and act on the notion that, although things might be as they are, they do not have to remain that way. And, it is always easier to ascribe the causes of unpleasant conditions or events to a mysterious and deterministic history or Nature than it is to unravel the complications of a political economy that spans the globe while reaching into every nook and cranny where there are human beings.

Markets, the state, and war are not "natural," and to believe or act otherwise is to affirm the status quo as the best of all achievable worlds. All three are human institutions and, as such, are constructed and mutable. This is why water wars and water markets can be so easily juxtaposed in the language and reasoning of liberalism and neoclassical economics, even though creating open, transborder markets in water will not necessarily lead to "water peace." After the dust settles, it will probably be more "efficient" for Palestine to sell its water to Tel Aviv than use it for West Bank agriculture. Water will then flow across borders, becoming scarce on one side and plentiful on the other, thanks to control by markets rather than the military. How the people of Hebron and Nablus will feel about that remains to be seen.

6❖
THE SOCIAL CONTRACTION

Since the end of the Cold War, culture and identity have become prominent explanatory variables in international politics (see, e.g., Lapid and Kratochwil, 1996). Among the proponents of this notion are Benjamin Barber (1995), Robert Kaplan (1996), and Francis Fukuyama (1995a, 1995b). The best known, perhaps, is Samuel P. Huntington (1993; 1996), with his "clash of civilizations." He (1996:19, 20) argues that

> the years after the Cold War witnessed the beginnings of dramatic changes in peoples' identities and the symbols of those identities. Global politics began to be reconfigured along cultural lines. . . . In the post–Cold War world flags count and so do other symbols of cultural identity, including crosses, crescents, and even head coverings, because culture counts, and cultural identity is what is most meaningful to most people.

In this and other recent works, both culture and identity have been invoked in essentialist terms, as factors that are as invariant as the earth on which they stand. States once came into conflict over raw materials (or so it is said; see Lipschutz, 1989; Westing, 1986); today they are liable to go to war over unfinished idea(l)s. Straits, peninsulas, and archipelagos were once the objects of military conquest; today religious sanctuaries, languages, and national mythologies are the subjects of occupation and de(con)struction. The result appears to be a new type of geopolitics, one that invokes not the physical landforms occupied by states but the mental platforms occupied by ethnies, religions, and nations.

In line with such geoculturalism, most of the forty or so wars that have erupted since 1989 have been characterized, both analytically and in the popular press, as "ethnic" or "sectarian," oriented largely around conflict between cultures. Ordinarily, the origins of such wars are pictured as too ancient and arcane for the citizens of the modern world to understand, inasmuch as the "irrational" cultural factors deemed to be their cause have changed very little over time and no longer make any sense. The most that can be done, according to such logic, is to let them "burn out." For the most part, however, such categorizations serve more to expel combatants from "history" than to explain what is going on, why such wars are taking place, or what might be done to stop or prevent them.

More to the point, not only are essentialist cultural explanations unhelpful, they are wrong. So-called ethnic and sectarian conflict are artifacts of changes within states driven, to no small degree, by forces associated with recent social transformations linked to global integration and external pressures for economic liberalization. Moreover, the fragmentation afflicting "weak" states, such as those in the Balkans, Central Asia, and Africa (Kaplan, 1996), is only the very visible tip of an iceberg that includes even those "strong" countries that are so prominent in the new global economy, including the United States (Rupert, 1997; Crawford and Lipschutz, 1998). As I suggested in chapter 2, political fragmentation and integration are part and parcel of the same process; they are part of a dialectic whose overall consequences cannot, as yet, be foreseen.

I begin this chapter with a discussion of standard explanations of recent civil wars and conflicts, and offer a somewhat different account of why such wars have broken out. I then take up the matter of state survival in an era of economic competition, liberalization, and deregulation, discussing the ways in which these economic processes foster *both* integration and fragmentation, and how this dialectic plays itself out in many places, threatening, perhaps, a proliferation of statelike entities. Next, I ask how many states are enough? Whereas, from the perspective of already existing states, there are too many to permit the creation of more, from the vantage of proto-states there are too few states, and reopening the books is an absolute necessity.

The key question is, of course, too many or too few for what? I suggest here that, perhaps, there are too many states from the security perspective, and too few from the economic and cultural perspectives. Finally, I address the structural difficulties posed by those rules and norms of the international state system governing the establishment of new states. As posed in chapter 3, those rules are premised on exclusivity—indeed, the state system *requires* exclusivity if it is to operate as an anarchy—and, short of a return to a full-service welfare state that can overcome the centrifugal forces inherent in the pursuit of individual self-interest, we are faced here with an insoluble situation in which units of exclusivity will only get smaller and smaller until they can no longer divide.

Is There Ethnic Conflict?

For our purposes, it is possible to identify five general "theories" of ethnicity that have something to say about the conflicts that result "when ethnies collide."[1] The first suggests that ethnicity is *biological.* Proponents of this view argue that ethnic tensions are, somehow, "natural." Observes one scholar, "people reflexively grasp at ethnic or national identifications or what passes for them" (Rule, 1992:519). An alternative formulation, which falls back on sociobiology, argues that "the urge to define and reject the other goes back to our remotest human ancestors, and indeed beyond them to our animal predecessors" (Lewis, 1992:48).

Another view, enunciated some years ago by then-secretary of state Warren Christopher, reiterated by Huntington (1993; 1996), and invoked by President Clinton (1999) to explain the bombing of Yugoslavia in 1999 cites "long histories" and *primordiality,* accounting for the emergence of ethnic politics and violence by invoking "centuries" of accumulated hatreds among primordial "nations." Such hatreds, goes the argument, have exploded into war as a consequence of the end of the Cold War and the disappearance of the repressive mechanisms that kept them from boiling over for four decades. Indeed, as can be seen in the cases of Croatia and Serbia, Kosovo, South Asia, and other places, such invocations, akin to a form of historical materialism, serve to "naturalize" ethnic consciousness and conflict almost as much as do genetic and biological theories. Inasmuch as we cannot change historical consciousness, according to this view, we must allow it to work its logic out to the bitter end.

A third perspective, most closely associated with Benedict Anderson (1991), but elaborated by others, is the idea of the *imagined community*. This view suggests that ethnicity and ethnic consciousness are social constructions best understood as the "intellectual projects" of a bourgeois intelligentsia. These projects arise when elites, using new modes of communication, seek to establish what Ernest Gellner (1983) has called a "high culture" that is distinctive from other, already existing ones (see also Mann, 1993). Such individuals are, not infrequently, to be found in the peripheral regions of empires or states, excluded from the ruling apparatus by reason of birth or class. Because they are highly educated, peripheral intellectuals may be offered opportunities to assimilate into the ruling class, but to reach the top levels, they must renounce completely all of their natal culture. At the same time, these elites are also often aware of the cultural and political possibilities of an identity distinct from that of the center, in which they can play a formative role. Ethnicity, from this view, is cultural, and not inherently violent. But violence may develop when two ethnies, such as Jews and Palestinians, claim the same territory.

A fourth perspective is the *defensive* one (Lake and Rothchild, 1998). Here, the logics of the state and state system begin to come into play. Historically, states have been defined largely in terms of the territory they occupy and the resources and populations they control. Hence, the state must impose clearly defined borders between itself and other states. To do this, the state must plausibly demonstrate that other states and groups pose a physical and ideological threat to its specific emergent "nation." Herein, then, lies the logic for the politicization of group identity, or the emergence of "ethnicity" and "ethnic conflict": self-defense.[2]

The last view is *instrumental*: Ethnicity is the result of projects meant to capture state power and control. But such a project is not, as we shall see, totally ahistorical, as rational-choice theory might lead us to believe. Rather, it is a response to the logics of the state system and globalization, drawing on historical and cultural elements already present (and sometimes free floating) within societies, and invoking "threats" (usually imagined) posed by other real or emergent ethnicities as a reason for its own formative and offense-oriented activities (Ra'anan, Mesner, Armes, and Martin, 1991). One might ask why such antagonisms are necessary; wouldn't communal autonomy suffice? Efforts to provide national/cultural autonomy to ethnic and religious groups were tried in the Ottoman and Hapsburg empires, but failed ultimately because they did not provide to these groups the power accorded to the dominant identity group in those empires and their subunits (Gagnon, 1995). Once the European state system became well-established and spread, only through a "state of one's own" was it possible and desirable to acquire such power and position (Lipschutz, 1998a).

All of these theories focus on cultural difference as the source of conflict and violence, and this view reaches its apotheosis in the work of Huntington (1996:21), who argues that

> people define themselves in terms of ancestry, religion, language, history, values, customs and institutions. They identify with cultural groups: tribes, ethnic groups, religious communities, nations, and, at the broadest level, civilizations. People use politics not just to advance their interests but also to define their identity. *We know who we are only when we know who we are not and often only when we know whom we are against.* (Emphasis added)

[handwritten margin note: Problem we face in the Middle East]

In Huntington's schema, culture, identity, and what he calls "civilization" are defined not through associational values, but in terms of *enemies* and what people are *not*. This is problematic for two reasons. First, there are many cases of cultures coexisting peacefully for extended periods of time. Second, Huntington assumes cultures not only to be stable but also static.

While anthropologists continue to have serious disagreements about the definition of culture, we can define it here as the combination of social factors—norms, rules, laws, beliefs, relationships necessary to the reproduction of a society—with material factors that help produce subsistence and foster accumulation. Cultural functionalism is largely out of style in anthropology because it seeks to explain all features of a culture and its development by their specific purpose in production and reproduction. But such functionalism lies at the core of the geocultural perspective, whose advocates see ethnicity and culture as roughly equivalent to other countries' supplies of raw materials and military technology. Huntington's elements of culture fit this schema, although he regards those elements as basic and functionally common to *all* societies, rather than contextual and contingent. In addition to objecting to such deterministic functionalism, the anthropologist would also point out that cultures are neither static nor stagnant, and that major changes in internal and external environments are likely to disrupt an apparently stable society and make it into something else (as I argued with respect to security in Chapter 3). Huntington, however, seems to believe that cultures and civilizations, like continents and oceans, are immutable and forever (see Gray, 1990).

The parallels between classical geopolitics and geocultural politics have been noted in a number of places (see, e.g., Tuathail, 1997). As I suggested in chapter 5, the classical geopolitics of Mahan, Mackinder, and Spykman operated as a discourse of power and surveillance, a means of imposing a hegemonic order on an unruly world politics. Cold War geopolitics divided the world into West and East, good and evil, with perpetual contestation over the "shatter zones" of the Third World (adrift in some cartographic purgatory of nonalignment). Today, these neat geographic boundaries can no longer be drawn between states and across continents, and the shatter zones are to be found within countries as well as consciousnesses. Yet, Huntington's book (1996:26–27) offers tidily drawn maps whose geocultural borders, with a few exceptions, follow modern boundaries between states (a few oddities do show up hither and thither: an outpost of "Hindu civilization" in Guyana; Hong Kong remains "Western" in spite of its then forthcoming reunification with China; Circumpolar Civilization is entirely missing).

There is yet another paradox here: In spite of its very material *objectives* (and, we must assume, substructure), geoculture, according to Huntington's conceptualization, seems to lack any *material* basis. To be sure, geoculture is connected to great swaths of physical territory, "civilizations" much larger than the states that occupy those spaces, but neither geoculture nor these civilizations have any evident material or even institutional existence. The Islamic *umma* imagined by some and feared by others is much larger than the states it encompasses but, between Morocco and Malaysia, it is riddled by sectarian, political, economic, and social as well as cultural differences, even down to the local level.

Geoculture shows no such variegation. People simply identify with those symbols—"crosses, crescents, and even head coverings"— that "tell them" who they are. Culture and identity, twinned together, thereby come to operate as a sort of proto-ideology, almost a form of "false consciousness." And because ideologies are, of necessity, mutually exclusive, they must also be unremittingly hostile to one another. The inevitable conclusion is the "clash" predicted in Huntington's title, and the replacement of the Cold War order with a new set of implacable enemies driven by an incomprehensible (and "irrational") system of beliefs.

The imputation of such explanatory power to geoculture is not only theoretically invalid, it is also empirically incorrect. Most of the violent conflicts underway around the world today are domestic and involve often-similar ethnic, religious, or class-based groups, struggling to impose *their* specific version of order on *their* specific societies. Such social conflicts do appear to be contests for hearts, minds, and bodies, and combatants seem to feel no remorse in eliminating those whom they cannot convert—indeed, conversion is rarely an option. While most observers and policymakers view these wars as manifestations of chaos that must be "managed" (as detailed in Crocker and Hampton, 1996), it is perhaps more illuminating to see them as very much a product of contemporary (or even "postmodern") times (Luke, 1995). What passes for culture in these wars is, at best, an instrumental tool for grabbing power and wealth.

Postmodern social warfare has thus been mistakenly characterized as war between "cultures." Huntington (1996) goes so far as to use the carnage in Bosnia as an archetype for his predictions of "clashes between civilizational cultures," pointing to the "fault line" between Western and Orthodox Christianity as one of the "flash points for crisis and bloodshed." Yet the tectonic metaphor is flawed. Just as earthquake faults are often notable for their invisibility prior to an event, such cultural fractures in Bosnia were, according to most reports, hardly apparent prior to 1990 (Gagnon, 1995). Moreover, except for periodic and usually infrequent tremors, faults tend to be very quiet. Drawing on Freud's notion of the "narcissism of small differences," it appears that culture wars are more likely to erupt between those whose ascriptive differences are, initially, minor but that can be magnified into matters of life and death and then reified so as to seem eternal and immutable (Lipschutz, 1998b).

Still, how else are people to decide who is deserving of good? How else can one account for success and failure? And what else is one to do when success and failure seem to contradict the rules and expectations of one's experience? As one scholar of the "ideology of success and failure" in Western societies puts it,

> Society is considered to be "in order" and justice is considered "to be done" when those individuals, in general, attain success who "deserve" it, in accordance with the existing norms. If this does not happen, then people feel that "there is no justice" or that something is basically wrong. (Ichheiser, 1949:60, quoted in Farr, 1987:204)

At the extreme, rationalization of such displacement may take one of two forms: self-blame or scapegoating. Self-blame is more common in the United States, given the high emphasis placed on individualism and entrepreneurism, but self-blame can also generate anger that is externalized onto scapegoats. Who or what is attacked—other countries, minorities, immigrants, or particular economic or political interests—depends on how the causes of displacement are explained and understood, and which narratives carry the greatest logical weight (Hajer, 1993). Academic models that explain job loss by comparative advantage and other such theories are, generally speaking, unintelligible to all but trained economists. Putting the blame on specific individuals or groups is much easier and has "the function of replacing incomprehensible phenomena by comprehensible ones by equating their origins with the intentions of certain persons." (Groh, 1987:19).

Nevertheless, what ultimately happens in a specific country or place is permitted, but *not* determined, by overarching macrolevel structures. Violence is not inevitable. Such structures function, rather, by imposing certain demands *and* constraints on domestic possibilities. In such situations, people are offered the opportunity to make meaningful choices about their future, choices that do not involve constrained identities (Todarova, 1998). The problem is that political and economic changes of virtually any type usually cut against the grain of prior stratification and corporatism. From the perspective of those who have benefited from such arrangements, any change is to be opposed.

If Not "Culture," What Then?

The problem with the views and theories offered above is that, taken individually, each is incomplete. To be sure, ethnicity, religion, and culture *have* played prominent roles in Bosnia, Rwanda, Sri Lanka, Kashmir, Nigeria, Algeria, Georgia, Angola, Kosovo, Chechnya, and so on, but they are better understood as contingent factors, rather than either fundamental triggers of intrastate wars or ends in themselves. Each theory provides some element of the whole, but none, taken alone, is sufficient. Moreover, each assumes that the phenomenon we call "ethnicity" or "sectarianism" is, necessarily, the same today as it was 50, 200, or even 1,000 years ago. But the systems within which these phenomena and wars have emerged in recent years have not been static and, to the extent that systemic conditions impose changing demands and constraints on domestic political configurations, today's "ethnicity" must be different from even that of 1950. But how?

As indicated by a growing body of research (Crawford and Lipschutz, 1998), we must look beyond the five arguments to account for the implosion of existing states and the drive to establish new ones out of the pieces of the old. The causes of recent and ongoing episodes of social conflict are obviously correlated with the end of the Cold War,[3] but they have been fueled in no small part by large-scale processes of economic and political change set in train long before 1989. Specifically, as I argued in chapter 2, changes in the international "division of labor," economic globalization, and the resulting pressures on countries to alter their domestic economic and political policies in order to more fully participate in the "community of nations"—all processes that began *during* the Cold War—have had deleterious effects on the relative stability of countries long after its end.[4]

As I noted in earlier chapters, Barry Buzan (1991) has argued that the state is composed of three elements: a material base, an administrative system, and an idea. He suggests that the "idea" of the state is equivalent in some way to nationalism, although he does not examine closely the role of the state itself, or its elites, in creating and sustaining this idea. What has become more evident in recent years is that nationalism (or "patriotism," as it is called in the United States) is only the public face of a very complex citizen/civil society/state relationship. In industrialized, democratic countries, flag waving, anthem singing, and oath taking are public rituals that visibly unite the polity with the state. Such rituals can extend even to sports and similar activities, as evidenced by the nationalist hoopla that surrounds the supposedly internationalist Olympic Games.

There is, however, more to this relationship than just ritual; there is a substructure, both material and cognitive, that might be called a "social contract."[5] This is an implicit understanding of the quid pro quos or entitlements provided to the citizen in return for her loyalty to the idea, institutions, and practices of the state (see chapter 8). All relatively stable nation-states are characterized by political and social arrangements that have some form of historical legitimacy. The idea of the "social contract" is, conventionally, ascribed to Rousseau (1968) and Locke (1988), who argued that the state is the result of what amounts to a contractual agreement among people to yield up certain "natural" rights and freedoms in exchange for political stability and protection. Locke went so far as to argue that no state was legitimate that did not rule with the "consent of the governed," a notion that retains its currency in the contemporary Washington consensus for "democratic enlargement" (Clinton, 1997; Mansfield and Snyder, 1995, offers a more skeptical view of this proposition). Rousseau's theory of the origin of the state owed much to the notion of consent, as well, although he recognized that some sovereigns ruled through contempt, rather than consent, of the governed. Both philosophers also acknowledged the importance of material life to the maintenance of the social contract.

My use of the term here is somewhat different, in that it does not assume a necessarily formalized expression of the social contract. Sometimes, these contracts are codified in written constitutions; at other times, they are not inscribed anywhere, but are found instead in the political and social institutions of a country (as in the United Kingdom or Israel). In either case, a social contract structures the terms of individual citizenship and inclusion in a country's political community, the rules of political participation, the political relationship between the central state and its various regions, and the distribution of material resources within the country and to various individuals. Social contracts also tend to specify the roles that people may occupy within the country and society, and the relationships between these roles.

Quite often, these social contracts are neither just, equitable, nor fair. They are nevertheless widely accepted, and people tend not to dispute them actively, if only because such opposition can also affect their own material position and safety. The social contract is, therefore, a constitutive source of social and political stability within countries, and its erosion or destruction can become the trigger for conflict and war. I do not claim that these social contracts are necessarily respectful of human rights or economically efficient; only that, as historical constructs, they possess a certain degree of legitimacy and authority that allows societies to reproduce themselves in a fairly peaceful manner, over extended periods of time.[6]

Within the frameworks established by such social contracts, we often find stratified hierarchies, with dominators and dominated, powerful and powerless. Frequently, these roles and relationships have what we would call an "ethnic" or "religious" character as, for example, in the traditional caste system in India, or the "ethnic divisions of labor" once found throughout the lands of the former Ottoman Empire, institutionalized in the *millet* system, and still present throughout the Caucasus and Central Asia (as well as in some American cities; see Derlugian, 1998). Historically, these hierarchies have tended to change only rather slowly, on a generational scale, unless exposed to sudden and unexpected pressures such as war, invasion, famine, economic collapse, and so on.

What is crucial is that these arrangements help to *legitimate*, in a Gramscian sense, the political framework within which a society exists, thereby reinforcing the citizen/civil society/state relationship. External threats to the nation and its inhabitants—whether real or imagined—can help to consolidate these social contracts as well as to facilitate changes deemed necessary for the continued reproduction of state and society. Threats make it possible to mobilize the citizenry in support of some national "interests" as opposed to others. Threats also help to legitimate domestic welfare policies and interventions that might, under other circumstances, be politically controversial and disruptive.

The introduction into societies of radical changes that take effect over shorter time spans can, however, destabilize, delegitimize, and dissolve long-standing, authoritative, and authoritarian structures and relationships very quickly, as in Central and Eastern Europe in 1989, Yugoslavia in 1991, and Indonesia in 1998. A transition to market organization or democracy represents one such change; the collapse of a kleptocracy, another. The former provides, for example, an economic environment within which some individuals and groups can, quite quickly, become enriched, while others find themselves being impoverished, as in the case of post-Communist Russia. But even where markets and democracy are long established, as in the United States, economic liberalization, certain forms of deregulation (and reregulation), and hyperliberalism can also have the effect of undermining social stability and generating political dissatisfaction and alienation. These kinds of changes disrupt the rule-governed basis of people's behavior and expectations, sending them in search for new rules, old rules, or no rules (Lipschutz, 1998a, 1998b). The past beckons at those times when change is pervasive; the present becomes illegitimate, nostalgia replaces reasoned discourse, politics becomes venal and, sometimes, violent.

To make the point once again: it is not that external pressures are wholly to blame; rather, the political and social changes required of countries whose leaders and elites, both old and new, wish to participate more fully in the changing global economy tend to destabilize the "social contracts" and make them vulnerable to particular types of political mobilization and violence. As Georgi Derlugian (1995: 2) has put it, the causes of conflicts usually labeled "ethnic" are

> to be found in the prevailing processes in a state's environment, that may be only tenuously divided into "external"—the interstate system and the world economy—and "internal" which, according to Charles Tilly, shapes the state's structure and its relation to the subject population and determines who are the major actors within a particular polity, as well as how they approach political struggle.

But the consequent dynamics are almost wholly internal. Serge Moscovici (1987:154) has argued that

> everyone knows what constitutes the notion of conspiracy. Conspiracy implies that members of a confession, party, or

ethnicity . . . are united by an indissoluble bond. The object of such an alliance is to foment upheaval in society, pervert societal values, aggravate crises, promote defeat, and so on. The conspiracy mentality divides people into two classes. One class is pure, the other impure. These classes are not only distinct, but antagonistic. They are polar opposites: everything social, national, and so forth, versus what is antisocial or antinational, as the case may be.

And Dieter Groh (1987:1) points out that

human beings are continually getting into situations wherein they can no longer understand the world around them. Something happens to them that they feel they did not deserve. Their suffering is described as an injustice, a wrong, an evil, bad luck, a catastrophe. Because they themselves live correctly, act in an upright, just manner, go to the right church, belong to a superior culture, they feel that this suffering is undeserved. In the search for a reason why such evil things happen to them, they soon come upon another group, an opponent group to which they then attribute certain characteristics: This group obviously causes them to suffer by effecting dark, evil, and secretly worked out plans against them. Thus the world around them is no longer as it should be. It becomes more and more an illusion, a semblance, while at the same time the evil that has occurred, or is occurring and is becoming more and more essential, takes place *behind* reality. Their world becomes unhinged, is turned upside down, [sic] in order to prevent damage to or destruction of their own group (religion, culture, nation, race) they must drive out, render harmless, or even destroy those—called "conspirators"—carrying out their evil plans in secret.

That such conspiracies are bizzare, imagined, or socially constructed hardly matters if and when shooting starts. Bullets do kill.

Political Entrepreneurs and Social Contraction

Faced with pressures and processes that mandate change in domestic arrangements, both those who would lose status *and* those who would grasp it tend to see power in absolute and exclusionary terms. In order to limit the distribution of potential benefits, and to mobilize political constituencies in support of their efforts, such people often fall back on social/cultural identities that do incorporate ethnic, religious, and class elements. Rapid social, economic, and political changes create new opportunity structures for those who are in a position to take advantage of them.[7] These "political entrepreneurs" are usually well-educated members of the professional classes or intelligentsia. As David Laitin (1985:302) puts it, they know

> how to provide "selective incentives" to particular individuals to join in the group effort. Communal groups will politicize when there is an entrepreneur who (perhaps instinctively) understands the constraints to organization of rational individual behavior.

In other words, a political entrepreneur is one who is able to articulate, in a coherent and plausible fashion, the structure of opportunities and constraints that face a specified group of people as well as the potential costs of *not* acting collectively. Such appeals have been especially persuasive in "times of trouble," when societies are faced with high degrees of uncertainty, and particular groups within societies see their economic and social prospects under challenge. It is under these conditions that we find domestic differences emerging and developing into full-blown social conflict and warfare.

To put the argument more prosaically, in social settings that are "underdetermined"—where rules and institutions have broken down or are being changed—opportunities often exist for acquiring both power and wealth. There are material benefits to social solidarity. Kinship can function as a form of social capital, establishing relations of trust even where they have not existed previously (Fukuyama, 1995a, 1995b). The political mobilization of ethnic, religious, and cultural identities is one means of taking advantage of such opportunities. Consequently, people do not grasp "reflexively" for their essential ethnic identity when political power and authority crumble. Instead, exclusive and oppositional identities, based on ethnic, religious, and class elements whose meaning is never too clear, are politically constructed and made virulent as those in power, or those who would grasp power, try to mobilize populations in support of their struggles with other elites for political power, social status, and economic resources (Laitin, 1985; Brass, 1976; Crawford and Lipschutz, 1998).

As René Lemarchand (1994:77) has written in his insightful study of conflict and violence in Burundi,

> The crystallization of group identities is not a random occurrence; it is traceable to specific strategies, pursued by ethnic entrepreneurs centrally concerned with the mobilization of group loyalties on behalf of collective interests defined in terms of kinship, region or ethnicity. . . . Clearly, one cannot overestimate the part played by individual actors in defining the nature of the threats posed to their respective communities, framing strategies designed to counter such threats, rallying support for their cause, bringing pressure to bear on key decision makers, and, in short, politicizing ethnoregional identities.

And, he (1994:77) continues,

> The essential point to note is the centrality of the state both as an instrument of group domination and as an arena where segments of the dominant group compete among themselves to gain maximum control over patronage resources. So from this perspective the state, far from being a mere abstraction, emerges as a cluster of individual contestants and cliques actively involved in the struggle for control over the party, the army, the government, the civil service, and parastatal organizations. . . . *Access to the state thus becomes a source of potential rewards for some groups and deprivations for others.* (Emphasis added)

Of course, political settings are never quite this simple. Many of the societies where political entrepreneurs are, or have been, at work are already characterized by class and social differences that parallel ethnic ones (Derlugian, 1998). The exacerbation of these differences, through an appeal to chauvinistic ideologies of identity, becomes a means for these elites to extract or negotiate for more economic resources, status, and power within a "state of their own." In this fashion, political entrepreneurs are able to transform "ethnic" identities into tools of political mobilization and opposition. The collapse of Yugoslavia falls into this pattern,[8] but it is apparent in any number of countries afflicted by ethnic conflict. Indeed, there is reason to think that even democratic capitalist countries could fall victim to this process (Lipschutz, 1998b).

There is nothing particularly new or novel about these arguments, or about the impacts of international economic change on the domestic politics of countries at different levels of development; Alexander Gerschenkron (1962) wrote about this in the early 1960s (see also Crawford, 1995). What *is* different now is that the processes of economic liberalization and integration, thought so important to national competitiveness and growth, have, on the one hand, undermined critical responsibilities of the state even as they have, on the other hand, created a whole set of demands for "new" states or comparable political entities. In a very real sense, however, this explanation of the sources of ethnic conflict does not account for the ways in which opportunities for social and political mobilization come into being; rather, it takes for granted that political communities can, and do, implode. What creates the necessary, if not sufficient, conditions for implosion is less clear.

Breaking Up Is Not So Hard to Do

The difficulty in explaining so-called ethnic and cultural violence may arise because of (1) our inability to see any kind of political formation other than the state; (2) a continuing ontological commitment to and epistemological fascination with the state and state system; and (3) our reluctance to see certain contradictions that inhere to both. Not only are states considered to be the "highest" form of political organization in existence today—at least, as scholars of international relations argue—they are also signifiers of legitimate power that, as Lemarchand notes above, bring wealth and status to individuals simply by virtue of the capacity to occupy dominant roles within them.

Two consequences follow. First, in the contemporary world, legitimate representation can arise only through a state; no other form of political status or autonomy quite fits the bill (see chapter 8). Second, as indicated above, control of a state also provides access to a considerable flow of wealth and power, via rents that can be extracted from domestic constituencies and international sources of finance. Not

everyone takes advantage of political power for these "corrupt" ends—
we like to think that Western democracies are, in particular, immune
from such corruption[9]—but those who do do this in an overt fashion are
more likely to find themselves ruling a potentially unstable country.

There is a tendency among analysts and policymakers, moreover,
to take for granted the fundamental ontological reality of the state and
its ability to exercise meaningful control over what goes on within and
across its borders (Mearsheimer, 1994), although the growing reach of
the global economic system puts paid to this fantasy, even if not in the
way that is commonly believed (Strange, 1996). Interdependence theory
is, by now, almost a cliché, reaching a preposterous extreme in Kenichi
Ohmae's (1991) "borderless" world of nearly 6 billion atomized consumers. But realists continue to argue that states *remain* states and could,
if they wished, reassert their hegemony over transnational economic,
social, and cultural processes (Thomson, 1995). Interdependendistas,
conversely, speak sorrowfully of the "erosion" of sovereignty, as though
the material base of the state is carried away through slowly growing
ravines, while leaving the mountains largely intact.

Such theories cannot explain, however, how and why states might
fall apart into smaller units, inasmuch as they largely ignore two critical factors. First, as Buzan's conceptualization indicates, the state is a
cognitive as well as a material construct, and it relies heavily on citizen loyalty for legitimacy, authority, and continuity. Second, in the
absence of mechanisms for reinforcing loyalty, such as nationalism,
the introduction of markets can exacerbate rather than eliminate already existing social and cultural schisms even as it further undermines the basis of loyalty to the state (as indicated by the collapse of
the Soviet Union; Crawford, 1995). Conversely, as seen in the People's
Republic of China, nationalism can become a powerful tool for maintaining loyalty to the state when markets are eroding older bases of
state legitimacy (Wehrfritz, 1997).

To repeat: for historical reasons and as discussed above, societies
and states are usually organized along lines that tend to privilege some
groups over others. Such privileges often have much to do with the
national, ethnic, or even regional constitution of state and society. Many
states have struggled to mute or eliminate such hierarchies, with varying
degrees of success and failure, through juridical relief, internal resource
transfers, and administrative fiat. Under appropriate conditions, markets

can be efficient allocators of investment. They are, however, largely indifferent to national and ethnic distributions of power and wealth, except insofar as they delineate specific niches for production, services, and sales (Reiff, 1991; Elliott, 1997). And because markets do require rule structures to operate, those who can establish the rules are often able to do so to their individual or collective advantage. Moreover, as markets and economies are liberalized and opened to greater competition from abroad, conditions also favor those who have begun the new game with greater factor endowments. As any investor knows, you have to have money to make money. Left to its own devices, therefore, the market provides greater and more remunerative opportunities to those who are already well-off, and leaves farther behind those who are less wealthy and begin with fewer initial advantages.

    Beyond this, as noted in earlier chapters, integration and fragmentation are linked consequences of the further globalization of capitalism, rather than independent phenomena as is sometimes assumed. The origins of global economic integration are to be found in the mid-nineteenth century, with the rise of English liberalism and the doctrine of free trade as propogated by the Manchester School (some argue that it began even earlier, in the sixteenth century). With fits, starts, and retreats, such integration has reached into more and more places in the world, creating myriad webs of material and cognitive linkages. The fact that such integration has become so widespread does not mean that all places in the world share in the resulting benefits (nor does it necessarily imply a fading away of the state).

Indeed, it is uneven development, and the resulting disparities in growth and wealth, that make capitalism so dynamic. And, as I noted in chapter 2, it is the constant search for new combinations of factors of production and organization, and not states, that drives innovation, competition, and the rise and fall of regions and locales.[10] The fact that there are multiple economic "systems" present in any one location simply adds to the dynamism of the process.[11] Today's comparative advantage may become tomorrow's competitive drag.

The larger political implications of this process have not been given much thought. Comparative advantage is no longer a feature of states as a whole—it never really has been, in any event—but, rather, of region and locale, where the combination of material, technological and intellectual, is, perhaps, only briefly fortuitous (Noponen, Graham, and Markusen, 1993; Smith, 1989). The specific advantages of a place such as Silicon Valley—in many ways, a historical accident arising as much from the war in the Pacific as the result of deliberate policy[12]—may have only limited spillover in terms of a country as a whole. The specific conditions that give rise to such development poles, moreover, seem not to be so easily reproduced wherever there is land available for a "science park."[13]

Holders of capital can choose locations in which to invest. Cities, communities, places—and to a certain degree, labor—control a much more limited set of factors through which they can attract capital. Because the supply of capital is seen as limited (and probably is), competition among places to attract investment and jobs becomes more of a zero-sum game than the positive sum one argued by advocates of comparative advantage. For a country as a whole, where wealth is produced is thought to be immaterial; for towns and cities, it can be a matter of life or death. This point is not lost, for example, on those American states and cities that have established foreign trade offices and regularly send trade missions abroad (Shuman, 1992, 1994). Nor have the business opportunities arising from such competition been ignored; according to one article in the *San Francisco Examiner* (Trager, 1995) describing the activities of a consulting firm providing city and regional marketing programs for economic development, its activities resemble those

> of an international arms dealer—selling weapons to one ruler and then making a pitch to the neighboring potentate based on the new threat. Part of the pitch for these [economic development] programs is that a region needs its own program to survive against the rival programs of other areas.

This could become the cause of considerable political antagonism against the neighbors who win and the authorities who are deemed responsible for the loss.

As discussed above, how these particular dynamics play themselves out depends on the history and political economy of the specific state and society under consideration and preexisting social and political "differences" that, under the pressures of real, potential, or imagined competition, become triggers of antagonism. The critical point is that the disjunctures between past and future, and between places and regions within countries, can have politically destructive consequences for the state, because it can also delegitimate the cognitive and ideological basis for loyalty to state and society. As pointed out in chapter 2, the notion that individual self-interest can serve the social welfare is only valid under rather narrow conditions. Much of the time (and to a growing degree), the newly wealthy see no reason to contribute to state and society. The newly–poor and those with declining prospects see that the state cares less and less about them. Both groups become alienated from state and society, although the former retreat into private enclaves while the latter seek to restore the status quo ante. Both moves contribute to the fragmentation and dissolution of the public political sphere. The result is that, with the global economic integration that reaches into more and more corners of the world, we find ourselves faced with dialectically linked integration *and* fragmentation that can play itself out in a number of different ways (see, e.g., Sakamoto, 1994).

In the United States, for a number of historical reasons, potential divisions are geographical as well as class- and ethnicity-based. While it is difficult to envision the secession of individual states, not a few parts of the country have been abandoned by the rest as a result of integration and competition (Lipschutz, 1998b). In other countries, such as the former Yugoslavia, the boundaries between jurisdictions were intended to be administrative, but were drawn up in ethnic or national terms. In yet other places, the dividing lines are linguistic, religious, clan-based, "tribal," or even vaguely cultural (Derlugian, 1998). It goes without saying that those places in which people have fallen to killing each other have nothing to offer global capital—they have, quite literally, fallen out of "history"—but those places able to break away from the political grip of larger polities, as Slovenia escaped the competitive drag of Serbia, might be well-placed to participate in the global economy. Conversely, as seen in the tentative moves of Catalonia to assert its place among the "regions" of Europe, and the interminable discussions in Quebec about whether it would be better off alone than in the Canadian federation, the number of potential states or statelike entities appears to be quite large.

How Many Are Enough?

How many of the potential nations existing in the world are likely to seek a state? Approximately 50 countries signed the United Nations charter in 1945. In theory, those 50 represented virtually all of the population of the Allied countries and empires, inasmuch as the European powers fully expected to regain control over colonial territories occupied by the Axis or lost, for a time, to domestic insurgencies. By the mid-1970s, with the first wave of postwar decolonization just about over, UN membership had climbed to more than 150. Following the collapse of Yugoslavia and the Soviet Union, the number of states belonging to the UN passed 190. There is little reason to think the count will stop there, as suggested by an article in the *Wall Street Journal* (Davis, 1994) entitled "Global Paradox: Growth of Trade Binds Nations, but It Also Can Spur Separatism." The author pondered whether we might see a world of 500 countries at some time in the future. Another piece in the *San Francisco Chronicle* (Viviano, 1995), "World's Wannabee Nations Sound Off," told of the many ethnic, indigenous, and sectarian groups seeking political autonomy. Finally, there are World Wide Web sites listing hundreds of "microstates" and "micronations," some serious, others not.

In principle, there are few limits to the number of independent states that might come into being in the future; some have suggested the world's 2,000-odd languages or 5,000-odd potential ethnies stand as an upper limit. In practice, however, there is considerable reluctance on the part of already existing countries to recognize new ones that have not been created with the consent of both government and governed, even though this specific requirement is quite elastic (see Bierstecker and Weber, 1996). As testified to by efforts to reassemble shattered states, such as Cambodia and Somalia, there may also be a *sub-rosa* fear that successful nonstate forms of political community could be disruptive of the current structure of international politics. In other words, for the time being, the only normatively acceptable form of political community at the international level is the state. A proliferation of clans, tribes, city-states, trading leagues, social movement organizations, transnational identity coalitions, diasporas, and so on could raise questions of legitimacy and representation that might very well undermine the status of existing states, not to mention well-established hierarchies of power and wealth (see chapter 8).

But there are also limits beyond which the "international community" will apparently not go to in order to preserve existing international borders. The Bosnia "peace settlement" signed at Dayton, Ohio, in late 1995 suggests one such limit. With all of its inherent flaws and contradictions, the agreement seemed to recognize that, in this case at least, juridical borders would make not the slightest difference to ethnic politics after fragmentation. The agreement maintained the fiction of a unitary Bosnia, albeit as a confederation of federations comprised of what are by now largely ethnically pure, semiautonomous territories. Provisions permitting repatriation to their former homes of refugees of ethnicity different than the dominant one have, for the most part, gone unfulfilled, although municipal elections have taken place, with displaced refugees being allowed to vote in their former towns of residence.

The reality appears to be, however, that the Bosnian Croats treat mostly with Zagreb, and the Bosnian Serbs mostly with Belgrade. There is not much in the way of border controls between the respective ethnic zones and the mother countries, whereas there might well develop increasingly stronger controls between the ethnic zones within Bosnia. And the Bosniak (Muslim) government in Sarajevo will do what it can to maintain itself and expand. If a relative degree of peace can be established and maintained within the fiction of a state—as seems to be happening—the United States and Europe will be satisfied. A precedent will have been established that can be cited by others seeking a similar settlement (Campbell, 1997).

From the perspective of the industrialized powers, and especially the United States, there are also both military and economic reasons to limit the number of independent states occupying the planet's surface. While the United States once pursued a policy of "divide and conquer" in its efforts to dismember the European colonial powers, it has never had a real national interest in a proliferation of juridically sovereign states. For one thing, managing a highly fragmented world system is quite complicated and expensive—as evidenced in reductions in the number of U.S. embassies and consulates abroad. For another, the transaction costs of dealing with even a single new national government can be considerable, especially if it is located in a politically sensitive region.

Too many states also pose a strategic nightmare (a point made implicitly by Chase, Hill and Kennedy, 1996). During the Cold War, each new country had the potential of becoming another cockpit of East-West conflict and, therefore, each existing state required minute attention (and control) lest the Soviets gain another salient into the West. This militated against changes in borders. Now, each additional *Current* state is one that could fall under the control of "rogues" or putative *Problem* terrorists or into threatening disorder. The reported presence of Iranian and Afghani *mujuhadeen* on Bosniak territory during the civil war there gave nightmares to NATO commanders, the National Security Council, and the U.S. Congress (whether such fears were justified or not). But practically speaking, there is little to prevent the establishment of new states except the ability of more powerful countries to stop the process through active intervention and economic boycotts, something few of them have so far indicated a willingness to do, the intervention by NATO on behalf of Kosovo not withstanding.

But maybe more *is* better. From the economic and cultural perspectives, there is no reason *not* to have a world of 500 or more statelike political entities. In the past, big was preferable. Because the military prowess of a Great Power rested on its material and economic base, and the autonomy of that base required relatively high levels of self-reliance, large territories could provide both economies of scale and security. Neomercantilism made sense. This was the logic behind states with continental or even transcontinental scope, such as the United States, the Soviet Union, and European colonial empires. Nowadays, however, within the structure of the new global division of labor, and the apparent prospects for global (if not local) peace, prosperity rests more than ever on comparative advantage and market niches (a point also argued in Rosecrance, 1996).

The difficulties involved in getting the single European currency up and running—in part, exacerbated by the differential levels of wealth and development from northern to southern and western to eastern Europe—also suggest that such economies of scale may no longer matter as much as they once did. Fordist production for mass markets—both raw materials as well as consumer goods—leads to overcapacity, ruinous competition, and, perhaps, national bankruptcy; niche strategies allow regions and locales in industrialized countries to trade in similar, although not identical, goods and services, without having to broadly share the wealth with less-fortunate compatriots in other parts of their country. The result can only be detrimental to the political cohesiveness of existing nation-states.

Every House a State?

In one sense, the state has come full circle in its travels from Westphalia to "McWorld" (as Benjamin Barber puts it; 1995). When the original documents constituting state sovereignty were formulated and signed in the seventeenth century, the princes and their noble colleagues were seeking to protect *themselves*. States (and populations) were sovereign property, not the autonomous actors we imagine them to be today and, inasmuch as royal sovereignty was coterminous with territory, prince and state were the same. In essence, the Westphalian agreement said, "What is mine is mine, what is yours is yours, and we leave each other's property alone." Exclusion of the Other was, therefore, the watchword, for this was the best way to ensure that one's property would be left alone. This did not rule out wars, of course, for there was nothing and no one to enforce such agreements. As often as not, self-interest and family feuds overrode social niceties (Elias, 1994).

The transition from royal state to nation-state was a gradual one, though well under way by the end of the eighteenth century. Still, the fundamental principle of state *exclusivity* did not change. Indeed, without it, the state as an entity with sole jurisdiction over a defined territory could not exist, precisely as it did not exist in this form prior to the Westphalian revolution. In its absence, we would be faced now, as then, with a form of "neomedievalism," characterized by overlapping but differentiated political realms, governed by multilevel and sometimes coterminous authorities, with inhabitants confessing loyalty to several different units, depending on circumstances (see, e.g., Elias, 1994; Bull, 1977:264–76).

As events turned out, the nation-state came to be defined by a shared, if artificial or imagined, nationality that was also exclusive: the citizen could not confess loyalty to more than one state at a time (even today, dual citizenship is rarely permitted by national authorities). The nation-state thus became, on the one hand, a container for all those who fit within a certain designated category and, on the other hand, a barrier to keep out those who did not fit within that category. It also became a means for the accumulation of power at the center as well as the division of power with other similar centers.

To reinforce the claim to centralized power and generate exclusive allegiance to a single center, the state had to accomplish two ends. First, it had to eliminate competing claimants to legitimacy from within its putative jurisdiction; ethnic cleansing was state practice long before CNN began to transmit news stories and film from Bosnia and Rwanda. Turning "peasants into Frenchmen" (Weber, 1976)—or whatever—could lead either to assimilation of peripheral nations into the nationality of the center, or it could result in the ruthless extermination of minorities by the center (Elias, 1994). Second, the state had to generate in those under its jurisdiction a parallel resistance to the attractions of other centers, that is, other nation-states and nationalities. Keeping with the precise demarcation of state territories beginning in the nineteenth century, it also became necessary to demarcate precisely the same boundaries within the minds of those living within the lines on the ground and to discipline those who, somehow, violated those boundaries (a point to which I return in the next chapter).

Nationalism—and distinctions among types is irrelevant here—was, with very few exceptions, formulated as a doctrine of collective superiority and absolute morality vis-à-vis other nations, thereby serving to bind citizens to the state and to separate them from other states. This was not a one-way deal, of course; the state promised to provide security and political stability to those who signed up with it and not with another (not unlike the deals offered by competing phone and Internet Service Providers companies today). This system of national exclusivity reached its apogee during the middle of the twentieth century, when some countries became, in effect, sealed containers from which there was no possibility of escape. The end of the Cold War not only unsealed the containers but provided the permissive conditions for new containers to be established, as groups of people found themselves both dispossessed from their position within the nation-state and increasingly resentful of their dispossession.

Where might the processes of state fragmentation and social contraction stop, once they have been put into motion? Here, the contradictions between the nation-state and the market become critical. To repeat briefly what has been said above as well as many times before:

the liberal doctrine of self-interest calls into question the relationship between the self-interested actor and the larger context within which that actor finds him/her/itself, be it society and state or individual and society. At the international level, this tension is resolved through the dual fictions of anarchy and self-help; at the domestic level, however, taking the logic of self-interest to an extreme risks civil or social warfare and the replication of a Hobbesian "state of nature" at the neighborhood, household, or even individual level. All that is lacking, it would seem, are entrepreneurs with the military force to challenge the center. Given the chaos in some places around the world, and the growing obsession with "gang violence" in the United States and Europe, some might argue that this situation already holds in more places than we would care to acknowledge (Enzenberger, 1994).[15]

7❖
THE PRINC(IPAL)

On March 3, 1983, President Ronald Reagan appeared on American television to announce the end of the nuclear threat. A new military program, designed to protect the country against the possibility of a first-strike attack by Soviet nuclear-tipped intercontinental ballistic missiles, was about to be launched. The Strategic Defense Initiative (SDI), or "Star Wars" as it was almost immediately tagged by its detractors, was proffered to an increasingly restive public as a means of overcoming the moral dilemma inherent in mutual assured destruction (MAD): the holding hostage of one's people to potential nuclear annihilation as a means of preventing the enemy from even contemplating such an attack. This particular dilemma had already created political disorder throughout Europe and America, manifested most clearly in the Nuclear Freeze movement, the Catholic Bishops' statement on nuclear weapons, and massive antinuclear protests throughout Western Europe (Meyer, 1990; Wirls, 1992). Reagan, seizing on citizens' fears of nuclear war, offered SDI as an alternative means of protecting them, thereby attempting to render ineffective and impotent the arguments of "freezniks," bishops, and other antinuclear activists.

There were numerous critics of SDI. Most chose not to contest the program on moral grounds but, rather to launch an attack on its technological (in)feasibility (see, e.g., Drell, Farley, and Holloway, 1985). This, they hoped, would blast to bits what some saw as a dangerous and destabilizing attempt to gain a viable first-strike capability against the Soviet Union, a capability that might trigger the very eventuality that everyone wished to avoid. But here SDI's critics faced an insoluble dilemma: inasmuch as one could never prove conclusively that an effective shield could not be built, how could one justify halting a project that promised such an enticing vision?[1] Ultimately, the defense sectors of the United States and its allies managed to absorb tens of billions of dollars in a largely fruitless attempt to develop the required technologies, although this has not deterred various parties from continuing to argue that a strategic defense system is feasible, desirable, and necessary or the Clinton Administration and U.S. Congress deciding to proceed with an SDI Junior (Rowny, 1997; see also Mandelbaum, 1996).

What was largely ignored in the long-playing, choleric exchange over SDI was its essentially *moral* purpose. SDI became a tool of the American state in providing an impenetrable shield not so much against missiles and accidental nuclear launches (whether from friend or foe) as in opposition to notions of detente, disarmament, and other indicators of declining determination and credibility vis-à-vis the USSR. In offering SDI, Ronald Reagan was promising to build a barrier that would redraw the wavering lines between the Free World and its unfree *doppelgänger*, between democracy and totalitarianism, between the "Evil Empire" and the "City on the Hill." Indeed, SDI was a moral statement but, more than that, it was also a reimagining and reinforcing of the borders between nations, between liberal and socialist nationalisms, between what was to be permitted and what was absolutely forbidden.

In this chapter, I explore these matters. I begin by describing the features of the *moral-state*, as I call it, and review briefly the antecedents to this phenomenon, beginning prior to 1648 with a specific focus on the ways in which states, as constituted following the Thirty Years War, also functioned as moral authorities. In historical terms, this authoritative role was first expressed through the person of the sovereign. Following the collapse of the universal moral authority of the Roman Catholic Church, the sovereign's mandate to rule the state invoked God's authorization. Although most contemporary democracies do not seek legitimacy through theocracy, these deeply buried roots nevertheless retain considerable influence.

This is seen, in particular, in the emergence of nationalism—the "civil religion" of the state—as a new source of moral authority, a topic I address in the second section of the chapter. The emergence of state-centered nationalisms was a product of the secular Enlightenment—many of whose acolytes nevertheless subscribed to the authority of "Nature" and natural law (see Noble, 1997). The state now came to provide bounded containers of moral authority within which some practices were prescribed in the name of national solidarity while others were proscribed on pain of ostracism or expulsion. At the limit, as discussed in chapter 6, some national elites found it expedient to eliminate whole classes and categories of people within their states' borders, or to engage in large-scale civil warfare in order to establish domestic moral discipline.

In the third section of the chapter, I examine the emerging contradiction between the moralities of nationalism and the rise of liberal individualism, especially as it developed after 1945. As I argued in earlier chapters, containment of the "Free World" *and* the "Soviet bloc" throughout the Cold War specified the perimeters of two dominant orders and thereby united two great polities, each within its own "sphere of moral influence." Populations were disciplined not so much by the threat of physical punishment—although this was forthcoming in certain situations—as the fear of being cast outside the "Realm of Order" into moral ambiguity (and damnation?). President Reagan's invocation of the "Evil Empire" was thus as much an allusion to Satan and his legions as Stalin and his. More recently, the United States has attempted to reimpose its global moral authority by way of what I called, in an earlier chapter, "disciplinary deterrence," both at home and abroad, via public relations, demonstration, and, if necessary, public punishment.

Finally, I address the collapse of state-centered moral authority in the New World Order of global liberalization. As I argued in chapter 2, old (b)orders have dissolved under the pressures of the global market, which, in turn, has become a sink for, rather than a source of, moral authority. The ever-more-frantic search for new sources of moral authority therefore proceeds through a great number of channels—social, political, economic, ethnic, identity-based—but none is likely to provide the means for reestablishing borders and order. I conclude with a discussion of efforts to restore (b)orders, and speculate on the implications of such an impossible task for twenty-first century global politics.

Real-State or Moral-State?

The end of the Soviet Union destroyed utterly and finally the conceptual border between the good of the Free World and the evil of the "bad bloc," thereby exposing the American people to all sorts of pernicious, malevolent, and immoral forces, beliefs, and tendencies. It should be no cause for wonder, consequently, that the domestic politics of morality, especially in the United States, have become so pronounced and full of inconsistencies ("get the government off of our backs but into the bedrooms of teenage mothers") and have been extended ever more strongly into the international arena.[2] Paradoxically, perhaps, the fundamental causal explanations for these contradictions are to be found not in domestic politics, as is conventionally thought; rather, the roots of this phenomenon lie in the very nature of the nation-state itself, in its somewhat uncertain place in the so-called international system, and in the spread of the norms and practices of political and economic liberalism, a point I have argued in earlier chapters. Far from being *amoral*, as is so often claimed, state behavior, as encoded in the language and practices of realism, nationalism, state-centricity, and anarchy, exemplifies *morality* in the extreme, with each unit representing a self-contained, exclusionary moral-state.

How can this be? In contemporary international relations theory, the conventional perspective on the nation-state is largely a realist, functionalist one. The state serves to protect itself and its citizens against external enemies, and to defend the sanctity of contracts and property rights from internal ones. Morality, as George Kennan (1985/86) and others have never tired of telling us, should play no role in the life of the *real-state*, for to do so is to risk both safety and credibility. But *can* the state stand simply for the protection of material interests and nothing else (Hirsch, 1995; Ellis and Kumar, 1983)? After all, the essential constitutive element of the nation-state—the *nation*—represents the eternal continuity of specific myths, beliefs, and values, usually with a teleological character. Conversely, the defeat of those elements, whether in war *or* peace, represents a mortal wound to the nation as well as to the authority and legitimacy of the state that protects it.

This aspect of the state is largely ignored by the conventional wisdoms of both realism and liberalism (not to mention Marxism). Their advocates fail to historicize the state, seeing it as having no genealogy and thereby omitting from their stories of international politics one critical element: the European state, as heir to the authority of the Catholic Church, was originally constituted as a *moral order*, defining a prescriptive standard of legitimate authority through containment of its citizens within well-defined physical *and* moral (b)orders. And, with some changes, this remains the practice today. The legitimacy of the state does not grow simply out of material power; it also rests on the presumption that the state's authority is both *good* and *right* (Brown, 1992: chaps. 2-3). And, although legitimacy is normally addressed only within the context of domestic politics (if then), history from the Thirty Years War on nonetheless illustrates that domestic legitimacy matters in international politics, too.

One might argue, of course, that that was then and this is now. The contemporary state no longer fulfills this moral role, and has not done so for many decades. Contemporary threats to state and polity are almost wholly material: terrorists throw bombs, illegal immigrants take resources, diseases trigger illness. I argue to the contrary: the modern nation-state acts not only to protect its inhabitants from threatening material forces, it also acts to limit their exposure to noxious ideas by establishing boundaries that discipline domestic behavior and beliefs. After all, what is a "terrorist" but someone with bad ideas? What is an "illegal" immigrant except someone who knowingly violates public norms? A state that cannot maintain such (b)orders becomes a prime candidate for disorder. And, as I shall argue below, it is in no small part the collapse of these moral borders that is responsible for much of the political disorder throughout the world today.[3]

More specifically, the *kulturkampf* that has wracked the United States (and other countries) since the end of the Cold War, and probably longer, is a struggle over where, and on whom, these moral borders should be inscribed. It is not a simple matter, however, of the moral versus the immoral (or amoral) within the confines of the 15 members of the European Union, the 50 American states or the world's 190-odd countries. Rather, the question is more properly understood as: Are the borders of our contemporary moral community to be national or global? If pernicious forces have free reign across formerly impermeable borders, how can the struggle stop at the water's edge? And, if such miscreants threaten to penetrate the body politic with their black helicopters, Gurkha troops, and Soviet tanks, how can we not carry the culture war into the international realm (as Samuel Huntington and others have done)?

Consequently, on the one side of this struggle are those who would reinscribe the national, excluding or expelling all who do not live up to the moral standards of the Founding Fathers of the United States (there are no Founding Mothers), and extending the borders of that morality abroad through example and discipline (U.S. congressional prohibitions on family-planning funds to certain countries and the Helms-Burton Act restricting dealings with Cuba come to mind here). On the other side are those who, for better or worse, by virtue of choice or via the chances of change, find themselves swept up or away by the disintegration of national *and* moral (b)orders. This latter group is not identical with those captive to the contemporary events that give rise to refugees, migrants, and the casualties of wars and markets; its members freely make choices among and in support of difference in ways that the culture warriors resolutely abjure. And, as I noted above and in chapter 4, these struggles are not restricted to the domestic domain; in the global realm, moral conflict, disguised as "cultural" or religious difference, has come to replace the ideological blocs of the Cold War. In these struggles, the United States has taken on the role, not of world policeperson, as it is often said, but global dominatrix (both mistress and vice-princ(ipal)). But how can this be?

What Was Westphalia?

For most international relations (IR) scholars, and for mainstream IR theory, the defining moment of contemporary world politics was 1648, when the Treaty of Westphalia brought an end to the Thirty Years War. As David Campbell critically observes, accounts of this history "offer nothing less than an edifying tale of modernization in which we witness the overcoming of chaos and the establishment of order through the rise of sovereign states" (Campbell, 1992:47). There is good reason to believe that the signers of Westphalia, and its precedessor, the Treaty of Augsburg, had nothing of this sort in mind at the time. It is only through the contingent and contextual lenses of subsequent centuries that such an orderly meaning was imposed on those events.

Today, this teleological story of the state offers two central signifiers: *anarchy* and *sovereignty*. Through anarchy, we are told, the princes who put their names to the two treaties agreed that a universal authority—the Roman Catholic Church—would no longer stand over them. Through sovereignty, each prince would come to constitute the highest authority within each state and, enjoined from interfering in the affairs of any other, would have no authority anywhere outside of his state. This state of affairs, with its distinction between domestic "order" and the interstate "nonorder," was subsequently reified through realist Hobbesianism, that is, *hard* interpretations of the writings of Thomas Hobbes and others (Walker, 1992).

The princes were probably not very concerned about this particular inside/outside distinction; we might say that, in 1648, there was more concern with affairs of family than matters of state. Indeed, if we look at a map of sixteenth- and seventeenth-century Europe, we discover that relations between polities were much more *intra*familial than *inter*national. Moreover, relations *within* domestic orders—often scattered about the continent in discrete tracts—had as much to do with *which* branch and member of a family ruled over a specific territory as with each branch and individual's religion (a point best illustrated by the intrafamily wars among British royalty and nobility; see Elias, 1994).

Hence, while Westphalia did not put an end to these intrafamily squabbles, it did for the most part do away with the remaining vestiges of feudal authority, replacing a confused medieval order with a clear hierarchy that placed prince or king above duke and lord, and invoked the moral authority of God, whether Protestant or Catholic, to bless and legitimate the new arrangements.[4] Westphalia, in other words, was a social contract for European society with an embedded morality defining "good" behavior. It lacked many of the elements of domestic orders, to be sure, including a sovereign, but it did provide moral principles in place of an actual ruler. Those principles were frequently violated (although probably more often observed than not), but they did form the basis for a continent-wide society.

Not altogether unintentionally, most late-twentieth-century mainstream IR theorists have been little concerned with the domestic implications of anarchy and sovereignty and have, instead, addressed the functional significance of the two practices for relations among states. Anarchy is said to imply "self-help," or self-protection, while sovereignty is said to imply "self-interest" or, in its modern mode, accumulation (Inayatullah, 1996). I will not belabor these two points, inasmuch as they are the staple of every IR text published over the past 150 years (Schmidt, 1998). I will point out, however, that as practices, both presuppose modes of transnational regulation rather than the absence of rules and norms so often associated with them.[5] More than this, both sovereignty and anarchy can be regarded as expressions of a state-centric *morality* that presumes a legitimate order within and illegitimate disorder without.

The first point is best seen in Kenneth Waltz's well-known (albeit flawed) invocation of the market as a structurally anarchic parallel to international politics (Waltz, 1979). In invoking the headless market, Waltz draws on Adam Smith's famous "invisible hand" to explain outcomes of relations between states but fails to recognize that the "invisible foot" of international politics might well produce results quite unlike the orderly outcome posited by Smith. The error committed by Waltz is to regard both markets *and* international politics as self-regulating, driven by no more than self-interest or power (Smith, by contrast, hoped that religious beliefs would constrain people's appetites; see Hirsch, 1995).

As social institutions, markets are subject to both implicit and explicit regulations. The market is governed, first of all, by the command "Thou shalt not kill." Other rules follow. Walter Russell Mead (1995/96:14) makes a similar point about airports and air travel when he argues that, "Cutthroat competition between airlines coexists with common adherence to traffic and safety regulations without which airport operations would not be possible." So it is between states. The two principles of anarchy and sovereignty are both constitutive of the international system as it is conceived and regulative of it, and they constitute moral boundaries for the state that preserve the fiction of *international* (dis)order and *domestic* order (Brown, 1992: chap. 5).

On reflection, it also becomes clear that sovereignty and anarchy have *moral* and, in consequence, *legal* implications for domestic politics, too. As Hobbes (1962:132) put it,

[T]he multitude so united in one person, is called a COMMON-WEALTH, in Latin CIVITAS. This is the generation of that great LEVIATHAN, or rather, to speak more reverently, of that *mortal god*, to which we owe under the *immortal God*, our peace and defense. (Emphasis added)

By establishing borders between states and permitting rulers to be sovereign within them, princes were granted the right to establish within their jursidictions autonomous systems of law with both functional and moral content. These systems enjoined certain activities in order to prevent consequences that would be disruptive of the order of the state—that is, order as the way things should be, according to the individual prince's vision. Or, as Hobbes (1962:113) argued, "But when a convenant is made, then to break it is *unjust*: and the definition of INJUSTICE, is no other than *the not performance of covenant.*" Violation of the convenant is, therefore, not simply the breaking of the law; it is repudiation of the underlying moral code of the society.

Hobbes argued that coercive power, entrusted to Leviathan, was necessary to ensure "performance of covenant" and the safety and security of each man who subscribed to that covenant. But even though the seventeenth century was quite violent, overt coercion was still relatively uncommon. Rather, it was the *possibility* of discipline and ostracism by the state (and the other subscribers to the covenant) as a result of a violation of order—not repeated day-to-day punishment—that kept subjects from violating the prince's laws or the convenant (and continues to do so today).[6] Most, if not all, of the legal systems of the time acknowledged, moreover, the hegemony of Christianity—later manifested in the "divine right of kings"—even if they disagreed on which particular version of the religion was to be practiced.[7] Hence, although princes opposed a universal morality or empire that could impose sanctions on them against their wills, they sought to foster such an order within their own jurisdictions, based on their right to do so under God.

The fact that war and interstate violence among princes did not cease after Westphalia does not mean, however, that morality was absent from their relations or that combatants were motivated by merely functional needs or appetites. The moral basis of a political entity—its ontology—provides a justification for its existence as well as the implication that other entities are morally illegitimate if they reject the ontology of the first. John Ruggie (1989: 28) argues that Westphalia defined who had the "right to act as a power," thereby including within its purview the numerous small and weak German principalities and states. The treaty acknowledged both a *right of existence* for these units and the right of each prince to impose *his* morality on *his* subjects.

Westphalia did not, however, command that each prince recognize, accept the rule, or adopt the morality of others. War could thus be understood as both a moral *and* material event. To be conquered was punishment for immoral domestic beliefs and practices; to conquer was reward for moral domestic beliefs and practices.[8] By agreement, therefore, although Westphalia commanded domestic morality and international amorality (the latter a rule rather than a condition), this did not prevent princes from trying to extend the boundaries of their domestic morality to engulf the domains of other, "immoral" princes.

The original Westphalian system lasted only about 150 years, if that long. Although the royal sovereign was invested with authority via a mysterious God, Enlightenment efforts to introduce rationalism into political rule succeeded all too well, especially in Western Europe. Whereas some of the early empirical scientists, such as Newton, saw their work as illuminating the workings of a universe created by God (Noble, 1997), others took a more physicalist view. Gradually, religious morality was undermined by scientific experimentation and explanation, and philosophers and theorists sought to justify political order by reference to Nature (which some still equated with God, albeit a distant one; a somewhat exaggerated view of this change can be found in Saul, 1992). From this tendency there emerged what came to be called "nationalism."

From *Corpus Christii* to *Corpus Politicum*

The first true nation-states, it is usually agreed, were Britain and France. In Britain, the modern "nation" emerged out of the Civil War of the seventeenth century, as Parliament fought with the king over the right of rule and the power of the purse. The Puritan Revolution represented an effort to impose on the state a moral order that was both Christian and a forerunner of capitalist individualism but that nonetheless had no external sources or referents of authority apart from God. Hence, the Puritans portrayed Rome and its adherents (including, putatively, any Catholic English sovereigns) as mortal enemies of Cromwell's Commonwealth and England.

This effort to purify the body politic of religious heresy was doomed to fail, however, so long as heretics could not be expelled from the nation's territory or eliminated through extermination (a familiar problem even today).[9] The Restoration, which put Charles II on the British throne, was as much a recognition of the intractability of the moral exclusion of a portion of the body politic itself as a reaction against the harshness of the Commonwealth and its attacks on certain elites. The emergence of the British nation during the following century—and the renewal of war with France during the 1700s—redrew the moral boundaries of society at the edges of the state, and established loyalty to king and country as a value above all others.

In France, the Revolution launched a process whereby the source of state legitimacy was transferred from an increasingly discredited (and eventually dead) sovereign to the "people." The French nation did not, however, attempt to establish a new moral order; that was left to the various and successive leaderships in the two centuries that followed. But the French Revolution did mark a major change in the ontology of the moral order of the state. Whereas the princely state derived authority from God, the new French state derived its authority from a "natural" entity called the "nation." Enlightenment rationalism sought explanations for the workings of the universe in science; even Hobbes looked to Nature to explain politics and provide a model for the Commonwealth. What could be more logical than to look for the origins of the nation in Nature? By the end of the nineteenth century, even though the very concept was less than a century old, nations had been transmorgrified into constructs whose origins were lost in the dim mists of antiquity but whose continuity was attributed to the their connections to specific territories and the "survival of the fittest" (Dalby, 1990; Agnew and Corbridge, 1995).

As I have noted in earlier chapters, this new age of moral imperialism was rooted in Darwin's ideas about natural selection, but ex-

tended from individual organisms as members of species to states
(Darwin, himself, had no truck with these ideas). Members and leaders
of nations that fifty years earlier had not even been imagined (Anderson, 1991) now competed to see whose history was more ancient and
who had survived greater travails for longer periods of time. This
became a means of establishing greater legitimacy and authority (a
process that continues, even today, in places such as Kosovo, Rwanda,
and Israel/Palestine). A more antideluvian history, in turn, established
the moral right to occupy particular territorial spaces, and delegitimated
the rights of all others to remain in those spaces (Berend and Ránki,
1979:80–96).

Inherent, too, in such national organicism was a notion of "purity," not only of origins but also of motives. Long-term survival could
not be attributed simply to luck; it had, as well, to be a matter of
maintaining one nation's moral distinctiveness from those who were
not of the nation, and of accounting for survival with a teleological
national mythology. Maintenance of such distinction through culture
was not, however, enough; there also had to be dangers associated
with difference. These dangers, often as not imagined into being (rather
than being "real" in any objective sense), made concrete those borders
separating one state from another.[10] Those living in borderlands were
forced to choose one side or the other. Anyone on the wrong side of
such a border were, quite often, forcibly made to migrate across them,
as with Native Americans during the nineteenth century, Greeks and
Turks after World War I, Germans after World War II, Hindus and
Muslims in 1947, Palestinians on the wrong side of the moving "Green
Line" between 1947 and 1949, and many others since. Once again, a
form of moral order was invoked and moral purity maintained.

The apotheosis of this politics of danger took place during World
War II in those areas of Europe that fell under Nazi rule. To the
national socialist regime, guardian of the moral and biological purity
of *all* Germans, whether within the Third Reich or not, races of a
lower order were threats to both (Pois, 1986). The Nazi moral hierarchy could live with Slavs restricted to their place (although it intended
eventually to eliminate them or force them to move further to the east).
It could not tolerate Jews, Gypsies, and homosexuals, all of whom
tended toward high mobility across social, geographical, and sexual
borders, and who treated with what the national socialists regarded as

"impure" ideas and practices (e.g., "Jewish science"). Inasmuch as containment in ghettos and camps was insufficient to protect the German nation from these impurities, extermination came to be seen as a necessity. And, so, millions died.

Ethnic cleansing thus serves a double purpose. Whereas forced transfer leaves alive aggrieved populations whose territorial claims might, at some time in the future, gain international legitimacy and recognition, genocide does not. Not only does it remove contenders for title to property, it also eliminates all witnesses to the deadly actions of the "moral community"—and, at times, as in towns and cities in the former Yugoslavia and other partitioned or cleansed territories, all physical traces, too.[11] Any who are left behind will testify to the evil intentions of those Others who have so conveniently been eliminated or erased from the scene.

Nothing Succeeds like Success

In the United States, attacks on "liberals," right-wing violence against the federal government and the "New World Order," and conservative and religious fervor for "family values" (Bennett, 1998) can be understood as an attempt to reimpose a nationalistic moral frame on what some think is becoming a socially anarchic society (Lipschutz, 1998b; Rupert, 1997). The *kulturkampf* at home is paralleled by the transformation of state practice from military-based to discipline-based behavior, especially where U.S. foreign policy is concerned (see chapter 4). A closer look suggests that the two are of a piece, as in the convergence of a draconian welfare policy with an increasingly vocal movement against immigrants—whatever their legal status—and their countries of origin.

Welfare is deemed to sap the moral vitality of the poor, to foster promiscuity and illegitimacy and, more generally, to be a form of immoral "theft" from righteous citizens. Although statistics suggest that most welfare recipients are U.S. citizens, much political ire and fire has been directed at immigrants, whose moral claim to be in the United States is deemed to be weak or nonexistent (a sentiment held by some against immigrants in other countries, too; see Crawford and Lipschutz, 1998). The film *Independence Day*, in which a disciplinary environmental sensibility (*RECYCLE*) complements a plot warning of "aliens stealing our resources," nicely illustrates how domestic and foreign policy have come together around the extension of morality from the private (domestic) to the public (international) sphere (and further into the solar system and even interstellar space).[12]

How can we explain such behaviors? While the demise of social (and moral) discipline has been instrumental in the erosion of the citizen-state relationship (Drainville, 1995; see also chapter 8), this is a proximate rather than a primary cause. To explain the sources of social disorder—in this instance, the decline of the state's moral authority—we must again look back to the immediate post–World War II period and the establishment of the Bretton Woods regime, which put in place the basis for the current social crisis. As I proposed in earlier chapters, the fundamental contradiction in the American and British goal of liberalizing the world economy was that the interests of citizen and state would coincide so long as there existed a threat against which only the state could protect the citizen. By extending the American economic system abroad, throughout the "Free World," but pointedly drawing lines around the always threatening Soviet bloc, this arrangement generated broad support among Western publics and largely eliminated the security dilemma inside of the Free World's borders.[13]

At the end of World War II, of course, the Free World was not yet "free,"[14] inasmuch as the Soviets had not yet been definitively tagged as the new enemy. Harry Truman's felicitous doctrinal phrasing concerning "free peoples everywhere" provided the label; the imperialism of the dollar and the fear of Reds did the rest. As the ex cathedra pronouncements of politicians, pundits, and pastors, and novels and films such as *The Manchurian Candidate* and *Invasion of the Body Snatchers* suggested, communism was a pathology of Nature, not an ideology of men; it took you over, you did not take it on (Lipschutz, 1997b: chap. 3). Keeping the enemy out and contained meant, therefore, not only imposing secure boundaries around the world but also imposing limits on one's own self and behavior.

The domino theory was not only about the fall of states; any rupture of containment could breach the individual self and expose it to evil. As I noted in chapter 3, the success and survival of the Free World depended on extending boundaries around a natural community

(Stone, 1988) that had not, heretofore, existed. *But in order to maintain its sovereignty and autonomy, this natural community had to be juxtaposed against another.* Thus, on one side of the boundary of containment was to be found a unit (the Free World) whose sovereignty depended upon keeping out the influences of a unit on the other side (the bloc). The Free World could never have existed without the corresponding "unfree world."

Within the borders of the Free World, however, there remained a problem: the protection of state sovereignty and autonomy—heretofore regarded as the natural order of things—threatened to undermine the integrity of the whole. This was especially difficult from the American point of view, as illustrated in the famous confrontation between so-called isolationists and internationalists.[15] The solution to the dilemma was a form of multilateral economic nationalism (Ruggie, 1983a; 1991, 1995). Inside the boundaries of the Free World, states were granted the right to manage their national economies, but only so long as they agreed to move toward and, eventually, adopt the tenets of an internationalized liberalism. With respect to the area outside the boundaries, however, the Free World would, to the extent possible, remain neomercantilistic and self-contained, antagonistic to those who refused to "come in from the cold" (Pollard, 1985; Lipschutz, 1989; Crawford, 1993).

Already in the late 1950s, the morality of this arrangement, and the security strategy based on nuclear "massive retaliation," was being challenged by so-called peace movements opposed to the threat-based logic of East-West relations (Deudney, 1995). By the early 1980s, the Free World's social contract was becoming fragile as a result of détente, a growing international emphasis on human rights, and the economic troubles that had begun during the 1970s. The former two threatened to undermine moral order within the Free World by turning friends into enemies and vice versa; the latter—especially inflation—threatened to undermine moral order within the United States. It required the renewal of a really cold Cold War during the 1980s to reestablish the moral polarities of East and West, and to excuse the vile behaviors of American allies in the name of meeting the greater moral threats of Soviet adventurism and loss of faith in America.

Alas, to no avail! The subsequent collapse of Communism, and the much-trumpeted triumph of liberalism and democracy, fully undermined the moral authority of the West, inasmuch as there was no longer a global "evil" against which to pose a global "good." As earlier chapters have shown, the efforts of some to reestablish a moral divide—as, for example, Samuel Huntington (1993, 1996) with his clashing civilizations—have not, so far, been conspicuously successful.

To restore its moral authority in times to come, the nation-state must redraw the boundaries of good and evil, replacing disorder with new (b)orders. The United States government is attempting to restore order at home and abroad in two ways. First, the notion of "democratization and enlargement," offered during the first Clinton administration, represents an attempt to expand the boundaries of the "good world" (see Clinton, 1997). Those who follow democracy and free markets subscribe to a moral order that makes the world safe for Goodness (which, in turn, supports the now-conventional wisdom that democracies never go to war with each other; but see Mansfield and Snyder, 1995). Second, as described in chapter 4, *disciplinary deterrence* is being directed against so-called rogue states, terrorists, and others of the "bad bloc," who are said to threaten the good world even though they possess only a fraction of the authority, influence, and destructive power of the latter.[16] Ordinary deterrence is aimed against any state with the capabilities to threaten or attack. Disciplinary deterrence is different. It is an act of national morality, not of national interests.

Bondage, Domination, Discipline

To repeat the point made in chapter 4, disciplinary deterrence is warfare by other means: through demonstration, through publicity, through the equivalent of corporal punishment. The difficulty with disciplinary deterrence is that there is no there there, and it does not work very well. It is largely conducted against imagined enemies, with imagined capabilities and the worst of imagined intentions. Two men with explosives or cults with gas hardly pose a threat to the whole of the physical body politic; it is their ability to undermine faith in state authority that is so fearsome to those in power. And, as pointed out in earlier chapters, *where* "rogues" and other such enemies might choose to issue a challenge, or *why* they would do so, is not at all evident (see also Lipschutz, 1999b). But that these enemies represent the worst of all possible moral actors is hardly questioned by anyone.

Disciplinary deterrence is not, however, limited to renegades outside of the United States; it has also been extended into the domestic arena. For most of the Cold War, the threat of Communist subversion, and the fear of being identified as a Pinko Comsymp in some police agency's files, were sufficient to keep U.S. citizens from straying too far from the Free World straight and narrow. Red baiting continued long after the Red Scares of the 1950s—one can even find it today, in the excoriation of so-called liberals (*San Francisco Chronicle*, 1997) and Marxist academics (Lind, 1991)—although the language of discipline and exclusion has become somewhat more sophisticated with the passage of time. Still, since the collapse of the Soviet Union it has been difficult for political and social elites to discipline an unruly polity; that things can get out of hand without strong guidance from above is the message of South Central (Los Angeles), Oklahoma City, Waco, and Ruby Ridge.

Consequently, warnings routinely issued from on high that the "world is a dangerous place" serve to replace the disciplining threat of Communism (Kugler, 1995). Such warnings are, however, unduly vague. We are told that weapons of mass destruction—nuclear, biological, chemical—could turn up in a truck or suitcase (Myers, 1997). We are informed that laptop cyberterrorists are skulking around the Internet. We are instructed that some country's missiles are bound, eventually, to land in Alaska, Hawaii, or even Los Angeles. Therefore, we must rely on and trust the authorities to prevent such eventualities, even though the damage done by one or several such devices would never approach the destructive potential that still rests in the arsenals of the nuclear weapons states (Lipschutz, 1999b).

Unnamed terrorists—often implied to be Muslim—are discussed and dissed, but some of the most deadly actors turn out to be the "boy or girl next door" (Kifner, 1995). The Clinton administration further sows paranoia, seeking funding to track such neighbors by

creat[ing] a special computer tracking system to flag, or "profile," passengers and identify those with suspicious travel patterns or criminal histories. . . . The names addresses, telephone numbers, travel histories and billing records of passengers would be run through a giant database that might lead to a search of the luggage of those deemed suspicious. (Broeder, 1996)

In a move reminiscent of CONTEILPRO, the FBI establishes "counter terrorism task forces" in a dozen major U.S. cities that, according to a draft memorandum, are "dedicated full time to the investigation of acts of domestic and international terrorism and the gathering of intelligence and [sic] international terrorism" (Rosenfeld, 1997). The Justice Department disseminates funds for cities to prepare for biological terror attacks. Domestic police departments acquire military-type guns and armored vehicles and, as events in New York, Los Angeles, and elsewhere suggest, take on the role of occupying army. And the fearful mayor of New York City, convinced that he might be a target for foreign malcontents, barricades City Hall so that no citizen can enter without official permission. Clearly, disorder knows no borders.

Every Wo/man a State!

The state possessed by the siren song of its own moral efficacy is not yet an artifact of history; as illustrated by international indignation over Rwanda, Bosnia, and Kosovo, the acts of purification required by extreme nationalism are not so willingly accepted in today's world as they once might have been. Interventions—on those rare occasions when they do take place—are still usually explained, however, by old statist moralities—the "balance of power" or some such—rather than humanistic ones. At the same time, moreover, a new phenomenon has emerged to challenge the logic of realism: the morality of the *market* has begun to displace the morality of the *state*. One might easily say, of course, that the market has no morality. Driven by an ethic of self-interest, the individual is motivated only to consume as much as possible, within the constraints of the combined limit of her debit and credit cards. And yet, and yet. . . .

There *is* a quite explicit morality associated with discourses of market liberalism and economic growth. According to Smithian principles, the behavior of individuals in free exchange, when taken together, leads to the collective betterment of society without the intervention of politics or power. The market is often offered as a "natural" institution, whose organic expansion is not unlike that of the Darwinian states of yore. Indeed, the contemporary mantra of economic competitiveness fuses the Social Darwinism of geopolitics with the Social Darwinisn of the market: as always, only the fittest will survive. Those old welfare-state ideas of community are not only passé, they are the sure path to failure (see, e.g., Cohen, 1997). Hence, the unfettered market generates an unequivocal *good* that, logically, must also be morally desirable. Conversely, the intervention of politics or power obstructs this generation of good by being "inefficient," and such meddling must therefore be immoral. The paradox that follows is that any equity brought about by politics comes to be regarded as *bad* (and immoral), while the inequities consequent on marketization are deemed regrettable but the natural consequence of human nature and *good* for those who get the short end of the stick (Himmelfarb, 1995; see also Szerszynski, 1996).

In his 1973 biography of Eisenhower's first secretary of state, John Foster Dulles, Townsend Hoopes (1973:286) wrote that Dulles believed that "American economic and technical superiority rested in large part on the *moral* superiority of the free enterprise system" (emphasis added). This was not an isolated belief, then or now. According to the President's Materials Policy Commission (1952:1)—the Paley Commission—established by President Truman in 1952 to examine the problem of raw materials supplies:

> The United States, once criticized as the creator of a crassly materialistic order of things, is today throwing its might into the task of keeping alive the spirit of Man and helping beat back from the frontiers of the free world everywhere the threats of force and of a new Dark Age which rise from the Communist nations. In defeating this barbarian violence *moral values* will count most, but they must be supported by an ample materials base. Indeed, the interdependence of moral and material values has never been so completely demonstrated as today, when all the world has seen the narrowness of its escape from the now dead Nazi tyranny and has yet to know the breadth by which it will escape the live Communist one—both materialistic threats aimed to destroy moral and spiritual man. The use of materials to destroy or preserve is the very choice over which the world struggle today rages. (Emphasis added)

Such ideas, originating with the Calvinist notion of the elect, have been repeated again and again in countless political jeremiads (Bercovitch, 1978) and presidential speeches, of which Bill Clinton's 1997 Inaugural Address is only one recent expression (and which his successor will, undoubtedly, repeat on January 21, 2001).

There is a difference between Calvinism and consumerism, however. In times past, one's material success was indicative of one's moral superiority; today, one's material consumption is indicative of one's contribution to the moral uplifting of the world. Indeed, we might say that, in the emerging global moral economy, consumption becomes not only an *individual* good, but a *collective* moral and utilitarian "good," too. Consumption fosters prosperity, prosperity improves people's well-being and contentment with the status quo, and the resultant stability of social relations is a morally desirable outcome. As President Clinton (1997) put it in "A National Security Strategy for a New Century,"

> As we enter the twenty-first century, we have an unprecedented opportunity to make our nation safer and more prosperous. Our military might is unparalleled; a dynamic global economy offers increasing opportunities for American jobs and American investment; and the community of democratic nations is growing, enhancing the prospects for political stability. . . .

Or, modifying slightly the late Deng Xiaoping's dictum, "It is glorious to consume."

The dissemination throughout the world of liberal market principles, including liberalization, privatization, and structural adjustment, thus begins to acquire the character of a teleological moral crusade rather than the simple pursuit of national or self-interest. Public ownership and welfare spending are condemned as inefficient and wasteful and proscribed by international financial bodies and investors. Venal and bloated governments expend resources on projects that contribute to corruption and indolence, and undermine individuals' efforts to improve their own position and status by dint of moral reasoning and good works. The discipline of the market rewards those who hew to its principles, whether state, corporation, or individual. And those who cannot or will not do so must be left to suffer the consequences of their economic apostasy.

It's the Economy, Stupid!

Stephen Gill (1995) has written perceptively about the ways in which the "global panopticon" of liberal markets act to impose their peculiar morality on the both the credit-worthy and credit-risky. As I argued above, as the nation-state and nationalism have lost the moral authority they once commanded, such authority has shifted increasingly to the market and its disciplines (Strange, 1996). And there is more religion to the market than meets the eye. Those who don't adhere to the standards of the credit-givers (and takers!)—whether individual or state—are cast out of the blessed innermost circle of the global economy. To be readmitted requires a strict regimen of self-discipline, denial, and reestablishment of one's good name.

But even those with triple-A credit ratings and platinum plastic are not free of this moral regime. Inundated daily with bank offers of new credit cards and below-market interest rates, the credit-worthy are kept to the straight and narrow by fear of punishment should they violate the code of the credit-rating agencies. The proper response to such offers is, of course, "Get thee from me, Satan!" (although not everyone can rise above such temptation; ballooning consumer debt and growing numbers of bankruptcies in the United States indicate that backsliding is on the increase). Nonetheless, we see here the true genius of a globalized credit system. Whereas Church authority was akin to statist regulation—the same rules for everybody, with damnation bestowed through the collective judgement of the community—market-based morality relies on *self-regulation* (and self-damnation). Pie can be had now (none of that "by and by in the sky" stuff) and temporal salvation is keyed to individual capacity to carry the maximum credit load that s/he can bear—different strokes for different folks. As many of us know from experience, however, self-regulation is a weak reed on which to base a social system. Moreover, the desire to consume to the maximum of one's individual credit limit does carry with it a larger consequence: the domestic social anarchy that arises from self-interest as the sole moral standard to which each individual consumer hews.

Faced with this New World morality, can the nation-state recapture its moral authority and reimpose the borders of order? In some places, such as the former Yugoslavia, the agents of virulent ethnonationalisms have tried, but only with limited success. More recently, in places such as Israel and Guatemala, the lure of riches in the market have come to outweigh the certainty of riches by forced appropriation (Lipschutz, 1999a). In other places, such as the United States and Europe, culture wars have become the chosen means to discipline those who would deviate from "traditional" social norms, in a forced effort to bring the heretics back in. But hedonism, cultural innovation, and social reorganization are hallmarks of the market so loved by the very conservatives who have launched these very domestic battles (Gabriel, 1997; Elliott, 1997).

Short of reimposing a kind of quasi-theocratic autarchy on their societies—which, in any case, would be vigorously opposed by the cosmopolitan economic elites that benefit from globalization, and lead to disruption and upheaval on a massive scale—the nation-state has little to fall back on in facing this new world. National borders might be guarded by armies, navies and police armed to the teeth, but the borders of nationalist moralities, drawn in the minds of the "nation," have always been fluid and difficult to demarcate. And imagination knows no boundaries. Carried to an extreme, the market will turn each of us into a nation of one, every man and woman a state, a world of 10 billion atomized, consuming countries. Then, indeed, will we enter into the "borderless world."

8❖
POLITICS AMONG PEOPLE

One may also observe in one's travel to distant countries the feelings of recognition and affiliation that link every human being to every other human being.
—Aristotle, *Nicomachean Ethics*

The pictures I have painted throughout this book are none too attractive; they might be pleasing to the logical eye but cannot be very appealing to the emotional one. Yet, such scenes of gloom, doom, conflict, war (and "liberal" peace; Lipschutz, 1999a) do not encompass the entire world. As Kenneth Boulding (1977) once pointed out, at any particular moment, the number of people living peaceful lives is much, much greater than the number who are not. Why, then, focus on the bad to the exclusion of the good or promising? Why not try to portray positive possibilities rather than a bleak futurescape?

We pay greater attention to social disorder, violent conflict, and war precisely because they are so outside the norm of everyday experience, because they "sell" in the media, and because they make us feel a need to do *something*. The result, however, is that we are left with the belief that the world truly *is* "a dangerous place," that we are under constant threat, and that there is little that we, as individuals or members of our small groups and organizations, can *do*. To be sure, there are matters of pressing importance that could, under certain circumstances, seriously undermine the viability of human civilization but, except for nuclear war or an errant asteroid, none of them is likely to erupt very suddenly or have an instantly terminal effect.

The critical question thus remains, as it was put at the beginning of the twentieth century: What is to be done? But "done" about what? And who is to decide? There are many problems, more than can possibly be addressed. It might seem odd, then, to assert that we do not lack for solutions to most of these problems, that we do "know" what to do. But, by and large, the solutions are primarily technical ones, in the sense that they propose to grow, make, or provide more: more food, more energy, more democracy, more capitalism, more peace agreements, more carbon dioxide sequestered in the ocean so that we can drive more cars.

When the time comes to apply these solutions, however, things turn out not to be quite so simple (Stone, 1988). To put the matter prosaically, it is often easier to make a horse drink than to change the customary social behaviors of both groups and individuals (Scott, 1999). Furthermore, when faced with a menu of possible choices about "what to do," not every individual or group will select that option most desired by policymakers, economists, or psychologists. "Rational choice" does not mean singular possibilities, and even "irrational" choices usually have a purpose behind them.

Later in this chapter, I offer a somewhat reflective perspective on the future of citizenship, political action, and civil society in a globalizing world, in the view that authority is possible only when people are members of a social institution whose goals they actively support (Drainville, 1996; Thomas, 1997). I also provide some thoughts about what "belonging" and "membership" might mean under these various arrangements. I argue there that, although the concept of global civil society has been underdefined, for a variety of reasons it remains a useful concept in terms of the matter of "after authority." Drawing on the work of Michael Mann (1993), Steven Gill (1993, 1995), Sakamoto (1994), and others, I attempt to offer a more concrete conceptualization, illustrating parallels between the emergence of the modern national state, citizenship, and domestic civil society, and a growing system of global governance and global civil society.

Making the claim that global civil society is important to the future of global politics does not imply some sort of teleological "triumph" of reason or a world state, if only because not all of the transnational networks, coalitions, and actors making up global civil society are supportive of this postnational project. Some act through these networks in order to resist the state, while others engage in attacks on states as collaborators with institutions of global governance such as the United Nations. Moreover, those economic actors deeply involved in hyperliberal globalization—primarily corporations and institutions of capital—also constitute an arm of a "global civil society" in their efforts to regulate politics at the transnational level and, in some instances, to intervene in domestic settings through sponsorship of functional projects at the local level. How these actors might view postnational politics and citizenship is not entirely clear.[1] Finally, the ultimate form of these mutually constitutive "entities" is, as yet, underdetermined; a collapse back into a more traditional international state system cannot be ruled out, although it is highly unlikely, as I have made clear throughout this book. The growth of various mechanisms of transnational governance, strongly driven by processes linked to economic globalization, suggest otherwise.

Prior to that discussion, however, I consider the question of choices: What choices are available; what might we do? I begin with a brief summary of my argument in this book and then ask: What happens after authority? Next, I turn to questions about the future of the nation-state: Will it survive? What will it do? Will something replace it? I discuss how the diffusion of jurisdictional authority from the state to other actors is both fragmenting and integrating global politics, but not in the conventionally understood territorial sense. Finally, I raise a challenge to the conventional "state/nonstate" dichotomy that characterizes the international relations and global politics literature, and propose that we need to go far beyond this binary if we are to understand and act on our future.

After Authority

In the preceding chapters of this book, I have argued that the basic problem we face is best understood as a disjunction between contemporary social change and people's expectations about their individual and collective futures. Changes in modes of production and reproduction have exposed us to what is, except during periods of war, a historically high rate of social innovation and reorganization. This change has progressed to the point that uncertainty has come to dominate politics, both domestic and global, in ways that were rarely the case, at such a large scale, in earlier times. We regard predictability (if not stability) as central to contemporary life. It is predictability that allows us to be reasonably certain that we can accomplish in the future what we have planned today; it is predictability that lets us go beyond fatalism to action.[2] Or, to put the point another way, we expect both our actions and the actions of others to be sufficiently patterned and predictable that we do not have to live in a "State of Nature" in which neighbors are enemies and no one can be trusted.[3]

Hobbes (1962) thought it necessary to create a Leviathan that would prevent such a situation by imposing its authority on society. Already more than three hundred years ago, he recognized in the English Civil War the potential disorder inherent in the methodological individualism that followed the collapse of centralized religious authority and the rise of capitalism. He therefore sought to discover a new source of rule—possibly based in Nature's mathematics or science—that could contain such disorder. But the joke, it turns out, has been on us. All along we have been told that the mythical "war of all against all," in which life was "nasty, brutish, and short," was a description of an antediluvian time, *before* authority and society, and that it was only the morality of state and society that brought humanity to a civilized condition.[4] Instead, the State of Nature turns out to be our *future,* a condition that, unwittingly or not, Leviathan itself has let loose on the world.

In this instance, I have argued, it is the globalization of markets that is undermining the state, a process set in train by the United States after World War II, a process that may soon approach its apotheosis in the "borderless world" (Ohmae 1991, 1995). This is hardly a new or innovative argument—that the spread of market forces destroys the basis for the social contract that Hobbes and others thought so necessary to restrain human nature (Polanyi, 1944/1957)—and it is one that is harshly critiqued by any number of analysts (see the *The Economist,* 1997; for counter arguments, see Hirsch, 1995; Ellis and Kumar, 1983). What *is* new is, perhaps, the inversion of the sequence of events, followed by the query: Who or what is to decide on an "authoritative allocation of values" in the absence of authority? The World Federalists sought (and continue to seek) global federation. William Ophuls (Ophuls and Boyan, 1992) and Robert Heilbroner (1991) proposed something akin to world dictatorship. George Bush's New World Order rested on American hegemony and discipline. Perhaps in the future wealth or corporate tonnage will become the basis of authority, in which case Bill Gates might become the global "Grand Poobah" or Exxon-Mobil a new superpower. Or, conceivably, each individual and her appetite will become her sole source of authority; if so, even the corporation as we know it might not survive. Hyperbole, perhaps, but in some places not so far from the truth.

What, then, *is* our future after authority? Most analysts peering into the future try to describe the big picture: The world will be richer. It will be happier. It will be poorer. It will be crowded. It will be violent. It will be wired. To be sure: it may be all of those. But such global generalizations, encapsulating in very short sound bites the actions of the six (now) or 10 billion (by 2050 or so) individuals populating the Earth, do not tell us very much about what those people are up to, or will be up to. Yet, if the individual has become the new sovereign, as I have argued in this book, what people do *will* matter, whether they do it alone or in groups, whether they do it peacefully or violently, whether they do it for self-interest or the community. And *why* they do what they will do will matter, too, because, in the final analysis, *their* sources of authority for *their* actions will be important to politics.

In making this point, I do not mean to suggest that many of the problems that give rise to both clichés and questions of rule and rules are, somehow, *not* transnational, transboundary, or world-encompassing in nature, or that national, cultural, and class differences are *not* implicated in them. I do mean to argue, however, that these problems, factors, and forces are not implicated in world politics in the ways that the Huntingtons, Barbers, Fukuyamas, Ohmaes, or Kaplans of our day might claim they are. Indeed, it is more probable that, after authority, authority will originate less in the actions of "great women and men" of state than in the patterns of everyday politics, of politics among people, locally and globally. These patterns will have less to do with hegemonic stories of a dangerous world and the actions that follow, and more to do with fairly mundane matters, with everyday questions of governance, citizenship, and even civic virtue: Who rules? Whose rules? What rules? What kind of rules? At what level? In what form? Who decides? On what basis?

It is fair to say that these questions, and other similar ones, are already being answered. People's responses to them are evident in their patterns of behavior in a number of political arenas, in the reorganization of politics around functional issues such as environmental restoration and protection, human rights, gender, indigenous peoples, labor, and culture, as well as trade, investment, property rights, and product standards. While some of these patterns and tendencies might seem contradictory (and are), in that their orientations and consequences are often in opposition, they are all part of what I have called, elsewhere, "global civil society" and global governance (Lipschutz, 1996)[5] and they are all generating new types of institutional roles and relations, memberships, and categories of belonging (indeed, were we speaking of nation and state, we might call these roles "citizenship"). To a growing degree, it is in functional arenas such as these, and the ways in which people act toward them and with each other, that we must look in order to see the emerging outlines of twenty-first century politics among people.

The skeptical reader might rightfully ask, "What is the evidence for this global civil society and these new forms of citizenship? The state, after all, remains the most powerful and authoritative actor in global affairs. Moreover, if such things do exist, what do they presage?" Would they mean the disappearance of the state-system and a true "postsovereign, postinternational" world politics, as James Rosenau (1990; 1997) has put it? Are not "sovereignty-free" transnational networks and actors so dependent on the structures created and supported by states that they cannot exist without them? How could a global politics function if its basic units were not defined in territorial terms? And, are global civil society and new forms of citizenship plausible in the face of the communitarian and ethnic forces tearing apart so many countries? Can there be a truly democratic, transparent, and representative global politics without the state?

The State(s) of Our Future

In recent years, speculation about the "future of the state" has been rife (as evident from this book and others cited throughout). What is most conspicuous, and provides the basis for solid skepticism about the unchanging nature of world politics, are seemingly contradictory tendencies evident in world politics, as we have seen in earlier chapters.[6] On the one hand, we are offered the notion of a single world, integrated via a globalizing economy, in which the sovereign state appears to be losing much of its authority and control over domestic and foreign affairs (Ohmae, 1991; 1995; Strange, 1996; Woodall, 1995). These trends appear to point toward an eventual world state or federation, along the lines of the European Union, only bigger. On the other hand, and contrary to the expectations of neofunctionalists and others, we have seen once-unified countries fracture into war-ridden fragments, in which an ever shrinking state exercises sovereignty over diminishing bits of territory. Both processes involve, as Susan Strange (1996) put it, a "retreat of the state," albeit in quite different ways. But they also suggest that integration will not lead to a world federation of states and regions even as fragmentation does not presage a return to national sovereignty and a more traditional international relations among five hundred or more states. So, what is going on?

In *The Great Transformation,* Karl Polanyi (1944/57) argued that the self-regulating market was an ideal that could not be fully achieved, lest it destroy human civilization; the two world wars almost accomplished this task (and the Third World War that never happened, but might yet, would surely do so). In recent decades, we have tended to forget his prescient warnings.[7] The globalization of production and capital over the past half century has been accompanied by liberalization and, at the rhetorical level at least, a commitment to the deregulation of markets. But in deregulation lies an apparent paradox of our times: a liberal economy cannot exist without rules—so, where are they? Indeed, as I noted in chapter 7, markets *require* rules in order to function in an orderly fashion (Mead, 1995/96; Attali, 1997).

In the late nineteenth and early twentieth centuries, the first steps toward globalization were brought to a halt by national governments and elites who saw threats to their autonomy and prerogatives. The same pattern followed in the 1930s, and there are a few signs that this may be happening again, today. Free traders and their economist supporters decry the protectionist trends they see developing in trade relations among the industrialized economies, warning that the world is going down the same path it has trodden before (Bergsten, 1996).

Perhaps they are correct, perhaps not. It is certainly not beyond the realm of possibility that competitive geopolitical blocs could (re)emerge in the future, as feared by some observers of the European Union, the North American Free Trade Area, and the once-feared and now dormant New Asian Co-Prosperity Sphere under Japanese tutelage. There remains, however, enough residual collective memory, and the World Trade Organization, to suggest that such an outcome might be avoided.

But there are good reasons, too, for arguing that contemporary international economic relations bear little if any resemblance to the 1930s. As I have noted throughout this book, nation-states are caught in a contradiction of their own making and, for all the parallels to the past, are treading down a path they have *not* walked before. On the one hand, they are decentralizing, deregulating, and liberalizing in order to provide more attractive economic environments for financial capital and, as they do so, dismantling the safety net provided by the welfare state. That safety net, it should be noted, includes not only assurance of health and safety, environmental protection, public education, and so on, but also standard sets of rules that "level the economic playing field" and ensure the sanctity of contracts, the latter two both desired by capital. On the other hand, the shift of regulation from the national to the international level is creating a new skein of rules and regulations.

Even the British-governed international economy of the nineteenth century, often idealized by gold bugs and free traders, was not a free-for-all. It *was* regulated, if only by the constraints of the gold standard and the resultant behavior of financiers in London and New York. Today's markets are hardly self-regulating, either. While "deregulation" is the mantra repeated endlessly in virtually all national capitals and by all international capitalists, it is *domestic* deregulation vis à vis other producers that is desired, not the wholesale elimination of all rules (Vogel, 1996; Graham, 1996). Selective deregulation at home may create a lower-cost environment in which to produce, but deregulation everywhere creates uncertainty and economic instability. Hence, transnational regulation and global welfarism—the successors to Bretton Woods—are becoming increasingly important in keeping the global economic system together and working.[8] The difficulty with the globalization of rules is, to repeat an earlier point: What rules and whose rules? Who pays for them? Who decides what they will say? And how are those decisions made?

There is another important problem here. With national economies, there was at least the possibility of addressing domestic maldistribution; a global economy hardly permits even this. As deregulated capitalism works its way within countries, the economic playing field develops pits, holes, and undulations, and the distribution of wealth both within and between countries, groups, and classes becomes more and more uneven. This, as might be expected, can pose political problems both domestically and internationally (see, e.g., Pollack, 1997; Kapstein, 1996). For example, in the United States and other industrialized countries, groups of small-scale fixed capitalists, property owners, workers, and others chafe under the new economic environment. But individual countries cannot move to reregulate because there are strong interests who benefit from domestic deregulation, and to reimpose political management might also be to give up a competitive advantage to other countries and their firms.

The future does not, however, lie with petty capitalists or labor who operate within the limits of subnational economies; these groups are, generally speaking, of little interest to Wall Street—except for their role in domestic consumption—and they are rarely a locus of technological and organizational innovation.[9] Profits are to be found in the high-tech and information industries, in transnational finance and investment, and in flexible production and accumulation. This means looking beyond national borders for ways in which to deploy capital, technology, and design in order to maximize returns and access to foreign markets. One obstacle to such moves is that the transaction costs associated with having to deal with 50- or 150-odd sets of national regulations can be quite high. High–tech, financial, and transnational sectors would, therefore, prefer to see the playing field made level *among* countries—preferably as inexpensively as possible, but level nonetheless—through single sets of rules that apply to *all* countries, much as is supposed to be the case within the European Union or among the members of international regimes (Vogel, 1995).

And so, although it is often argued that there is no global government, and that regulatory harmonization is not only difficult but also unfair (Bhagwati, 1993), global regulations have been and are being promulgated all the time. The General Agreement on Trade and Tariffs, and its successor, the World Trade Organization, provide examples of regulatory harmonization for the benefit of capital and country. The

Montreal Protocol on Substances that Deplete the Ozone Layer is a regulatory system designed to harmonize rules governing production of ozone-damaging substances. The Nuclear Non-Proliferation Treaty is intended to regulate the production and use of atomic bombs and fissile materials by its signatories. The human rights regime is meant to set a standard for the fair and just treatment of citizens by their states and governments as well as by their fellow citizens. International meetings such as the Conference on Population and Development in Cairo aim at the promulgation of a globally shared set of norms and rules. The ISO 14000 rules recently issued by the International Organization for Standardization are meant to provide a framework for "green" management by corporations. And even international financial institutions, such as the World Bank, are becoming involved in the provision of health and welfare services, albeit as a supplement to the large-scale projects they traditionally support.

Indeed, the raft of regimes and international institutions associated with the United Nations system and other transnational groups might be said to constitute something of an incipient international regulatory system (although there are many holes in this "safety net"). As such, it serves two critical functions. First, it sets in place norms and rules that are meant to apply everywhere, even though these standards are sometimes less rigorous than the citizens of particular countries would like, and observation and enforcement remain very problematic. Second, the system makes it possible for national governments to tell their citizens that a particular problem *is* being addressed but that they—both citizen and representatives—have no control over the content of the rules, and that domestic politics must not be permitted to intrude into either the promulgation or functioning of the rules. Note that political intervention into the market system is taking place here, albeit out of reach of domestic interest groups, lobbyists, and logrolling. The absence of accountability on the part of these global institutions is not so easily shrugged off and serious questions are being raised about this matter (Gill, 1993, 1995). Nevertheless, we see here the beginnings of global governance (and taxation) although, as yet, not representation.

There is little question that the "state" will remain a central actor in world politics for some time to come, by virtue of its capabilities, its material and discursive powers, and its domination of the political imaginary. Nevertheless, what has been regarded as the hard core of *jurisdictional authority* of the state—a naturalized fiction if ever there was one—is diffusing away throughout an emergent, multilevel and quite diverse system of globalizing *and* localizing governance and behavior.[10] Some have suggested that these changing patterns constitute a "new (or neo) medievalism"; others have proposed as organizing principles "heteronomy"[11] or "heterarchy."[12] In discussing the first of these three concepts, Ole Wæver (1995: note 59) argues that

> for some four centuries, political space was organized through the principle of territorially defined units with exclusive rights inside, and a special kind of relations on the outside: International relations, foreign policy, without any superior authority. There is no longer one level that is clearly *the* most important to refer to but, rather, *a set of overlapping authorities*. (First emphasis in original; second emphasis added)

What is critical here is not political *space*, but political *authority*, in two senses: first, the ability to get things done, and second, recognition as the legitimate source of jurisdiction and action (as opposed to one's ability to apply force or coercion in the more conventionally understood sense). As John Ruggie (1989: 28) has pointed out, in a political system—even a relatively unsocialized one—*who* has "the right to act as a power [or authority] is at least as important as an actor's *capability* to force unwilling others to do its bidding" (emphasis added). In this neomedieval world, authority will arise more from the control of knowledge and the power that flows from that control than outright material capabilities. The power to coerce will, of course, remain important, but most people do not need to be coerced; they want to be convinced.

This is meant neither as a teleological nor a necessarily progressivist argument. The eventual content of global governance and an international regulatory system could serve the interests of a narrow stratum of political and economic elites and prove profoundly conservative and reactionary (Gill, 1995). The result might be a repetition of previous catastrophes, as the pain of globalization bites deeply at home (Kapstein, 1996). There are disquieting trends to which one can point— such as the globalization of surveillance through information technologies and struggles to construct new, albeit bankrupt, states. Still, the future is not (yet) etched in stone.

Aux Armes, Citoyen?

What this discussion has not, so far, defined is the relationship between individuals and the new forms of political action inherent in the globalization of functional authority. That discussion requires an inquiry into the nature of membership in a political community, that is, *citizenship*. In its standard form, citizenship is defined as a collection of rights and obligations that give individuals a formal legal identity within a state and society. The Westernized (and, some would argue, masculinized) philosophical problem of how individuals come together to form political collectives in which they are members has puzzled political philosophers for centuries. The apparent tension between human beings as highly individualistic entities and the societies they nevertheless have created led historically to such propositions as Leviathan, the Social Contract, the Watchman State, Civil Republicanism, the Welfare State, and even the Invisible Hand. Indeed, the problem of how State and Society came to be remains something of a puzzle to Western theorists, even today.

These are not, however, the only ways to conceive of citizenship. As Bryan Turner (1997:5) puts it in the introduction to the first issue of a journal called *Citizenship Studies,* "[T]hese legal rights and obligations [of citizenship] have been put together historically as sets of social institutions such as the jury system, parliaments and welfare states." Turner goes on to argue that a "political" conception of citizenship is typically focused on "political rights, the state and the individual," whereas a "sociological" definition involves the nature of people's entitlements to scarce resources, confers a particular cultural identity on individuals and groups, and includes the "idea of a political community as the basis of citizenship . . . typically the nation-state." That is,

> when individuals become citizens, they not only enter into a set
> of institutions that confers upon them rights and obligations, they
> not only acquire an identity, they are not only socialized into civic
> virtues, but they also become members of a political community
> with a particular territory and history. (Turner, 1997:9)

The advantage of this definition is that it ties together the material substructure of citizenship with the superstructure of rules, rights, behaviors, attitudes, and obligations that constitute the citizen vis-à-vis other citizens and the state. The market is part of this institutional structure and, historically, the rules underwriting and functioning of markets have been guaranteed by the authority and activities of the state.[13]

In "normal" times, the contradictions between substructure and superstructure are minimal—or are either not very evident or are foisted off on the poor and powerless as "natural"—and citizenship is a relatively stable construct. Under those circumstances, people follow the rules and expect to receive commensurate rewards in return (see chapter 6). Less and less, however, are these "normal" times, as I have argued throughout this book. For better or worse, then, the tensions between globalization and fragmentation cannot be addressed by attempts to establish exclusive domains of society and citizen, either by philosophy or force. Such solutions attempt to "imagine communities" (Anderson, 1991) into being without taking into account the material forces that are, on the one hand, keeping imaginary communities from becoming "real" and, on the other hand, pulling real ones apart.

The core problematic here is that the forces of globalization are disrupting the boundaries that, for the past two centuries, contained societies and national communities and provided the basis for contextual forms of citizenship and belonging (Shapiro and Alker, 1996). Attempts to reestablish these boundaries and the civic communities within them through disciplinary measures, whether domestic or foreign, risk reproducing the logic of antagonistic nation-states in a much more fragmented form, as newly imagined communities resist the hegemony of the old one (see the essays in Crawford and Lipschutz, 1998).

If territorial units are no longer the logical focus for political loyalty, can some other form of political community substitute? What can replace the citizen's allegiance to state as the new basis for politics? If the rampant individualism of the market is creating a world of 10 billion statelets, how can people come together to act collectively? In principle, states might be able to act against the tendency of marketization to diminish their authority within their national boundaries. In practice, and short of a repeat of a global crisis akin to the 1930s (which was, after all, one of the reasons for the post–World War II globalization project), it is difficult to imagine such a restoration taking place. For reasons I have discussed elsewhere, having to do with the notion of global governance (Lipschutz, 1996), we need to look beyond the nation-state to answer the questions posed above. In what follows, I want to suggest that there is a real problem with thinking about alternatives to citizenship, especially if we are focused on ways to restore them *within* the "iron cage" of the contemporary nation-state form.

In recent years, research into transnational social movements, nongovernmental organizations, global networks and coalitions, and global governance structures has represented the core of thinking about alternatives to the state among academics and intellectuals (see, e.g., Princen and Finger, 1994; Wapner, 1996; Mathews, 1997; Keck and Sikkink, 1998; Lipschutz, 1996 and the citations therein). Still, virtually all that has been written about these trends continues to use the language and framework of state and "nonstate" actors. As Paul Wapner and others have pointed out, this focus on the state and its "discontents" reflects a certain poverty of imagination about other types of nonnational, postnational political arrangements. In particular, this singular focus leaves out those other discussions that avoid or even ignore the state/nonstate dichotomy. It is at this very point that debates stall over the future of citizenship, politics, and authority under globalization.

Is there another way to think about alternatives to the state? To develop this line of thought, I draw on a body of theory that, at first glance, might appear far removed from international relations theory: the work of Judith Butler.[14] In her 1990 book, *Gender Trouble,* Butler uses the work of Michel Foucault to show how, in the case of gender, "juridical systems of power *produce* the subjects they invariably come to represent."

> The question of "the subject" is crucial for politics, and for feminist politics in particular, because juridical subjects are invariably produced through certain exclusionary practices that do not "show" once the juridical structure of politics has been established. In other words, the political construction of the subject proceeds with certain legitimating and exclusionary aims, and these political operations are effectively concealed and naturalized by a political analysis that takes juridical structures as their foundation. Juridical power inevitably "produces" what it claims merely to represent; hence, politics must be concerned with this dual function of power: the juridical and the productive. (Butler, 1990:2)

Butler (1990:2) goes on to argue that "the category of 'women,' the subject of feminism, is produced and restrained by the very structures of power through which emancipation is sought." Elsewhere in the book (112), she writes that "if gender is not tied to [biological] sex, either casually or expressively, then gender is a kind of action that can potentially proliferate beyond the binary limits imposed by the apparent binary of sex" (parenthetical term added).[15] Butler (1990:9–13) also points to the work of Luce Irigaray who writes that, in the hegemonic discourses of gender with which we are most familiar (even if not in agreement), women are not the *opposite* of men but, rather (if I understand the argument correctly) are *not-men* (my words). Butler (1990:11) puts it thus.

> The female sex is thus also *the subject* that is not one. The relation between masculine and feminine cannot be represented in a signifying economy in which the masculine constitutes the closed circle of signifier and signified. (Emphasis in original)

I quote Butler at length here because her analysis can be transposed from her focus on *women* (as "not-men"), and the term's always-casual pairing with "men," to what are conventionally called *nonstate actors* (i.e., not-state). The term "nonstate actors" is paired with "state" just as casually in international politics literature to denote those political collectivities that act in the inter/transnational realm but that lack specific reified attributes of the state—territory, sovereignty, legitimate monopoly of violence. Such collective actors have the same relationship to the "signifying economy in which the [state] constitutes the closed circle of signifier and signified," as the feminine has to the masculine. The state, in this "signifying economy," becomes a "naturalistic necessity" (Butler, 1990:33) against which other political actors are treated and evaluated in terms of their (nonnatural) inability to replicate the symbolic and functional roles of a state for lack of appropriate (natural) tools. The result is that international relations (IR) scholars are always asking, "Yes, but can nonstate actors *do* what the state does?" when a more appropriate query might be "Is what the state has been doing even necessary?"

To give an example, several years ago, as the war in Bosnia was nearing the end of its most violent phase, Michael Mandelbaum (1996), the "Christian A. Herter Professor of American Foreign Policy at the Paul H. Nitze School of Advanced International Studies, Johns Hopkins University, and director of the Project on East-West Relations at the Council on Foreign Relations," attacked the Clinton administration for conducting "foreign policy as social work." Responding to then-national security advisor Anthony Lake's questionable argument that "I think Mother Teresa and Ronald Reagan were both trying to do the same thing," Mandelbaum (1996:18) riposted:

> While Mother Teresa is an admirable person and social work a noble profession, conducting American foreign policy by her example [sic; it was *not* social work!] is an expensive proposition. The world is a big place filled with distressed people, all of whom, by these lights, have a claim to American attention.

Not only did Mandelbaum ignore the role of the American state in fostering the "noble profession" of social work, he also fell into the traditional realist trap of regarding such intervention as unworthy of state attention, presumably seeing it as an activity fit only for nonstate actors. The American state has military power for a purpose, and it must use it!

A further, and much more fundamental, consequence of this binary treatment of state/nonstate was raised in chapters 4 and 6. Not only must a nation have a state of its own (or, perhaps, vice versa), a nation without a state is incomplete and impotent. It cannot act in international politics in a fully capable (and male) fashion; it must not even accept anything less than a fully sovereign (and potent) state. To remain a "not-state" is to not exist. Such views, to put it mildly, are absolute nonsense. More than that, they cast the matter of after authority in quite a different light than a choice between micro states and macro markets, and suggest a program that is quite distinct from the integration/fragmentation dichotomy of the state/not-state binary.

To go beyond this, toward a "proliferation" of legitimate and authoritative actors in the inter/transnational realm, requires us to think (and act) quite differently where global politics are concerned; as Butler (1990:33) writes about gender

> To expose the contingent acts that create the appearance of naturalistic necessity . . . is a task that now takes on the added burden

of showing how the very notion of the subject, intelligible only through its appearance as gendered [or state/not-state], admits of possibilities that have been forcibly foreclosed by the various reifications of gender [state/not-state] that have constituted its contingent ontologies. (Parenthetical terms added)

In practice, this is a rather more difficult proposition to operationalize, but to the extent that theory informs practice (and practice informs theory), opening up for examination the possibilities beyond the binary can make a contribution to such a project. For the moment, it is incumbent upon us to recognize that even the term "state" is applied to many, rather different political entities. Such difference ought to be welcomed as providing openings for imagining communities, rather than being bemoaned or ignored. And, if we are to speculate on alternatives to citizenship *in* the nation-state, we ought first to look to the alternatives *to* the nation-state that already exist in some form. As Iris Marion Young (1990:234) argues, "A model of a transformed society must begin from the material structures that are given to us at this time in history."

Below, I discuss three alternatives, although these hardly exhaust the universe of possibilities. First, I expand on "global civil society," which builds on parallels between state and domestic civil society, without necessarily postulating the emergence of a global state. The second involves the emergence of counterhegemonic social movements, which could provide the basis for new and innovative forms of political organization and action. The third focuses on the partial deterritorialization of political identity and political community.

Global Civil Society

In the heteronomous (dis)order of the future, authority will likely be distributed among many foci of political action, organized to address specific issue-areas rather than to exercise a generalized rule over a specific territory (Lipschutz, 1996: chap. 8). Territorially based political jurisdictions will continue to exist, but they will be complemented by others whose responsibilities will lie elsewhere. As Crook, Pakulski, and Waters (1992:34–35) point out, the relationship between actors and jurisdictions might not necessarily follow logically from their apparent functions. Schools are as likely to engage in environmental restoration as environmental organizations are to become involved in education at the K–12 level (see also Lipschutz, 1996: chap. 5).

Elsewhere, I have argued that "global civil society" could represent a structure of actors and networks within which these new authorities emerge (Lipschutz, 1997c). As conventionally understood, civil society includes those political, cultural, and social organizations of modern societies that have not been established or mandated by the state or created as part of the institutionalized political system of the state (e.g., political parties). These groups are, nevertheless, engaged in a variety of political activities.[16] Globalizing the concept extends this arrangement into the transnational arena, where it constitutes a protosociety composed of local, national, and global institutions, corporations, and nongovernmental organizations. Global civil society can be understood as shorthand for both the actors and networks that constitute a "new spatial mosaic of global innovation" (Gordon, 1995:196) and the growth in neofunctional authority resulting from a "proliferation" of political actors beyond, above, and beside the state.

But civil society and the state are not formations independent of each other; "sovereignty-bound" and "sovereignty-free," as James Rosenau (1990) has put it, are not fully dichotomous conditions. A state relies on some version of civil society for its legitimacy, a civil society cannot exist without the authority conveyed by the state, whether it is democratic or not. Indeed, we might go so far as to say that the two are mutually constitutive and derive their roles and identities from their relationship with each other. Of course, civic associations such as bowling leagues do operate quite autonomously of the state, yet we would be hard put to claim that they have no relationship whatsoever with the state. The members of a bowling league play according to "official" rules, wearing clothes and using equipment that have been vetted for safety by state officials, paying with money printed by the state, playing in a building whose every basic feature has been mandated by state regulations and constructed by virtue of state-granted permits, having arrived there in licensed vehicles on roads built by the state, etc., etc.

By the same token, the state is continually reproduced by the beliefs and practices of civic associations, whether or not they are overtly political. The bowling league does little or nothing that deliberately and consciously helps to reproduce the state—aside, perhaps, from its individual members paying taxes and respecting its institutions. Nevertheless, the normal activities of the league's members serve to reproduce the normal existence of those conditions that legitimate the state. Bowlers, after all, rarely blow up state buildings or take up arms against the government (and were they to do so, they might actually intensify the state's presence and legitimacy). None of this is to argue that bowling leagues are authoritative, neofunctional entities, but neither are they mere venues for throwing balls and drinking beer.

Why does this matter? It matters because declining state authority will, in all likelihood, be supplemented or replaced by, or sublimated in, some kind of alternative political framework, which could be similar to a world state or very different. The late Richard Gordon's (1995) research suggested that the relationship of production to politics, and the politics of production, are changing rather radically from what they once were. The strategies of corporate actors and other holders of capital take less and less cognizance of the residual authority and power of individual states to regulate them. More and more, they engage in individual and collective attempts to self-regulate (as, for example, in the multifarious activities of the International Organization for Standardization—ISO) or to generate supranational regulation (as in the World Trade Organization).

These findings point also toward the fact that political community—even a federal state—is not restricted to discrete levels of government. As Theda Skocpol (1985:28) points out:

> On the one hand, states may be viewed as organizations through which official collectivities may pursue collective goals, realizing them more or less effectively given available state resources in relation to social settings. On the other hand, states may be viewed more macroscopically as configurations of organizations and action that influence the meanings and methods of politics for all groups and classes in society.

Skocpol offers here a conception of the state that is, perhaps, too broad in encompassing society, but her point is, in my view, an important one. The state is more than just its constitution, agencies, rules, and roles, and it is embedded, as well, in a system of governance. From this view, state and civil society can be seen as mutually constitutive and, where the state engages in *government,* civil society often plays a role in *governance.*

What is striking, especially in terms of relationships between nongovernmental organizations and institutionalized mechanisms of government, as well as capital and international regimes, is the growth of institutions of governance at and across *all* levels of analysis, from the local to the global (see, e.g., Leatherman, Pagnucco, and Smith, 1994: esp. pp. 23–28). This growth suggests, to repeat the argument made above, that even though there is no world government, as such, there may well be an emerging system of *global governance.* Subsumed within this system of governance are both institutionalized regulatory arrangements—some of which we call "regimes"—and less formalized norms, rules, and procedures that pattern behavior without the presence of written constitutions or material power.[17] This system is not a "state," as we commonly understand the term, but it is statelike, in Skocpol's second sense. Indeed, we can see emerging patterns of behavior in global politics based on alliances between coalitions in global civil society and various international governance arrangements (see, e.g., Wilmer, 1993, on indigenous peoples alliances).

What constitutes the equivalent of citizenship in such a system of global governance? The interests of transnational capital are represented, to some degree, in the international financial regimes but, so far, there is little if any global regulation for the rest of us (Lipschutz, 1999d). There are no mechanisms for representation of anything other than nation-states (although a number of groups and organizations do have observer status in the United Nations General Assembly). There are only a very few judicial fora in which actors other than nation-states can bring international legal actions (although, again, this situation is slowly changing). The idea of the "world" citizen is a rather empty one, while arguments about global "cosmopolitanism" rarely acknowledge just how few are the members of this class. For the moment, therefore, the answer to this question is less than clear. In the longer term, however, we might expect to see the issues of membership and representation become central to support for the institutions and mechanisms of global governance.

Counterhegemonic Social Movements

A second alternative is related to global civil society but focuses more on the emergence of what are called "counterhegemonic social movements." Robert Cox (1987) and Stephen Gill (1993, 1994), among others, have used a Gramscian framework to speculate on the political possibilities of organized opposition to the hegemonic tendencies of global capital and authority. They argue, in essence, that contemporary progressive social movements represent social forces challenging the "historic bloc" that comprises the contemporary nexus of power rooted in states and capital. According to Gill (1994:195)

> Counter-hegemonic social movements and associated political organizations must mobilize their capabilities and create the possibility for the democratization of power and production. . . . [W]e might witness a 1990s version of Polanyi's "double movement" as social movements are remobilized and new coalitions are formed to protect society from the unfettered logic of disciplinary neo-liberalism and its associated globalizing forces.

How these challengers will proceed is somewhat less clear, although Cox, Gill, and others believe that the growing discursive power of "organic intellectuals" may play a central role in mobilizing these movements.

There is nothing new about organic intellectuals, per se; what *is* new is the scale at which they must do their work. Michael Mann (1993), drawing on the writings of Antonio Gramsci, has written about the emergence of national states in Europe and North America during the 1700s and 1800s, and the economic, political, and social revolutions and changes that took place throughout the "long" nineteenth century. Put briefly, Mann sees the rise of organic intellectuals, who played an essential role in the creation of the modern state, as central to the transition from royal to popular sovereignty and contemporary conceptions of citizenship (they were all men, and were seeking to establish new loci of authority, so it is not surprising that citizenship was defined largely in male terms). They filled primarily a discursive role in a gradual process of social change, by developing and articulating the ideas and practices that animated the political and social upheavals of those times. Mann observes that, while material interests and needs were always central to popular mobilization, emotional and ideational incentives were at least as important.

More than this, the ideas and arguments of the organic intellectuals were framed in terms of "progress," promising a better future through political, economic, and social reorganization. Nationalism, liberalism, socialism, and other "isms" that reified the strong state were teleological ideologies produced by these organic intellectuals. Without their communicating these arguments and putting them into practice, the nineteenth century might have been a much quieter, but less democratic, time. As it was, the centralized nation-states that have dominated world politics for the past century were, for better or worse, legitimated by the ideas of these intellectuals, if not constructed by them. As Mann (1993:42) has argued:

> Capitalism and discursive literacy media were the dual faces of a civil society diffusing throughout eighteenth-century European civilization. They were not reducible to each other, although they were entwined. . . . Nor were they more than partly caged by dominant classes, churches, military elites, and states, although they were variably encouraged and structured by them. Thus, they were partly transnational and interstitial to other power organizations. . . . Civil societies were always entwined with states—and they become more so during the long nineteenth century.

Here I would propose that the "organic intellectuals" that operate within these counterhegemonic social movements constitute a transnational cadre that could help to create the "double movement" discussed by Polanyi and Gill.

I do not refer here to populist opposition to globalization, as put forth by both the left and the right. Such movements seek to restore the primacy of the nation-state in the regulation of spheres of production and social life, although they have rather different ideas about the ends of such a restoration. Rather, I refer to more nuanced critiques of current modes of transnational regulation and their lack of representation, transparency, and accountability. Globalization offers a space for political organizing and activism of which these organic intellectuals and the mobilizers and members of nascent political communities are well-positioned to take advantage.

Political Deterritorialization

Can we imagine political arrangements in which citizenship is possible yet not dependent on territorial units, such as the nation-state? A deterritorialized political community would have to be based not on space, but on flows; not on *where* people live, but *what* links them together. That is, the identity between politics and people would not be rooted in a specific piece of reified "homeland" whose boundaries, fixed in the mind and on the ground, excluded all others. Instead, to slightly revise Michael J. Shapiro, this identity would be based on "a heterogenous set of . . . power centers integrated through structures of communication" (Shapiro, 1997:206) as well as knowledge and practices specific to each community. Kathy Ferguson (1996:451–52) argues that

> collective identity based on control of territory sponsors a zero-sum calculation: either we belong here or they do. One can imagine collective identities that are deterritorialized, knit together in some other ways, perhaps from shared memories, daily practices, concrete needs, specific relationships to people, locations, and histories. Such productions would be more narrative than territorial; they might not be so exclusive because they are not so relentlessly spatial. Connection to a particular place could still be honored as one dimension of identity, but its intensities could be leavened by less competitive claims. Participation in such identities could be self-consciously partial, constructed, mobile; something one does and redoes every day, not a docile space one simply occupies and controls. Empathy across collective identities constructed as fluid and open could enrich, rather than endanger, one's sense of who one is.

This is, perhaps, the most difficult political alternative to conceptualize, and we do not yet have much to go on. There is much talk, these days, of "virtual communities," composed of "netizens" linked through the Internet and the World Wide Web, but this is hardly a *political* entity, even in its broadest definition (e.g., Aizu, 1998). While the networks through which individuals and groups are connected provide conduits for communication of knowledge and patterns of behavior, collective political action in specific places is mediated by the networks. The idea of a web-based political community acting collectively (as opposed to wielding influence or lobbying political authorities) remains problematic (Lipschutz, 1996: chap. 3).

A deterritorialized political community, it seems to me, must have a much stronger material base (Lipschutz, 1996: chap. 7). Iris Marion Young (1990:171) develops one such idea, offering an "egalitarian politics of difference," a "culturally pluralist democratic" politics through which "Difference . . . emerges not as a description of the attributes of a group, but as a function of the relations between groups and the interactions of groups with institutions." These groups would be *social groups,* that is, "collective[s] of people who have an affinity with one another because of a set of practices or way of life." Such groups would be provided with "mechanisms for the effective recognition and representation of distinct voices and perspectives of those . . . constituent groups that are oppressed or disadvantaged" (Young, 1990:186, 184). Young proposes (1990:184) that

> such group representation implies institutional mechanisms and public resources supporting (1) self-organization of group members so that they achieve collective empowerment and a reflective understanding of their collective experience and interests in the context of society; (2) group analysis and group generation of policy proposals in institutionalized contexts where decisionmakers are obliged to show that their deliberations have taken group perspectives into consideration; and (3) group veto power regarding specific policies that affect a group directly.

Such arrangements cannot, of course, be created *ex nihilo.* In the United States, the already-existing material structures are, Young argues, "large-scale industry and urban centers." Within this context, "neighborhood assemblies [could be] a basic unit of democratic participation, which might be composed of representatives from workplaces, block councils, local churches and clubs, and so on as well as individuals" (Young, 1990:234, 252). Saskia Sassen (1994, 1998) makes a somewhat similar argument in her work on global cities.

Although this vision is attractive and well within our capabilities to pursue, there are, nonetheless, both conceptual and practical problems that remain to be addressed. For example, it appears that, in Young's vision, such urban assemblies would remain part of a larger national unit, to which they would, presumably, profess some kind of loyalty and whose authority they would recognize as final. Sociologically, in the absence of national redistribution, dependence on locally available resources would render some cities relatively rich while others would be forced to struggle along in poverty (much as is the case within and between cities and countries today; for a critical look at notions of local autonomy, see Lipschutz, 1991). Without some kind of national group- or city-based assembly with real political power, national authorities would tend to ignore cities, as they already often do in the United States. Finally, how would such a scheme play out in other countries?

None of this is to suggest that a city or region-based political system could not emerge in parallel to the state system; some writers, such as Kenichi Ohmae (1995), propose that this is already happening. There is a long history of successful city-states as well as city-based leagues, and some cities and groups of cities are deliberately reviving those forms (albeit for mostly economic reasons). Many cities already pursue their own "foreign policies," both economic and political. And, the urban political machines of the late nineteenth and early twentieth centuries certainly provide a model for a city-based, sociological conception of citizenship. Whether the city can provide the basis for global democratization, citizenship, and new foci of authority—especially when capital is so footloose and fancy-free and cities are competing with each other for capital investment like neighboring countries buying military weapons (see chapter 7)—will be demonstrated only through theory *and* activism.

One World or Many?

Do the foregoing notions suggest a global future that might, just possibly, be less dismal than that of the realists and catastrophists? Perhaps. But such a future will not happen without deliberate action. In the final chapter of *The Great Transformation,* Polanyi pointed, once again, to the way in which the loosing of the self-regulating market on nineteenth-century society in the interests of certain elites led to the inevitable destruction of that society:

> Nineteenth century civilization . . . disintegrated as the result
> of . . . the measures which society adopted in order not to be, in

its turn, annihilated by the action of the self-regulating market. . . . [T]he elementary requirements of an organized social life provided the century with its dynamics and produced the typical strains and stresses which ultimately destroyed that society. External wars merely hastened its destruction. (Polanyi, 1944/1957:249)

He (1944/1957:254) nevertheless ended on a brighter note, foreseeing after World War II "economic collaboration of governments *and* the liberty to organize national life at will" (emphasis in original; this is a formula that sounds very much like John Ruggie's embedded liberalism; 1983a, 1991, 1995). This would require freedom to be extended and maintained under unbreakable rules.

Juridical and actual freedom can be made wider and more general than ever before; regulation and control can achieve freedom not only for the few, but for all. Freedom not as an appurtenance of privilege, tainted at the source, but as a prescriptive right extending far beyond the narrow confines of the political sphere into the intimate organization of society itself. (Polanyi, 1944/1957:256)

How might this be accomplished under contemporary circumstances?

In keeping with Polanyi's hopes for the post–World War II period, we should recognize the opportunities inherent in the Great Transformation now underway. During this post–World War II (née Cold War) period, we could be witness to the democratization of societies and states through mechanisms of global governance and the proliferation of authorities, as well as the emancipation of peoples and cultures as states lose their historical roles as defensive containers and iron cages and become distinctive and diverse communities within a global society. The path to such emancipation will require our active involvement at all levels of politics and government, an involvement that must go beyond parties, elections, and indirect representation.

Following this path also suggests that we will need to rethink the notion of "citizen" and "citizenship," and their relationship to new "authorities," as I suggested above. In the majority of democratic societies across the planet today, to be a citizen involves the exercise of a few civic duties mostly done grudgingly, if done at all, and a growing unwillingness to contribute to the general well-being of the society in which s/he lives. Returning to the argument I made in the opening paragraph of this book, it is easy to see why this is so. As the state has lost interest in the citizen, letting the market get the upper hand, the loyalty of the citizen to the state has weakened. This is not necessarily a bad thing, but it has served to undermine bonds of community and social reciprocity and, in so doing, fostered a host of "solutions" that only exacerbate atomization and alienation.

The "ethnic" or "sectarian" solution to this problem—the creation of ever smaller and purer states—hardly seems viable in the longer term. The "globalist" answer—a world state or a planetary ethos—assumes what Dan Deudney (1993) has called "earth nationalism," one that will be broadly shared by all 6 or 10 billion of the world's present and future inhabitants. World federalists propose some combination of the two, akin to the civic identity we see in Catalonia, "a country in Europe" and a province in Spain. In speculating on the possibilities of citizenship under globalization, and the consequences for democracy and representation under just and equitable authority, perhaps it is best to return to the notion of "neomedievalism."

While the medieval world is hardly an attractive model on which to base a politics of the future, it nonetheless offers certain features worthy of notice. Power differentials were extreme and hierarchy was nearly absolute, but clients and patrons were enmeshed in a web of mutual rights and duties that bound them together and that could be called upon in specific situations. Moreover, the networks of relations and loyalties linking individuals were not all territoriality based; as Wæver (1995) notes, there was "a set of overlapping authorities" some of which had little to do with space. The multiple levels of "citizenship" developing in Europe, alluded to above, represent only one possible form of political community.

In a global political system of the future, we could imagine many political communities, some based on place, others on affiliations, but linked relationally rather than through domination by or loyalty to a single power. Such communities might be material as well as virtual, possessing, for example, the power to tax members, represent them in various political assemblies, and engage in functional activities such as provision of certain welfare services, environmental conservation, and education. A member, in turn, would hold "citizenship" in the community—and could simultaneously be a citizen of many such communities. Such citizens could be called on to serve their communities in specific political roles both within and in relation to other communities. Indeed, opportunities for "public service" at this scale might very well generate an efflorescence of involvement in democratic politics, to the benefit of all.

This will not happen automatically, nor is it likely to come about through the decisions of states and capital; agency is essential. Human beings are not bound to endlessly reproduce the forms and problems of the past, nor are they complete prisoners of the logics of the present. We are constrained by our histories, of course, and what we can do as a result might not always be what we would like to do. Nonetheless, along with constraints come opportunities and the possibility of imagining choices and them making them. More than ever, it is important to both individual *and* global politics that we recognize those choices and make them carefully. Our future might be better or worse as a result, but at least it will be a future that *we* have chosen.

Notes

Chapter 1. Theory of Global Politics

1. This is what happened in the old Soviet Bloc; today, it is taking place, as well, in the West.

2. I realize that the first date is arguable. I am using poetic license here.

3. Statements by former Soviet general Alexander Lebed, in September 1997, that one hundred nuclear "suitcase bombs" have gone missing in Russia can only further stir up fears along these lines. It is puzzling, however, that if they are truly unaccounted for, why none have turned up in the hands of miscreants. Are they, perhaps, in the possession of the United States?

Chapter 2. The Worries of Nations

1. Not everyone takes a dim view of the workhouses. Gertrude Himmelfarb (1995), for example, believes that ending the Poor Laws made people responsible for their individual well-being and fate. The concept of family solidarity has been examined by Francis Fukuyama (1995a, 1995b).

2. The Triffin Dilemma arose because U.S. dollars in the possession of foreign countries could be exchanged for gold. Unfortunately, by 1960, the

United States did not hold enough gold to redeem all of the dollars in circulation abroad. Were the demand for gold to outstrip U.S. gold stocks, the role of the dollar as an international reserve currency could be undermined or destroyed.

3. Again, it is important to recognize that the "self-regulating market" is a fiction; it must be supported by implicit or explicit agreements regarding rules of operation (Attali, 1997).

4. A conventional security-based account can be found in Gaddis (1982; 1987). An economic account is Pollard (1985). A revisionist economistic account can be found in McCormick (1996). A sophisticated and insightful analysis of the process discussed is Gill (1993: esp. 30–34).

5. In essence, this is the core of the so-called Washington consensus, the increasingly popular argument that democracies do not go to war with each other. For a critical assessment of this claim, see Mansfield and Snyder (1995).

6. The dollar was exchangeable for gold at the rate of $35/ounce. Americans could not hold gold bullion and only governments could officially request gold for their dollars. At this rate of exchange, Fort Knox held about $10 billion in gold.

7. Charles Tilly said "The state made war and war made the state." After World War II, the state made Cold War and Cold War made the state.

8. This was not the only reason underlying the extension of civil rights to African Americans and the implementation of affirmative action, of course. There was also a fear of urban revolt and a desire to show the world that the United States did not oppress its minorities.

9. This continues to be the case today, as evidence by the high proportion of non-U.S. citizens receiving doctorates in scientific and engineering fields. According to Joseph Nye and William Owens (1996:29), "American higher education draws some 450,000 foreign students each year."

10. For example, the Soviet Union's MIG fighters were as good or better than anything the United States had to offer, but its avionics used vacuum tubes rather than semiconductor devices. Tubes offered greater protection against the electromagnetic pulses associated with nuclear detonations, but the Soviets used them because they could not miniaturize the electronics.

11. The rise of the behavioralist model in the social sciences was part of this process, too.

12. To be entirely fair, Buchanan put the blame on free trade; that his analysis was, at best, partial and at worst, completely wrong, does not invalidate my argument here.

13. People might be offered *equal* opportunities to succeed, although even this is difficult to accomplish in practice. Even so, not everyone will seize those opportunities and succeed.

14. A fascinating essay on the commodification of consumer shopping habits can be found in Gladwell (1996), "The Science of Shopping." It is a simple matter to link the bar codes in a shopping cart to the name and address on the check or ATM card proffered in payment, enter them into a database, and sell the resulting information to the appropriate companies.

15. Stephen Kobrin (1997) argues that "e-money" poses a threat to the most fundamental perquisite of the state: taxation.

Chapter 3. The Insecurity Dilemma

1. Although, as a graduate student project during the mid-1980s, I tried to fit U.S. and Soviet nuclear missile deployments to different types of differential equations. I found that competition between the U.S. Navy and U.S. Air Force better explained the growth of American nuclear arsenals than did an arms race with the Soviet Union.

2. The hammer-nail conundrum is usually attributed to Abraham Maslow, who was supposed to have observed that "if all you have is a hammer, everything begins to look like a nail."

3. For an interesting list of "micronations" and hyperlinks to them, see http://www.execpc.com/~talossa/patsilor.html.

4. Border studies is a rapidly growing field; there is a Centre for Border Studies at the University of Wales, complete with peer-reviewed journal.

5. Ken Waltz attacked the idea of "peace through interdependence" almost thirty years ago, in "The Myth of National Interdependence" (1971).

6. Twenty years ago, Stephen Krasner (1978) and others argued that policymakers really did represent the singular interests of an autonomous actor called the "state." But even "strong" states no longer appear so unitary as they once might have been.

7. The intersubjectivity of national-security policy was never noted at this time. Threats were assumed to be real and objective; the state was assumed to protect society rather than itself. Under conditions of mutual assured destruction (MAD), preparations made for the continuity of state and government in the event of nuclear attack would have resulted, in all likelihood, in a state with no society to govern.

8. Although the literature on "redefining security" has proliferated over the past ten years, the two defining articles are probably Richard H. Ullman (1983) and Jessica Tuchman Mathews (1989).

9. Useful comparisons can be found in the Japanese and German economic spheres of the 1930s and 1940s; for a discussion of the latter, see Hirschman (1980).

10. It does not qualify as bona fide structural adjustment because the dollar remains dominant in the global economy and the United States has not yet been forced to reduce its budget deficits. But, it would be interesting to compare the effects of somewhat similar policies on labor in the United States and former Socialist countries.

11. For example, "electronic classrooms" may make it possible for one professor to lecture to many classrooms at the same time, thereby reducing labor costs for universities. See Marshall (1995b) and *The Economist* (1995a).

12. This is Huntington's (1997) argument, as well. The question is whether the "loss of enemies" is really such a problem.

13. Note that one of the most wide-ranging of such incidents to date occurred as the result of satellite failure. For a couple of days, tens of millions of pagers and thousands of computerized gas pumps went off the air. For an insightful analysis of what can and does go wrong with computer-run complex systems, see Rochlin (1997).

14. As Karl Marx said, "Adam Smith's contradictions are of significance because they contain problems which it is true he does not resolve, but which he reveals by contradicting himself."

15. Of course, "reality" is a loaded word. Inasmuch as the world and its condition are described by language, there are limits to a truly objective description. You and I can agree that that thing over there is a tank, but I say it is for defensive purposes only, while you say it is for offensive purposes.

16. These are questions ordinarily not asked. Either definitions of security are taken to be objective and nonproblematic, or the state is reified even as security and anarchy are treated as intersubjective constructs.

17. This is, in essence, the argument put forth by Alexander George in *Bridging the Gap* (1993), although he does acknowledge that images of the enemy are often inaccurate and that acting on such images may lead to undesirable outcomes. A rather different perspective is offered by Smithson (1996).

18. In other words, the enemy, and the threat it presents, possess characteristics specific to the society defining them. See, e.g., Weldes (1992), Lipschutz (1989), and Campbell (1990, 1992).

19. To this, the realist would argue: "But states exist and the condition of anarchy means that there are no restraints on their behavior toward others! Hence, threats must be material and real." As Nicholas Onuf (1989), Alex Wendt (1992), Mercer (1995), and Kubálková, Onuf, and Kowert (1998) have argued, even international anarchy is a social construction inasmuch as certain rules of behavior inevitably form the basis for such an arrangement (Lipschutz, 1992a).

20. This dialectical process is discussed rather nicely, albeit in a different context, by Harvey (1996).

21. This contradiction was apparent in the initial landing of U.S. Marines in Somalia in December, 1992. Demonstrably, there was a question of matching force to force in this case, but the ostensible goal of humanitarian assistance took on the appearance of a military invasion (with the added hyperreality of resistance offered only by the mass[ed] media waiting on shore).

22. Ordinarily, this dialectic might be expected to lead to a new social construction of or consensus around security. As I suggest below, for the United States at least, the contradictions are so great as to make it unlikely that any stable consensus will be forthcoming. See also Lipschutz (1999b).

23. This is not, however, to imply that state maintenance is the actual goal. Rather, the constructing of a nontraditional threat to security was seen during the last few years of the Cold War as a way of shifting resources away from the military and toward more socially focused needs. Some in the military—e.g., the Army Corps of Engineers—welcomed this shift as a way of redefining their mission, perhaps creating a "Green Corps" to send ashore in countries under environmental siege. For a detailed discussion, see Litfin (1998).

24. Often, borders are drawn down the middle of rivers running through valleys because they make such visible and convenient markers. Difference is thereby established even as the water and terrain on both sides are indistinguishable.

25. Star Wars would have drawn a line—or a surface—in the sky, a dome within which the self would be secure and secured, and outside of which would remain the eternal threat of the Other, but few believed that such a surface could be made, much less made secure (see chapter 7).

26. Now, threats emerge because the lines of security, drawn around Russian nuclear facilities, have literally dissolved, allowing fissile materials to become commodified and objects of exchange. In the market, there are no boundaries, only risks.

27. Although these are, apparently, what the United States has proposed as NATO's new objectives (Erlanger, 1998).

Chapter 4. Arms and Affluence

1. Another book by the same name is Oakes (1994).

2. Indeed, this point is demonstrated repeatedly in the opprobrium incurred by Bill Clinton for never having served (or being seen to have *wanted* to serve) in the military.

3. Indeed, the essential task of deterrence was to convince the other that they *would* be used, although one would never want to get to the point that they *might* be used. A typical bit of scenario building can be found in Paul Nitze's famous 1976 article, "Deterring our Deterrent." For a full-blown exegesis of this point, see Luke (1989).

4. The term "Finlandization" is worthy of an entire paper in itself. One used to hear people say that to be like Finland would not be so bad; today, no one wants to be like Finland, which is in an economic slump brought on by the collapse of trade with the former Soviet Union.

5. There was, at the time, some controversy over why the Soviets had put the SS-20s into Eastern Europe. On the one hand, some argued that it was done to take advantage of the escalatory gap. On the other hand, some pointed to the deployment as simply the arcane workings of the Soviet military-industrial complex, which had taken one stage off of an unsuccessful, solid-fueled intercontinental ballistic missile, thereby turning it into a working intermediate range one. The latter argument would, of course, have implied a state beset by bureaucratic conflict and irrationality, rather than one bent on conquering the West.

6. It might be noted, in passing, that the eventual impacts of the SS-20s and Euromissiles were greater at home than in enemy territory. The waves of protest against the missiles in the West was viewed with great alarm in many NATO capitals. In the East, the episode was the occasion of growing contacts between Western peace activists and Eastern dissidents that, in the long run, must have contributed to the revolutions of 1989 and 1991. See, e.g., Meyer (1993).

7. Retaliation against Sudan and Afghanistan for the August 1998 bombings of U.S. embassies in Kenya and Tanzania provides one answer to these questions, although it is less clear whether this had the intended effect.

8. In addition to the Iraqi invasion of Kuwait, the number of clear and blatant invasions of one country's territory by another since 1950 is small by comparison with minor border incursions and civil conflicts: Korea (1950), Southeast Asia (1950s–1970s), the Six Day War (1967), the Indo-Pakistani War (1971), the October War (1973), the Ogaden War (1977), Vietnam's invasion of Cambodia and the Chinese riposte (1979), the Soviet invasion of Afghanistan (1979), Israeli invasions of Lebanon (1976, 1982), Grenada (1983), Panama (1989).

9. The notion of "irrationality" tends to blend into cultural explanations, whereby irreconcilable differences among cultures become the provocation to conflict. On this point, see especially Huntington (1996).

10. For a somewhat distorted but nonetheless interesting exploration of the impact of cultural differences on diplomacy, see Cohen (1991).

11. Indeed, the dance has begun to seem like farce, to the point that a character on *The X-Files* (December 6, 1998) can plausibly claim that Saddam Hussein is a guy from Brooklyn who, put into power by the CIA, rattles his sabers whenever the U.S. government requires public distraction from other matters.

Chapter 5. Markets, the State, and War

1. This is not the precise wording of the document referred to. There, the author (Serageldin, 1995:2) writes, "Agreement on access to water is an important part of the peace accords between Israel and its neighbors. . . . As populations and demand for limited supplies of water increase, interstate and international frictions over water can be expected to intensify."

2. To name just a few: Starr and Stoll, 1988; Starr, 1991, 1995; Beschorner, 1992; Lowi, 1992, 1993, 1995; Bulloch and Dawish, 1993; Kally with Fishelson, 1993; Hillel, 1994; Isaac and Shuval, 1994; Gleick, 1994; Murakami, 1995; Starr, 1995; Wolf, 1995.

3. "Global deficiencies and degradation of natural resources, both renewable and non-renewable, coupled with the uneven distribution of these raw materials, can lead to unlikely—and thus unstable—alliances, to national rivalries, and, of course, to war" (Westing, 1986: introduction).

4. "We are . . . talking about maintaining access to energy resources that are key—not just to the functioning of this country but the entire world. Our jobs, our way of life, our own freedom, and the freedom of friendly countries around the world would suffer if control of the world's great oil reserves fell into the hands of Saddam Hussein" (President George Bush, 1990).

5. Although many scholars argue that wars between Israel and its neighbors have been about water, the evidence in support of this unicausal explanation remains thin.

6. The best example of this was the struggle over Alsace-Lorraine between France and Germany. Only the shedding of the nation's blood could redeem the lost pieces of the organic nation-state. See Elias (1994).

7. As opposed to political geography, which studies the "relationship between geographical factors and political entities" (Weigert, et al., 1957). Geography can be changed, of course, as evidenced for example by the case of the Panama Canal. Oddly, perhaps, the canal served to enhance American power—it was now possible for the Navy to move from one ocean to the other more quickly—while also exacerbating vulnerability: any other power gaining access to the canal could now threaten the opposite U.S. coast more quickly.

8. The dictum was: "Who rules East Europe commands the Heartland; Who rules the Heartland commands the World-Island; Who rules the World-Island commands the World" (Mackinder, 1919/1962:150; see also Mackinder, 1943).

9. Interestingly, as I noted in chapter 3 and discuss in chapter 6, culture has become the most recent refuge for many of those international relations scholars who are unable to account otherwise for the vagaries of world politics; see e.g., Fukuyama (1995b) and Huntington (1996).

10. More recent expressions of this still-common view can be found in Choucri and North (1975) and Organski and Kugler (1980).

11. Some writers, such as Richard Dawkins (1989), have gone so far as to argue that the appropriate unit of competition and survival is the individual "gene," and that humans (and, presumably, other species) are only containers for them. Of course, by that argument, bacteria and viruses are probably "bound to win."

12. Principle 21 abjures states to recognize the "responsibility to ensure that activities within their jurisdiction or control do not cause damage to the environment of other States or of areas beyond their national jurisdiction." Cited in Nanda (1995:86).

13. Do we ever speak of "ecological interdependence" with, say our children, spouses, significant others, or existing between California and Nevada?

14. Some have noted, of course, that renewable resources are not subject to this particular economic logic, inasmuch as their flows are large and their stocks small or nonexistent. But economists still argue that markets can prevent unsustainable depletion through the price mechanism. Unfortunately, by the time prices rise sufficiently to impel substitution, the renewable resource may be depleted beyond recovery.

15. The 1997–98 El Niño illustrated this proposition rather nicely: in the ocean, many species could follow the food from their normal feeding groups, and blue whales, tuna, and marlin were seen or caught off the coast of Northern California. Anchovy, being less able to go with the flows, died in droves off the coast of Peru.

16. And the invocation to "free up" markets does little to address the immediate needs of those who have no food.

17. The "double hermenutic" is a term used by Anthony Giddens to describe how scholars use the behavior of policymakers to formulate theories, and how policymakers, in turn, behave according to the dictates of theory; see the discussion in Dessler (1989).

18. Nor did they recognize that, given the nature of oil markets, even control of oil would not have prevented a generalized increase in prices; see Lipschutz (1992a).

19. Parallel to the argument about old married couples, divorce constitutes an effort to reestablish independence but usually serves to illustrate just how difficult it is to completely sever the bonds of matrimony.

20. This is best seen in discourses about population. The rich consume much more than the poor, but it is the rapidly-growing numbers of poor who the rich fear will move north and cross borders (thereby ignoring the fact that the rich moved south centuries ago).

21. This ignores the obvious point that human activities have *never* been "neatly compartmentalized."

22. The Newtonian "harmony of the spheres" remains with us today, even as ecologists warn us that ecosystemic balance and stability do not, for the most part, exist.

23. This is described as the "quantitative fallacy" by David Hackett Fischer (1970:90).

Chapter 6. The Social Contraction

1. The recent literature on ethnic conflict is enormous. Among them are: Lake and Rothchild (1998); Crawford and Lipschutz (1998).

2. Although he does not subscribe to this logic, R. B. J. Walker (1992) provides numerous insights into the contradictions and pitfalls of territory and sovereignty in *Inside/Outside: International Relations as Political Theory.*

3. Although it is a rather crude measurement, a search of the University of California's Melvyl bibliographic database under the subject category "ethnic relations" turned up 5,761 citations between 1987 and 1997, as compared to 3,197 prior to 1987 (with most of those being published during the 1980s).

4. "Stability" is obviously a tenuous concept. What appears to the outside or historical observer to be stable is usually quite dynamic. See, for example, the semifictional account of Visegrad, Bosnia, in Ivo Andric, *The Bridge on the Drina* (1977).

5. In the U.S. context, Huntington and others call it the "American Creed." See also Lipschutz (1998b).

6. Culture can be understood as a form of social contract within a group of people that shares certain types of social characteristics. Usually, such a form is called "tradition" or "custom."

7. The notion of actor choice in a structured context is discussed in Long and Long (1992).

8. V. P. Gagnon disagrees with me on this point; personal communication. See his article (Gagnon, 1995) as well as Woodward (1995).

9. Such rents accrue even in the absence of "corruption." For example, on September 15, 1997, "first student" Chelsea Clinton arrived at Stanford University, after having flown from Washington, D.C. on Air Force One with her parents. Surely this perk is available to very few other college freshpersons.

10. On this point, Kenichi Ohmae is correct; see *The End of the Nation State* (1995).

11. By this I mean that in any one location, there are economic systems of local, regional, national, transnational, and global extent. These are linked but not all of a single piece. Thus, for example, Silicon Valley is tightly integrated into the "global" economy, but some of its inhabitants are also participants in a service-based economy that, although coupled into global systems, is largely directed toward meeting "local" demand. For further discussions of the notion of "multiple" economies, see Gordon (1995). This section has also been informed by a conversation with Randall Germain of the University of Sheffield, April 20, 1996.

12. The term for such historical contingency is "path dependency." See the discussion of this point in Krugman (1994a: chap. 9).

13. How intentional or fortuitous is, of course, the key question. Silicon Valley was hardly the product of chance; rather, it was the result of intentional mobilization of resources by the state in its pursuit of national security. The difficulty of establishing such a development pole is evidenced by the numerous failed research parks that litter the United States; the problems of maintaining a pole once established were illustrated by the relative collapse of the high-tech center on Route 128 around Boston in the late 1980s. Some of the difficulties facing policymakers who might like to repeat such mobilization are discussed in Crawford (1995).

14. The Microstate Network is at www.microstate.net; the Micronations Page, at wwwl.execpc.com/~talossa/patsilor.htm.

15. One article (Hedges, 1995) on the Bosnian peace settlement suggested that "United Nations officials said that they expect NATO to initiate regional or neighborhood meetings to try and settle the complex claims and counterclaims that are sure to complicate the agreement."

Chapter 7. The Princ(ipal)

1. Which is why more than $20 billion have been spent on antimissile defense research and development, and why several hundred million dollars and more continue to be spent on it each year.

2. Susan Strange (1996) has also taken note of this phenomenon, but she ascribes it to the "retreat of the state."

3. Note that this is hardly a new argument and that in making it, I do not propose the restoration of theocracy or a return to Victorian values, as proposed by Gertrude Himmelfarb (1995). I do, however, believe that norms and ethics are important; see Hirsch (1995) and the essays in Ellis and Kumar (1983).

4. I do not mean to imply that the Treaty of Westphalia actually was the means of accomplishing this; rather, it put the stamp of legitimacy on an arrangement that had been developing for some time.

5. Barry Buzan (1991) acknowledges this in his schema of anarchies ranging from "immature" to "mature," but he retains survival in the state of nature as the rationale for movement toward greater maturity.

6. This point is evident, as well, in "traditional" societies and common-pool resource systems, where violation of the mutual bonds of obligation and responsibility can result in eviction from the community.

7. And this does not mean that we now subscribe to a secular order; see Bragg (1997).

8. The notion of "just war," which represented an effort to impose morality on the conduct of war, does not contradict this argument, I think. Civilians were the subjects of the prince and his morality, not the source of that morality.

9. The Jews, who had earlier been expelled from England, were sufficiently powerless and few in number to make this practical; there were altogether too many Catholics, however, for either expulsion or extermination to be practical.

10. Thereby creating an inversion of Benedict Anderson's (1991) "imagined communities," which we might call "unimaginable communities."

11. Although, as we see in claims being made against Switzerland and the former East Germany, extermination does not necessarily eliminate claims to property.

12. One is left to wonder what might happen should we make contact with non-terrestrial life, whether intelligent or not. Recent films (*Men in Black, Starship Troopers*) suggest, in particular, that "bugs" are the enemy, although some, such as *The Faculty,* warn us about our familiars, as well; see Leary (1997).

13. That is not to say that domestic security was not a concern; the ever vigilant search for ideological threats was pursued by a transnational network of intelligence and surveillance agencies whose capacity was often far in excess of any demonstrated need.

14. It was called the "Grand Area"; see Shoup and Minter (1977).

15. The distinction was never as great as claimed. The isolationists wanted to keep pernicious influences out; the internationalists wanted to keep them contained. Both aimed to avoid "contamination."

16. The defection of Yassir Arafat from the bad bloc to the good bloc clearly demonstrates how membership in both has more to do with morality than power.

Chapter 8. Politics among People

1. I note here, as well, Susan Strange's (1996) fierce attack on the notion of "global governance" in *The Retreat of the State,* which reminds us to always regard such neatly packaged concepts with a critical eye.

2. The very notion of cause and effect is rooted in the Enlightenment and the triumph of scientific reasoning, not to mention investment and rates-of-return. Even those who engage in risky, life-threatening activities expect to go back to work after their vacation is over.

3. The regime literature of the 1980s and 1990s (see, especially, Krasner, 1983) sought to discover and explain such patterned behavior among states in the "State of Nature."

4. Admittedly, liberalism recognizes only the authority of a "watchperson state" that does not seek to regulate human behavior. Still, this requires a very narrow definition of "state" and a great divide between it and "civil society."

5. For a general overview of perspectives on civil society, see Walzer (1995), and Cohen and Arato (1992). For essays on governance, see Rosenau and Czempiel (1992).

6. James Rosenau (1990; 1997) has taken the contrary tendencies into account by theorizing "sovereignty-bound" and "sovereignty-free" actors. This, I think, does not capture the entire dynamic, in that some of the actors in the latter category would dearly love to move into the former.

7. At least, this is true in the political and policy realms; Polanyi still has an ardent following in both academia and intellectual circles.

8. The author of the *Economist* survey cited earlier (1997) argues that the source of international economic instability remains too much domestic regulation and government intervention.

9. This does not mean that small companies are not innovative; rather, that the owners of fixed property and small service-oriented businesses face high social costs relative to revenues and find it difficult to liquidate their assets and invest them elsewhere.

10. Rosenau and others have tagged the trend "glocalization," although I find this term exceptionally grating.

11. Heteronomous: 1. Subject to external or foreign laws or domination; not autonomous. 2. Differing in development or manner of specializa-

tion, as the dissimilar segments of certain arthopods. My meaning here is the second, minus the detail about bugs.

12. The best-known discussion of the "new medievalism" is to be found in Bull (1977: 254–55, 264–76, 285–86, 291–94). The notion of "heteronomy" is found, among other places, in Ruggie (1983b: 274, n. 30). The term "heterarchy" comes from Bartlett and Ghoshal (1990), quoted in Gordon (1995: 181).

13. More to the point, as I have noted before, the "market" is not a free-floating institution whose operation is guaranteed by the "laws of Nature," as some would have it; it is underwritten by a set of embedded rules that are ideologically "naturalized" and that, consequently, seem to disappear.

14. In developing the following argument, I do not mean to ignore the growing body of literature by numerous scholars, both male and female, on the topic of feminism, gender, and international relations theory that has provided important insights into the constitution of world politics. See, for example, Tickner (1992), and Peterson and Runyan (1993).

15. I should note that this line of thought was triggered by Neil Easterbrook's use of Butler's work in "State, Heterotopia: The Political Imagination in Heinlein, Le Guin, and Delany" (1997).

16. By this definition, therefore, civil society includes social movements, various kinds of public interest groups, and corporations (although I am not explicitly discussing the last here), all of which do engage in politics of one sort or another. The state-civil society distinction is, sometimes, difficult to ascertain, as in the case of the World Wildlife Fund/Worldwide Fund for Animals and other similar organizations, which subcontract with state agencies.

17. This point is a heavily disputed one: To wit, is the international system so undersocialized as to make institutions only weakly constraining on behavior, as Stephen Krasner (1993) might argue, or are the fetters of institutionalized practices sufficiently strong to modify behavior away from chaos and even anarchy, as Nicolas Onuf (1989) might suggest.

Bibliography

Agnew, John, and Stuart Corbridge (1995). *Mastering Space—Hegemony, Territory and International Political Economy.* London: Routledge.

Aizu, Izumi (1998). "Emergence of Netizens in Japan and Its Cultural Implications for the Net Society." Institute for HyperNetwork Society and GLOCOM. Center for Global Communications, International University of Japan, at www.harvnet.harvard.edu/online/moreinfo/aizu.html, May 8, 1998.

Allison, Graham (1971). *Essence of Decision.* Boston: Little, Brown.

Anderson, Benedict (1991). *Imagined Communities: Reflections on the Origins and Spread of Nationalism.* 2d ed. London: Verso.

Andric, Ivo (1977). *The Bridge on the Drina.* Trans. L. F. Edwards. Chicago: University of Chicago Press.

Angell, Norman (1910). *The Great Illusion: A Study of the Relation of Military Power in Nations to Their Economic and Social Advantages.* London: W. Heinemann.

Arenson, Karen W. (1998). "Questions about Future of Those Many Ph.D.'s [sic]." *New York Times,* November 11, national edition, p. A28.

Attali, Jacques (1997). "The Crash of Western Civilization—The Limits of Market and Democracy." *Foreign Policy* 107 (summer):54–63.

Augelli, Enrico, and Craig Murphy (1988). *America's Quest for Supremacy and the Third World: A Gramscian Analysis.* London: Pinter.

197

Banerjee, Sanjoy (1991). "Reproduction of Subjects in Historical Structures: Attribution, Identity, and Emotion in the Early Cold War." *International Studies Quarterly* 35, no. 1 (March):19–38.

Barber, Benjamin R. (1995). *Jihad vs. McWorld.* New York: Times Books.

Barnet, Richard J. (1973). *Roots of War—The Men and Institutions Behind U.S. Foreign Policy.* Baltimore: Penguin.

Bartlett, C., and S. Ghoshal (1990). "Managing Innovation in the Transnational Corporation." In C. Y. Doz and G. Hedlund (eds.), *Managing the Global Firm* (pp. 215–55). London: Routledge.

Beck, Ulrich (1992). *Risk Society: Towards a New Modernity.* Beverly Hills: Sage.

Bennett, William J. (1998). *The Death of Outrage: Bill Clinton and the Assault on American Ideals.* New York: The Free Press.

Bercovitch, Sacvan (1978). *The American Jeremiad.* Madison: University of Wisconsin Press.

Berend, Iván T., and György Ránki (1979). *Underdevelopment and Economic Growth: Studies in Hungarian Social and Economic History.* Budapest: Akadémiai Kiadó.

Bergsten, Fred (1996). "Globalizing Free Trade." *Foreign Affairs* 75, no. 3 (May/June):105–20.

Bernstein, Richard, and Ross H. Munro (1997). *The Coming Conflict with China.* New York: Knopf.

Beschorner, Natasha (1992). *Water and Instability in the Middle East.* London: Brassey's for the International Institute for Strategic Studies.

Bhagwati, Jagdish (1993). "Trade and the Environment: The False Conflict?" In Durwood Zaelke, Paul Orbuch, and Robert F. Houseman (eds.), *Trade and the Environment: Law, Economics, and Policy* (pp. 159–60). Washington, D.C.: Island Press.

Biersteker, Thomas J., and Cynthia Weber (eds.) (1996). *State Sovereignty as Social Construct.* Cambridge: Cambridge University Press.

Block, Fred (1977). *The Origins of International Economic Disorder.* Berkeley: University of California Press.

Booth, Ken (1991). "Security in Anarchy." *International Affairs* 67, no. 3: 527–45.

Boulding, Kenneth (1977). *Stable Peace.* Austin: University of Texas Press.

Bragg, Rick (1997). "Judge Lets God's Law Mix with Alabama's." *New York Times,* February 15, national edition, p. A11.

Brass, Paul R. (1976). "Ethnicity and Nationality Formation." *Ethnicity* 3, no. 3 (September): 225–239.

Broeder, John M. (1996). "Clinton Seeks $1.1 Billion to Fight Terror." *Los Angeles Times,* September 10, p. A1.

Brown, Chris (1992). *International Relations Theory—New Normative Approaches*. New York: Columbia University Press.

Bull, Hedley (1977). *The Anarchical Society*. New York: Columbia University Press.

Bulloch, John, and Adel Dawish (1993). *Water Wars: Coming Conflicts in the Middle East*. New York: Victor Gollancz.

Bunce, Valerie (1985). "The Empire Strikes Back: The Evolution of the Eastern Bloc from a Soviet Asset to a Soviet Liability." *International Organization* 39, no. 1 (winter):1–46.

Burdick, Eugene, and Harvey Wheeler (1962). *Fail-Safe*. New York: Dell.

Burnham, James (1941). *The Managerial Revolution: What Is Happening in the World?* New York: John Day.

Bush, President George (1990). "Against Aggression in the Persian Gulf," *Dispatch* 1, no. 1 (August 15) (Address to employees of the Pentagon, Washington, D.C.).

Butler, Judith (1990). *Gender Trouble: Feminism and the Subversion of Identity*. New York: Routledge.

Buzan, Barry (1991). *People, States, and Fear*. Boulder, Colo.: Lynne Rienner, 2d ed.

Campbell, David (1997). " 'Ethnic' Bosnia and Its Partition: The Political Anthropology of International Diplomacy." Paper prepared for presentation at the annual meeting of the International Studies Association, Toronto, Canada, March 18–22.

——— (1992). *Writing Security*. Minneapolis: University of Minnesota Press.

——— (1990). "Global Inscription: How Foreign Policy Constitutes the United States." *Alternatives* 15:263–86.

Castells, Manuel (1996, 1997, 1998). *The Information Age*. 3 vols. Malden, Mass.: Blackwell.

Chase, Robert, Emily Hill, and Paul Kennedy (1996). "The Pivotal States." *Foreign Affairs* 75, no. 1 (January/February): 33–51.

Choucri, Nazli, and Robert North (1975). *Nations in Conflict*. San Francisco: W. H. Freeman.

Clancy, Tom (1987). *Red Storm Rising*. New York: Berkley Books.

Clinton, President Bill (1999). "President Clinton's Address on Airstrikes against Yugoslavia, *New York Times* (March 24, 1999), at: www.nytimes.com/032599clinton-address-text.html (3/25/99).

——— (1997). "A National Security Strategy for a New Century." Washington, D.C.: The White House, May, at: http://www.fas.org/man/docs/strategy97.htm.

Coats, A. W. (ed.) (1971). *The Classical Economists and Economic Policy*. London: Methuen.

Cohen, Eliot A. (1996). "A Revolution in Warfare." *Foreign Affairs* 75, no. 2 (March/April):37–54.

Cohen, Jean L., and Andrew Arato (1992). *Civil Society and Political Theory.* Cambridge: MIT Press.

Cohen, Raymond (1991). *Negotiating across Cultures.* Washington, D.C.: U.S. Institute of Peace Press.

Cohen, Roger (1997). "For France, Sagging Self-Image and Espirit." *New York Times,* February 11, national edition, p. A1.

Cox, Robert (1987). *Production, Power, and World Order: Social Forces in the Making of History.* New York: Columbia University Press.

Crawford, Beverly (1995). "Hawks, Doves, but No Owls: International Economic Interdependence and Construction of the New Security Dilemma." In Ronnie D. Lipschutz (ed.), *On Security* (pp. 149–86). New York: Columbia University Press.

――― (1993). *Economic Vulnerability in International Relations.* New York: Columbia University Press.

Crawford, Beverly, and Ronnie D. Lipschutz (1998). *The Myth of "Ethnic Conflict": Politics, Economics, and "Cultural" Violence.* Berkeley, CA: International and Area Studies, University of California, Berkeley.

Crocker, Chester A., and Fen Osler Hampton, with Pamela Aall (eds.) (1996). *Managing Global Chaos: Sources of and Responses to International Conflict.* Washington, D.C.: U.S. Institute of Peace Press.

Crook, Stephen, Jan Pakulski, and Malcolm Waters (1992). *Postmodernization: Change in Advanced Society.* London: Sage.

Dahlem Workshop (1993). *What Are the Mechanisms Mediating the Genetic and Environmental Determinants of Behavior? Twins as a Tool of Behavioral Genetics.* Chichester/New York: Wiley.

Dalby, Simon (1995). "Neo-Malthusianism in Contemporary Geopolitical Discourse: Kaplan, Kennedy, and New Global Threats." Paper prepared for presentation to a panel on "Discourse, Geography and Interpretation." Annual meeting of the International Studies Association, Chicago, February.

――― (1990). *Creating the Second Cold War: The Discourse of Politics.* London/New York: Pinter Guilford.

Davis, Bob (1994). "Global Paradox: Growth of Trade Binds Nations, but It Also Can Spur Separatism." *Wall Street Journal,* June 20, Western ed., p. A1.

Davis, Christopher Mark (1991). "The Exceptional Soviet Case: Defense in an Autarkic System." *Dædalus* 120, no. 4 (fall):113–34.

Dawkins, Richard (1989). *The Selfish Gene.* New ed. New York: Oxford University Press.

Dawson, Jane I. (1996). *Eco-Nationalism.* Durham, N.C.: Duke University Press.

Der Derian, James (1996). "Eyeing the Other: Technical Oversight, Simulated Foresight, and Theoretical Blindspots in the Infosphere." Talk given November 11, UC-Santa Cruz.

————— (1995). "The Value of Security: Hobbes, Marx, Nietzsche, and Baudrillard." In Ronnie D. Lipschutz (ed.), *On Security* (pp. 24–45). New York: Columbia University Press.

————— (1992). *Antidiplomacy: Spies, Terror, Speed, and War.* Cambridge, Mass.: Blackwell.

Derluguian, Georgi M. (1995). "The Tale of Two Resorts: Abkhazia and Ajaria before and after the Soviet Collapse." Berkeley, CA: Center for German and European Studies, University of California, Berkeley. Working Paper No. 6.2.

Dessler, David (1989). "The Use and Abuse of Social Science for Policy." *SAIS Review* 9, no. 2 (summer–fall):203–223.

Deudney, Daniel (1995). "Political Fission: State Structure, Civil Society, and Nuclear Weapons in the United States." In Ronnie D. Lipschutz (ed.), *On Security* (pp. 87–123). New York: Columbia University Press.

————— (1993). "Global Environmental Rescue and the Emergence of World Domestic Politics." In Ronnie D. Lipschutz and Ken Conca (eds.), *The State and Social Power in Global Environmental Politics* (pp. 280–305). New York: Columbia University Press.

————— (1990). "The Case against Linking Environmental Degradation and National Security." *Millennium* 19, no. 3 (winter):461–76.

Drainville, André C. (1996). "The Fetishism of Global Civil Society: Global Governance, Transnational Urbanism and Sustainable Capitalism in the World Economy." Paper presented at the annual convention of the American Political Science Association, San Francisco, Calif., August 29–September 1.

————— (1995). "Of Social Spaces, Citizenship, and the Nature of Power in the World Economy." *Alternatives* 20, no. 1 (January–March):51–79.

Drell, Sidney D., Philip J. Farley, and David Holloway (1985). *The Reagan Strategic Defense Initiative: A Technical, Political, and Arms Control Assessment.* Cambridge, Mass.: Ballinger.

Dreze, Jean, and Amartya Sen (1989). *Hunger and Public Action.* New York: Oxford University Press.

Easterbrook, Neil (1997). "State, Heterotopia: The Political Imagination in Heinlein, Le Guin, and Delany." In Donald M. Hassler and Clyde Wilcox (eds.), *Political Science Fiction* (pp. 43–75). Columbia: University of South Carolina Press.

The Economist (1997). "The Visible Hand: World Economy," September 21–27 (survey).

——— (1995a). "A World without Jobs?" February 11, pp. 21–23.

——— (1995b). "Flowing Uphill," August 12, p. 36.

Edmunds, John C. (1996). "Securities: The New World Wealth Machine." *Foreign Policy* 104 (fall):118–38.

Elias, Norbert (1994). *The Civilizing Process: State Formation and Civilization.* Trans. Edmund Jephcott. Oxford: Blackwell.

Elliott, Stuart (1997). "Advertising—The New Campaign for 3 Musketeers Adds Diversity to Portray Contemporary America." *New York Times,* February 12, national edition, p. C6.

Ellis, Adrian, and Krishan Kumar (eds.) (1983). *Dilemmas of Liberal Democracies.* London: Tavistock.

Enzenberger, Hans Magnus (1994). *Civil Wars: From L.A. to Bosnia.* New York: The New Press.

Erlanger, Steven (1998). "U.S. to Propose NATO Take On Increased Roles," *New York Times,* December 7, p. A1.

Farr, Robert M. (1987). "Self/Other Relations and the Social Nature of Reality." In Carl F. Graumann and Serge Moscovici (eds.), *Changing Conceptions of Conspiracy* (pp. 203–17). New York: Springer-Verlag.

Ferguson, Kathy (1996). "From a Kibbutz Journal: Reflections on Gender, Race, and Militarism in Israel." In Michael J. Shapiro and Hayward R. Alker (eds.), *Challenging Boundaries: Global Flows, Territorial Identities* (pp. 435–54). Minneapolis: University of Minnesota Press.

Fischer, David Hackett (1970). *Historical Fallacies: Toward a Logic of Historical Thought.* New York: Harper & Row.

Foster, Gregory (1994). "Interrogating the Future." *Alternatives* 19, no. 1 (winter):53–98.

Freedman, Lawrence (1983). *The Evolution of Nuclear Strategy.* New York: St. Martin's.

Friedberg, Aaron L. (1991). "The End of Autonomy: The United States after Five Decades." *Dædalus* 120, no. 4 (fall):69–90.

Fukuyama, Francis (1995a). "Social Capital and the Global Economy." *Foreign Affairs* 74, no. 5 (September/October):89–103.

——— (1995b). *Trust: The Social Virtues and the Creation of Prosperity.* New York: The Free Press.

Gabriel, Trip (1997). "Six Figures of Fun: Bonus Season on Wall Street." *New York Times,* February 12, national edition, p. A19.

Gaddis, John Lewis (1987). *The Long Peace: Inquiries into the History of the Cold War.* New York: Oxford University Press.

——— (1982). *Strategies of Containment.* Oxford: Oxford University Press.

Gagnon, V. P. (1995). "Historical Roots of the Yugoslav Conflict." In Milton J. Esman and Shibley Telhami (eds.), *International Organizations and Ethnic Conflict* (pp. 179–97). Ithaca, N.Y.: Cornell University Press.

Gaura, Alicia, and Bill Wallace (1997). "San Jose Seeks More Firepower for Cops: Mayor Wants to Buy Semiautomatic Guns." *San Francisco Chronicle*, March 15, p. A1.

Gellner, Ernest (1983). *Nations and Nationalism.* Ithaca, N.Y.: Cornell University Press.

George, Alexander (1993). *Bridging the Gap.* Washington, D.C.: U.S. Institute of Peace Press.

Gerö, András (1995). *Modern Hungarian Society in the Making: The Unfinished Experience.* Trans. James Patterson and Eniko Koncz. Budapest: CEU Press.

Gerschenkron, Alexander (1962). *Economic Backwardness in Historical Perspective.* Cambridge, Mass.: Belknap Press of the Harvard University Press.

Gill, Stephen (1995). "The Global Panopticon? The Neoliberal State, Economic Life, and Democratic Surveillance." *Alternatives* 2, no. 1 (January–March):1–50.

——— (1994). "Structural Change and Global Political Economy: Globalizing Elites and the Emerging World Order." In Yoshikazu Sakomoto (ed.), *Global Transformation: Challenges to the State System* (pp. 169–99). Tokyo: United Nations University.

——— (1993). "Epistemology, Ontology, and the 'Italian School'." In Stephen Gill (ed.), *Gramsci, Historical Materialism, and International Relations* (pp. 21–48). Cambridge: Cambridge University Press.

Gill, Stephen, and James Mittleman (eds.) (1997). *Innovation and Transformation in International Studies.* Cambridge: Cambridge University Press.

Gilpin, Robert (1987). *The Political Economy of International Relations.* Princeton, N.J.: Princeton University Press.

——— (1981). *War and Change in World Politics.* Cambridge: Cambridge University Press.

——— (1977). "Economic Interdependence and National Security in Historical Perspective." In Klaus Knorr and Frank N. Trager (eds.), *Economic Issues and National Security* (pp. 19–66). Lawrence, Kansas: Regents Press of Kansas.

Gladwell, Malcolm (1996). "The Science of Shopping." *The New Yorker* 72, no. 33 (November 4):66–75.

Gleditsch, Nils Petter (1997). *Conflict and the Environment.* Dordrecht: Kluwer.

Gleick, Peter (1994). "Water, War, and Peace in the Middle East." *Environment* 36, no. 3 (April):6–15, 35–42.

Goldstein, Joshua S. (1988) *Long Cycles—Prosperity and War in the Modern Age.* New Haven, Conn.: Yale University Press.

Gordon, Richard (1995). "Globalization, New Production Systems and the Spatial Division of Labor." In Wolfgang Litek and Tony Charles (eds.), *The Division of Labor—Emerging Forms of World Organisation in International Perspective* (pp. 161–207). Berlin: Walter de Gruyter.

Gowa, Joanne (1983). *Closing the Gold Window.* Ithaca, N.Y.: Cornell University Press.

Graham, Edward M. (1996). *Global Corporations and National Governments.* Washington, D.C.: Institute for International Economics.

Gray, Colin S. (1990). *War, Peace, and Victory: Strategy and Statecraft for the Next Century.* New York: Simon & Schuster.

——— (1988). *The Geopolitics of Super Power.* Lexington: University Press of Kentucky.

Groh, Dieter (1987). "The Temptation of Conspiracy Theory, or: Why Do Bad Things Happen to Good People?" In Carl F. Graumann and Serge Moscovici (eds.), *Changing Conceptions of Conspiracy* (pp. 1–37). New York: Springer-Verlag.

Hajer, Maarten A. (1993). "Discourse Coalitions and the Institutionalization of Practice: The Case of Acid Rain in Great Britain." In Frank Fischer and John Forester (eds.), *The Argumentative Turn in Policy Analysis and Planning* (pp. 43–76). Durham, N.C.: Duke University Press.

Hanley, Charles J. (1996). "Blood Money." *San Francisco Examiner,* April 21, p. A12. Associated Press wire service.

Harris, Judith Rich (1998). *The Nurture Assumption.* New York: St. Martin's.

Hartmann, H., and Robert L. Wendzel (1988). *Defending America's Security.* Washington: Pergamon-Brassey's.

Harvey, David (1996). *Justice, Nature, and the Geography of Difference.* London: Blackwell.

Hedges, Chris (1995). "Pentagon Confident, but Some Serbs 'Will Fight': In Sarajevo Suburbs, Talk of Resistance." *New York Times,* November 27, national edition, p. A6.

Heilbroner, Robert L. (1991). *An Inquiry into the Human Prospect: Looked at Again for the 1990s.* 3rd ed. New York: Norton.

Herrenstein, Richard, and Charles Murray (1994). *The Bell Curve.* New York: Basic Books.

Herz, John H. (1959), *International Politics in the Atomic Age.* New York: Columbia University Press.

Hillel, Daniel (1994). *Rivers of Eden: the Struggle for Water and the Quest for Peace in the Middle East.* New York: Oxford University Press.

Himmelfarb, Gertrude (1995). *The De-moralization of Society: From Victorian Virtues to Modern Values.* New York: Knopf.

Hirsch, Fred (1995). *Social Limits to Growth.* New ed. Cambridge: Harvard University Press.

Hirschman, Albert O. (1980). *National Power and the Structure of Foreign Trade.* Berkeley: University of California Press, expanded edition; original edition, 1945.

Hobbes, Thomas (1962), *Leviathan.* Ed. Michael Oakeshott. New York: Collier.

Homer-Dixon, Thomas F. (1995). "The Ingenuity Gap: Can Poor Countries Adapt to Resource Scarcity?" *Population and Development Review* 21, no. 3 (September):587–612.

Hoopes, Townsend (1973). *The Devil and John Foster Dulles.* Boston: Atlantic-Little Brown.

Huntington, Samuel P. (1997). "The Erosion of American National Interests." *Foreign Affairs* 76, no. 5 (September/October):28–49.

——— (1996). *The Clash of Civilizations and the Remaking of World Order.* New York: Simon & Schuster.

——— (1993). "The Clash of Civilizations." *Foreign Affairs* 72, no. 3 (summer):22–49.

Ichheiser, G. (1949), "Misunderstandings in Human Relations: A Study in False Social Perception." *American Journal of Sociology* 60 (suppl.).

Iklé, Fred C. (1996). "The Second Coming of the Nuclear Age." *Foreign Affairs* 74, no. 1 (January–February):119–28.

——— (1971). *Every War Must End.* New York: Columbia University Press.

Inayatullah, Naeem (1996). "Beyond the Sovereignty Dilemma: Quasi-states as Social Construct." In Thomas J. Biersteker and Cynthia Weber (eds.), *State Sovereignty as Social Construct* (pp. 50–80). Cambridge: Cambridge University Press.

Isaac, J., and H. Shuval (eds.) (1994). *Water and Peace in the Middle East: Proceedings of the First Israeli-Palestinian International Academic Conference on Water, Zurich, Switzerland, 10–13 December 1992.* Amsterdam: Elsevier.

Jackson, Robert H. (1990). *Quasi-states: Sovereignty, International Relations and the Third World.* Cambridge: Cambridge University Press.

Jervis, Robert (1978). "Cooperation under the Security Dilemma." *World Politics* 30, no. 2 (January):167–214.

Kahn, Herman (1965). *On Escalation: Metaphors and Scenarios.* New York: Praeger.

Kaldor, Mary (1990). *The Imaginary War: Understanding the East–West Conflict.* Oxford: Blackwell.

Kally, Elisha, with Gideon Fishelson (1993). *Water and Peace: Water Resources and the Arab-Israeli Peace Process.* Westport, Conn.: Praeger.

Kaplan, Robert D. (1996). *The Ends of the Earth: A Journey at the Dawn of the Twenty-first Century.* New York: Random House.

—— (1994). "The Coming Anarchy." *Atlantic Monthly,* February, pp. 44–76.

Kapstein, Ethan (1996). "Workers and the World Economy." *Foreign Affairs* 75, no. 3 (May–June):16–37.

Keck, Margaret E., and Kathryn Sikkink (1998). *Activists across Borders: Advocacy Networks in International Politics.* Ithaca, N.Y.: Cornell University Press.

Kennan, George F. (1985/86), "Morality and Foreign Policy." *Foreign Affairs* 64, no. 5 (winter):205–18.

Kennedy, Paul (1988). *The Rise and Fall of the Great Powers.* New York: Random House.

Keohane, Robert O. (1984). *After Hegemony: Cooperation and Discord in the World Political Economy.* Princeton, N.J.: Princeton University Press.

Keohane, Robert O., and Joseph S. Nye (1977/1989). *Power and Interdependence.* Boston: Little, Brown.

Kifner, John (1995). "Bombing Suspect: Portrait of a Man's Frayed Life." *San Francisco Examiner,* December 31, p. A4. *New York Times* wire service.

Kindleberger, Charles P. (1973). *The World in Depression, 1929–1939.* Berkeley: University of California Press.

Kobrin, Stephen (1997). "Electronic Cash and the End of National Markets." *Foreign Policy* 107 (summer):54–64.

Kotz, Nick (1988). *Wild Blue Yonder: Money, Politics, and the B-1 Bomber.* New York: Pantheon.

Krasner, Stephen D. (1993). "Westphalia and All That." In Judith Goldstein and Robert Keohane (eds.), *Ideas and Foreign Policy* (pp. 235–264). Ithaca, N.Y.: Cornell University Press.

—— (ed.) (1983). *International Regimes.* Ithaca, N.Y.: Cornell University Press.

—— (1978). *Defending the National Interest.* Princeton, N.J.: Princeton University Press.

Krause, Keith, and Michael C. Williams (1996). "Broadening the Agenda of Security Studies: Politics and Methods." *Mershon International Studies Review* 40, Suppl. 2 (October):229–54.

—— (eds.) (1997). *Critical Security Studies: Concepts and Cases.* Minneapolis: University of Minnesota Press.

Krugman, Paul (1994a). "Europe Jobless, America Penniless?" *Foreign Policy* 95 (summer):19–34.

——— (1994b). *Peddling Prosperity—Economic Sense and Nonsense in the Age of Diminished Expectations.* New York: Norton.

Kubálková, Vendukla, Nicholas Onuf, and Paul Kowert (eds.) (1998). *International Relations in a Constructed World.* Armonk, N.Y.: M.E. Sharpe.

Kugler, Richard (1995). *Toward a Dangerous World.* Santa Monica: RAND.

Kull, Steven (1988). *Minds at War: Nuclear Reality and the Inner Conflicts of Defense Policymakers.* New York: Basic Books.

——— (1985). "Nuclear Nonsense." *Foreign Policy* 58 (spring):28–52.

Laitin, David (1985). "Hegemony and Religious Conflict: British Imperial Control and Political Cleavages in Yorubaland." In Peter B. Evans, Dietrich Rueschemeyer, and Theda Skocpol (eds.), *Bringing the State Back In* (pp. 285–316). New York: Cambridge University Press.

Lake, David A., and Donald S. Rothchild (eds.) (1998). *The International Spread of Ethnic Conflict.* Princeton, N.J.: Princeton University Press.

Lapid, Yosef, and Friedrich Kratochwil (eds.) (1996). *The Return of Culture and Identity in IR Theory.* Boulder, Colo.: Lynne Rienner.

Larkin, Bruce (forthcoming). *War Scripts/Civic Scripts.* Manuscript in preparation.

Latour, Bruno, and Steve Woolgar (1986). *Laboratory Life—The Construction of Scientific Facts.* Princeton, N.J.; Princeton University Press; first edition, Sage, 1979.

Leary, Warren E. (1997). "Science Fiction's Microbe Peril from Mars is Unlikely but Possible, Panel Warns." *New York Times,* March 7, national edition, p. A10.

Leatherman, Janie, Ron Pagnucco, and Jackie Smith (1994). "International Institutions and Transnational Social Movement Organizations: Transforming Sovereignty, Anarchy, and Global Governance." Kroc Institute for International Peace Studies, University of Notre Dame, August. Working Paper 5:WP:3.

Lederer, William, and Eugene Burdick (1987). *The Ugly American.* New York: Fawcett; originally published in 1958.

Lemarchand, René (1994). *Burundi: Ethnocide as Discourse and Practice.* New York and Cambridge: Wilson Center and Cambridge University Press.

Levin, N. D. (ed.) (1994). *Prisms and Policy: U.S. Security Strategy after the Cold War.* Santa Monica, Calif.: RAND.

Lewis, Bernard (1992). "Muslims, Christians, and Jews: The Dream of Coexistence." *The New York Review of Books* 39, no. 6, March 26, pp. 48–52.

Libecap, Gary (1989). *Contracting for Property Rights.* Cambridge: Cambridge University Press.

Libicki, Martin C. (1996). "Technology and Warfare," Chap. 4 in Patrick M. Cronin (ed.), *2015: Power and Progress.* National Defense University, Institute for National Strategic Studies, July, at http://198.80.36/ndu/inss/books/2015/ ch4co.html.

Lind, William S. (1991). "Defending Western Culture." *Foreign Policy* 84 (fall):40–50.

Lipschutz, Ronnie D. (ed.) (1999a). *Beyond the Neo-liberal Peace.* Special Issue of *Social Justice* 25, no. 4, (winter).

——— (1999b). "Terror in the Suites: Narratives of Fear and the Political Economy of Danger." *Global Society* 14, no. 4 (October):409–437.

——— (1999c). "Members Only?" Citizenship and Civic Virtue in a Time of Globalization." *International Politics* 36, no. 2 (June):203–233.

———, with Cathleen Fogel (1999d). "Regulation for the Rest of Us—Global Civil Society and the Democratization of Global Politics." Paper presented at the Workshop on Global Civil Society/Global Democracy, Rutgers University-Newark, June 4–5.

——— (1998a). "Seeking a State of One's Own: An Analytical Framework for Assessing 'Ethnic and Sectarian Conflicts'." In Beverly Crawford and Ronnie D. Lipschutz (eds.), *The Myth of "Ethnic Conflict"* (pp. 44–77). Berkeley: Institute of International and Area Studies, UC-Berkeley.

——— (1998b). "From Culture Wars to Shooting Wars: Globalization and Cultural Conflict in the United States." In Beverly Crawford and Ronnie D. Lipschutz (eds.), *The Myth of "Ethnic Conflict"* (pp. 394–433). Berkeley: Institute of International and Area Studies, UC–Berkeley.

——— (1998c). "The Nature of Sovereignty and the Sovereignty of Nature: Problematizing the Boundaries between Self, Society, State, and System." In Karen T. Litfin (ed.), *The Greening of Sovereignty in World Politics* (pp. 109–138). Cambridge: MIT Press.

——— (1997a). "The Great Transformation Revisited." *Brown Journal of International Affairs* 4, no. 1 (winter/spring):299–318.

——— (1997b). *What Did You Do in the Cold War, Daddy? Reading U.S. Foreign Policy in Contemporary Film and Fiction.* Draft manuscript.

——— (1997c). "From Place to Planet: Local Knowledge and Global Environmental Governance." *Global Governance* 3, no. 1 (January–April):83–102.

———, with Judith Mayer (1996). *Global Civil Society and Global Environmental Governance.* Albany: State University of New York Press.

——— (1995a). "On Security." In Ronnie D. Lipschutz (ed.), *On Security* (pp. 1–23). New York: Columbia University Press.

———— (1995b). "Negotiating the Boundaries of Difference and Security at Millennium's End." In Ronnie D. Lipschutz (ed.), *On Security* (pp. 212–28). New York: Columbia University Press.

———— (1992a). "Reconstructing World Politics: The Emergence of Global Civil Society." *Millennium* 21, no. 3 (winter):389–420.

———— (1992b). "Strategic Insecurity: Putting the Pieces Back Together in the Middle East." In Harry Kreisler (ed.), *Confrontation in the Gulf* (pp. 113–26). Berkeley: Institute of International Studies, UC-Berkeley.

———— (1992c). "Raw Materials, Finished Ideals: Strategic Raw Materials and the Geopolitical Economy of U.S. Foreign Policy." In Martha L. Cottam and Chih-yu Shih (eds.), *Contending Dramas: A Cognitive Approach to International Organizations* (pp. 101–26). New York: Praeger.

———— (1991). "Wasn't the Future Wonderful? Resources, Environment, and the Emerging Myth of Global Sustainable Development." *Colorado Journal of International Environmental Law and Policy* 2:35–54.

———— (1989). *When Nations Clash: Raw Materials, Ideology, and Foreign Policy.* New York: Ballinger/Harper & Row.

Lipschutz, Ronnie D., and Beverly Crawford (1996). "Economic Globalization and the 'New' Ethnic Strife: What Is to Be Done?" Institute on Global Conflict and Cooperation, University of California, San Diego, May, Policy Paper #25.

Lipschutz, Ronnie D., and Ken Conca (1993). "The Implications of Global Ecological Interdependence." In Ronnie D. Lipschutz and Ken Conca (eds.), *The State and Social Power in Global Environmental Politics* (pp. 327–43). New York: Columbia University Press.

List, Friedrich (1856). *National System of Political Economy.* Philadelphia: J. B. Lippincott.

Litfin, Karen (ed.) (1998). *The Greening of Sovereignty in World Politics.* Cambridge: MIT Press.

———— (1994). *Ozone Discourses.* New York: Columbia University Press.

Locke, John (1988). *On Civil Government: The Second Treatise.* In Peter Laslett (ed.), *Two Treatises of Government.* Cambridge: Cambridge University Press, student edition.

Long, Norman, and Ann Long (eds.) (1992). *Battlefields of Knowledge: The Interlocking of Theory and Practice in Social Research and Development.* London: Routledge.

Lowi, Miriam R. (1995). "Rivers of Conflict, Rivers of Peace." *Journal of International Affairs* 49, no. 1:123–44.

———— (1993). *Water and Power: The Politics of a Scarce Resource in the Jordan River Basin.* Cambridge: Cambridge University Press.

———— (1992). "West Bank Water Resources and the Resolution of Conflict in the Middle East." Occasional Paper Series of the Project on Environmental Change and Acute Conflict no. 1 (September):29–60.

Luke, Timothy W. (1995). "New World Order or Neo-World Orders: Power, Politics, and Ideology in Informationalizing Glocalities." In Mike Featherstone, Scott Lash, and Roland Robertson (eds.), *Global Modernities* (pp. 91–107). London: Sage.

———— (1989). "On Post-War: The Significance of Symbolic Action in War and Deterrence." *Alternatives* 14:343–62.

Mackinder, Halford J. (1919/1962). *Democratic Ideals and Reality.* New York: Norton.

———— (1943). "The Round World and the Winning of the Peace." *Foreign Affairs* (July):595–605.

Malthus, Thomas Robert (1803). *An essay on the principle of population; or, A view of its past and present effect on human happiness; with an inquiry into our prospects respecting the future removal or mitigation of the evils which it occasions.* London, printed for J. Johnson, by T. Bensley; A new edition, very much enlarged.

Mandelbaum, Michael (1996). "Foreign Policy as Social Work." *Foreign Affairs* 75, no. 1 (January–February):16–32.

Mann, Michael (1993). *The Sources of Social Power: The Rise of Classes and Nation-States, 1760–1914.* Vol. 2. Cambridge: Cambridge University Press.

Mansfield, Edward, and Jack Snyder (1995). "Democratization and War." *Foreign Affairs* 74, no. 3 (May/June):79–97.

Marshall, Jonathan (1995a). "Electronic Classes Give Students More Options When Teacher Is Far, Far Away." *San Francisco Chronicle,* March 21, p. A1.

———— (1995b). "Don't Tie Anger to Low Wages." *San Francisco Chronicle,* May 29, p. D1.

Marx, Karl (1978). "Speech at the Anniversary of the *People's Paper.*" In Robert C. Tucker (ed.), *The Marx-Engels Reader.* 2d ed. (pp. 577–78). New York: Norton.

Massing, Michael (1998). *The Fix.* New York: Simon & Schuster.

Mastanduno, Michael (1991). "The United States Defiant: Export Controls in the Postwar Era." *Dædalus* 120, no. 4 (fall):91–112.

Mathews, Jessica Tuchman (1997). "Powershift." *Foreign Affairs* 76, no. 1 (January/February):50–66.

———— (1989). "Redefining Security." *Foreign Affairs* 68, no. 2 (spring):162–77.

McCormick, Thomas (1996). *America's Half-Century.* 2d ed. Baltimore: Johns Hopkins University Press.

Mcpherson, C. B. (1962). *The Political Theory of Possessive Individualism.* Oxford: Oxford University Press.

Mead, Walter Russell (1995/96). "Trains, Planes, and Automobiles: The End of the Postmodern Moment." *World Policy Journal* 12, no. 4 (winter):13–31.

Meadows, Dennis, et al. (1972). *Limits to Growth.* Cambridge: MIT Press.

Meadows, Donella H., Dennis L. Meadows, and Jorgen Randers (1992). *Beyond the Limits: Confronting Global Collapse, Envisioning a Sustainable Future.* Post Mills, Vt.: Chelsea Green.

Mearsheimer, John J. (1994). "The False Promise of International Institutions." *International Security* 19, no. 3 (winter):5–49.

——— (1990a). "Why We Will Soon Miss the Cold War." *The Atlantic* 266, no. 2 (August):35–45.

——— (1990b). "Back to the Future: Instability in Europe after the Cold War." *International Security* 15, no. 1 (summer):5–56.

Mercer, Jonathan (1995). "Anarchy and Identity." *International Organization* 49, no. 2 (spring):229–52.

Meyer, David S. (1993). "Below, Beyond, Beside the State: Peace and Human Rights Movements and the End of the Cold War." In David Skidmore and Valerie M. Hudson (eds.), *The Limits of State Autonomy: Societal Groups and Foreign Policy Formulation* (pp. 267–96). Boulder, Colo.: Westview Press.

——— (1990). *A Winter of Discontent: The Nuclear Freeze and American Politics.* New York: Praeger.

Milward, Alan S. (1977). *War, Economy, and Society, 1939–1945.* Berkeley: University of California Press.

Moravcsik, Andrew (1991). "Arms and Autarky in Modern European History." *Dædalus* 120, no. 4 (fall):23–46.

Moscovici, Serge (1987). "The Conspiracy Mentality." In Carl F. Graumann and Serge Moscovici (eds.), *Changing Conceptions of Conspiracy* (pp. 151–69). New York: Springer-Verlag.

Mueller, John (1989). *Retreat from Doomsday: The Obsolescence of Major War.* New York: Basic Books.

Murakami, Masahiro (1995). *Managing Water for Peace in the Middle East: Alternative Strategies.* Tokyo: United Nations University Press.

Myers, Laura (1997). "Art Imitates Life: Terrorism on Screen Has Some Validity." *Santa Cruz County Sentinal,* August 19, p. A-6 (Associated Press wire service).

Nanda, Ved. P. (1995). *International Environmental Law and Policy.* Irvington-on-Hudson, N.Y.: Transnational Publishers.

Nasar, Sylvia (1994). "More Men in Prime of Life Spend Less Time Working." *New York Times,* December 12, national edition, p. A1.

The New York Times (1996). "The Downsizing of America." March 3–9.

Nitze, Paul (1976–77). "Deterring Our Deterrent." *Foreign Policy* 25:195–210.

Noble, David F. (1997). *The Religion of Technology.* New York: Knopf.

Noponen, Heizi, Julie Graham, and Ann R. Markusen (eds.) (1993). *Trading Industries, Trading Regions: International Trade, American Industry, and Regional Economic Development.* New York: Guilford.

Nye, Joseph S., Jr. (1990). *Bound to Lead: The Changing Nature of American Power.* New York: Basic Books.

Nye, Joseph S., Jr., and William Owens (1996). "America's Information Edge." *Foreign Affairs* 75, no. 2 (March/April):20–36.

Oakes, Guy (1994). *The Imaginary War: Civil Defense and American Cold War Culture.* New York: Oxford University Press.

Ohmae, Kenichi (1995). *The End of the Nation State.* New York: Free Press.

——— (1991). *The Borderless World: Power and Strategy in the Interlinked Economy.* New York: HarperPerennial.

Onuf, Nicholas (1989). *World of Our Making: Rules and Rule in Social Theory and International Relations.* Columbia: University of South Carolina Press.

Ophuls, William, and A. Stephen Boyan, Jr. (1992). *Ecology and the Politics of Scarcity Revisited: The Unraveling of the American Dream.* New York: W. H. Freeman.

Organski, A. F. K., and Jacek Kugler (1980). *The War Ledger.* Chicago: University of Chicago Press.

Packenham, Robert A. (1973). *Liberal America and the Third World: Political Development Ideas in Foreign Aid and Social Science.* Princeton, N.J.: Princeton University Press.

Peluso, Nancy Lee (1993). "Coercing Conservation: The Politics of State Resource Control." In Ronnie D. Lipschutz and Ken Conca (eds.), *The State and Social Power in Global Environmental Politics* (pp. 46–70). New York: Columbia University Press.

——— (1992). *Rich Forests, Poor People—Resource Control and Resistance in Java.* Berkeley: University of California Press.

Peterson, V. Spike, and Anne Sisson Runyan (1993). *Global Gender Issues.* Boulder, Colo.: Westview Press.

Pois, Robert A. (1986). *National Socialism and the Religion of Nature.* London: Croom Helm.

Polanyi, Karl (1957). *The Great Transformation.* Boston: Beacon Press, original edition, 1944.

Pollack, Andrew (1997). "Thriving, South Koreans Strike to Keep It That Way." *New York Times,* January 17, national edition, p. A1.

Pollard, Robert A. (1985). *Economic Security and the Origins of the Cold War, 1945–1950.* New York: Columbia University Press.

President's Materials Policy Commission (1952). *Resources for Freedom.* Washington, D.C.: U.S. Government Printing Office.

Princen, Thomas, and Matthias Finger (eds.) (1994). *Environmental NGOs in World Politics.* London: Routledge.

Quadrennial Defense Review (QDR) (1997). Washington, D.C.: The Pentagon, at: www.fas.org/man/docs/qdr.

Ra'anan, Uri, Maria Mesner, Keith Armes, and Kate Martin (1991). *State and Nation in Multi-ethnic Societies: The Breakup of Multinational States.* Manchester: Manchester University Press.

Reich, Robert (1992). *The Work of Nations.* New York: Vintage.

Reiff, David (1991). "Multiculturalism's Silent Partner." *Harpers*, August, pp. 62–72.

Rochlin, Gene I. (1997). *Trapped in the Net: The Unanticipated Consequences of Computerization.* Princeton, N.J.: Princeton University Press.

——— (1985). "Shotguns and Sharpshooters: Command, Control, and the Search for Certainty in the U.S. Weapons Acquisition Process." Berkeley: Institute of Governmental Studies, University of California, Working paper 85–2.

Rosecrance, Richard (1996). "The Rise of the Virtual State." *Foreign Affairs* 75, no. 4 (July/August):45–61.

Rosenau, James N. (1997). *Along the Domestic-Foreign Frontier: Exploring Governance in a Turbulent World.* Cambridge: Cambridge University Press.

——— (1990). *Turbulence in World Politics: A Theory of Change and Continuity.* Princeton, N.J.: Princeton University Press.

Rosenau, James N., and Ernst-Otto Czempiel (eds.) (1992). *Governance without Government: Order and Change in World Politics.* Cambridge: Cambridge University Press.

Rosenfeld, Seth (1997). "FBI Wants S.F. Cops to Join Spy Squad." *San Francisco Examiner,* January 12, p. A1.

Rousseau, Jean-Jacques (1968). *The Social Contract.* Trans. by Maurice Cransto. Harmondsworth: Penguin.

Rowny, Edward L. (1997). "What Will Prevent a Missile Attack?" *New York Times,* January 24, national edition, p. A17.

Royal Institute of International Affairs (1936). *Raw Materials and Colonies.* London: Royal Institute of International Affairs, Information Department paper no. 18.

Rudolph, Susanne Hoeber, and James Piscatori (eds.) (1997). *Transnational Religion and Fading States.* Boulder, Colo.: Westview Press.

Ruggie, John G. (1995). "At Home Abroad, Abroad at Home: International Liberalisation and Domestic Stability in the New World Economy." *Millennium* 24, no. 3 (winter):507–26.

———— (1993). "Territoriality and Beyond: Problematizing Modernity in International Relations." *International Organization* 47, no. 1 (winter):139–74.

———— (1991). "Embedded Liberalism Revisited: Institutions and Progress in International Economic Relations." In Emanuel Adler and Beverly Crawford (eds.), *Progress in International Relations* (pp. 201–34). New York: Columbia University Press.

———— (1989). "International Structure and International Transformation: Space, Time, and Method." In Ernst–Otto Czempiel and James N. Rosenau (eds.), *Global Changes and Theoretical Challenges* (pp. 21–35). Lexington, Mass.: Lexington Books.

———— (1983a). "International Regimes, Transactions, and Change: Embedded Liberalism in the Postwar Economic Order." In Stephen D. Krasner (ed.), *International Regimes* (pp. 195–232). Ithaca, N.Y.: Cornell University Press.

———— (1983b). "Continuity and Transformation in the World Polity: Toward a Neorealist Synthesis." *World Politics* 35, no. 2 (January):261–85.

Rule, James B. (1992). "Tribalism and the State." *Dissent* 39, no. 4 (fall):519–23.

Rupert, Mark (1997). "Globalization and the Reconstruction of Common Sense in the U.S." In Stephen Gill and James Mittleman (eds.), *Innovation and Transformation in International Studies*. Cambridge: Cambridge University Press.

———— (1995). *Producing Hegemony: The Politics of Mass Production and American Global Power.* Cambridge: Cambridge University Press.

Said, Edward (1979). *Orientalism.* New York: Viking.

Sakamoto, Yoshikazu (ed.) (1994). *Global Transformation: Challenges to the State System.* Tokyo: United Nations University Press.

Sanders, Jerry W. (1983). *Peddlers of Crisis: The Committee on the Present Danger and the Politics of Containment.* Boston: South End Press.

Sandholtz, Wayne, et al. (1992). *The Highest Stakes: The Economic Foundations of the Next Security System.* New York: Oxford University Press.

San Francisco Chronicle (1997). "Conservative Accuses Gingrich of Cozying Up to Liberals," February 6, p. A8.

———— (1991a). "U.S. Pushing Language Studies," December 26, p. A3.

———— (1991b). "Security Threats," Editorial, December 28, p. A18.

Sassen, Saskia (1998). *Globalization and Its Discontents.* Princeton, N.J.: Princeton University Press.

———— (1994). *Cities in a World Economy.* Thousand Oaks, Calif.: Pine Forge Press.

Saul, John Ralston (1992). *Voltaire's Bastards: The Dictatorship of Reason in the West.* New York: Free Press.

Scheer, Robert (1982). *With Enough Shovels.* New York: Random House.

Schelling, Thomas (1966). *Arms and Influence.* New Haven, Conn.: Yale University Press.

Schlesinger, James (1991–92). "New Instabilities, New Priorities." *Foreign Policy* 85 (winter):3–24.

Schmidt, Brian C. (1998). *The Political Discourse of Anarchy: A Disciplinary History of International Relations.* Albany: State University of New York Press.

Schurmann, Franz (1987). *The Foreign Politics of Richard Nixon: The Grand Design.* Berkeley: Institute of International Studies, University of California, Berkeley.

———— (1974). *The Logic of World Power.* New York: Pantheon.

Schwartz, Stephen I. (ed.) (1998). *Atomic Audit: The Costs and Consequences of U.S. Nuclear Weapons Since 1940.* Washington, D.C.: The Brookings Institution.

Seaton, Jim (1994). "Social Warfare: The Setting for Stability Operations." Paper prepared for the ISA Annual Meeting, Washington, D.C., March 29–April 1.

Sen, Amartya (1994). "Population: Delusion and Reality." *New York Review of Books,* September 22, pp. 62–71.

Serageldin, Ismail (1995). *Toward Sustainable Management of Water Resources.* Washington, D.C.: The World Bank, August.

Shapiro, Michael J. (1997). *Violent Cartographies: Mapping Cultures of War.* Minneapolis: University of Minnesota Press.

Shapiro, Michael J., and Hayward R. Alker (eds.) (1996). *Challenging Boundaries: Global Flows, Territorial Identities.* Minneapolis: University of Minnesota Press.

Shoup, Laurence H., and William Minter (1977). *Imperial Brain Trust: The Council on Foreign Relations and United States Foreign Policy.* New York: Monthly Review Press.

Shuman, Michael H. (1994). *Towards a Global Village: International Community Development Initiatives.* London and Boulder, Colo.: Pluto Press.

———— (1992). "Dateline Main Street: Courts v. Local Foreign Policies." *Foreign Policy* 86 (spring):158–77.

Simon, Julian, (1996). *The Ultimate Resource 2.* Rev. ed. Princeton, N.J.: Princeton University Press.

———— (1981). *The Ultimate Resource*. Princeton, N.J.: Princeton University Press.

Skocpol, Theda (1985). "Bringing the State Back In: Strategies of Analysis in Current Research." In Peter B. Evans, Dietrich Rueschemeyer and Theda Skocpol (eds.), *Bringing the State Back In* (pp. 3–37). Cambridge: Cambridge University Press.

Smith, Neil (1989). "Uneven Development and Location Theory: Towards a Synthesis." In *New Models in Geography*. Vol. 1. (pp. 142–63). London: Unwin Hyman.

Smith, R. Jeffrey (1984a). "Missile Deployments Roil Europe." *Science* 223 (January 27):371–76.

———— (1984b). "Missile Talks Doomed from the Start." *Science* 223 (February 10):566–70.

———— (1984c). "Missile Deployments Shake European Politics." *Science* 223 (February 17):665–67.

———— (1984d). "The Allure of High-Tech Weapons for Europe." *Science* 223 (March 23):1269–72.

Smithson, Amy E. (1996). "Growth Industry: The U.S. Arms Control Bureaucracy in the Late 1980s." Ph.D diss., George Washington University. Washington, D.C.

Spykman, Nicholas J. (1944). *The Geography of the Peace*. Ed. H. R. Nicholl. New York: Harcourt Brace.

———— (1942). *America's Strategy in World Politics: The United States and the Balance of Power*. New York: Harcourt, Brace.

Starr, Joyce (1995). *Covenant over Middle Eastern Waters: Key to World Survival*. New York: H. Holt.

———— (1991). "Water Wars." *Foreign Policy* 82 (spring):17–30.

Starr, Joyce, and Daniel C. Stoll (eds.) (1988). *The Politics of Scarcity: Water in the Middle East*. Boulder, Colo.: Westview Press.

Steinbruner, John (1974). *The Cybernetic Theory of Decision*. Princeton, N.J.: Princeton University Press.

Stone, Deborah (1988). *Policy Paradox and Political Reason*. New York: HarperCollins.

Strange, Susan (1996). *The Retreat of the State*. Cambridge: Cambridge University Press.

———— (1983). "*Cave! hic dragones:* A Critique of Regime Analysis." In Stephen D. Krasner (ed.), *International Regimes* (pp. 337–54). Ithaca, N.Y.: Cornell University Press.

Szerszynski, Bronislaw (1996). "On Knowing What to Do: Environmentalism and the Modern Problematic." In Scott Lash, Bronislaw Szerszynski, and Briane Wynne (eds.), *Risk, Environment, and Modernity: Towards a New Ecology* (pp. 104–37). London: Sage.

Thomas, G. Dale (1997). "Historical Uses of Civil Society and the Global Civil Society Debate." Paper presented at the annual convention of the International Studies Association, Toronto, March 18–22.

Thompson, Michael (1979). *Rubbish Theory: The Creation and Destruction of Value.* Oxford: Oxford University Press.

Thomson, Janice E. (1995). "State Sovereignty and International Relations: Bridging the Gap between Theory and Empirical Research." *International Studies Quarterly* 39, no. 2 (June):213–33.

Thucydides (1954). *The Peloponnesian War.* Harmondsworth, U.K.: Penguin.

Tickner, J. Ann (1992). *Gender in International Relations.* New York: Columbia University Press.

Todarova, Maria (1998). "Identity (Trans)formation among Bulgarian Muslims." In Beverly Crawford and Ronnie D. Lipschutz (eds.), *The Myth of "Ethnic Conflict"* (pp. 471–510). Berkeley: International and Area Studies Press, UC-Berkeley.

Trager, Louis (1995). "All's Fair in Selling Growth to Cities," *San Francisco Examiner,* January 22, p. C-1.

Tuathail, Gearóid Ó (1997). "At the End of Geopolitics? Reflections on a Plural Problematic at the Century's End." *Alternatives* 22, no. 1 (January–March):35–55.

Turner, Bryan S. (1997). "Citizenship Studies: A General Theory." *Citizenship Studies* 1, no. 1 (February):5–18.

Uchitelle, Louis (1998). "Downsizing Comes Back, but the Outcry is Muted." *New York Times,* December 7, national edition, p. A1.

——— (1994). "Changing Economy Spawns 'Anxious Class'." *San Francisco Chronicle*, November 21, p. A6. *New York Times* wire service.

Ullman, Richard H. (1983). "Redefining Security." *International Security* 8, no. 1 (summer):129–53.

U.S. Senate (1996). *Hearings on Information Warfare and the Security of the Government's Computer Networks.* Senate Governmental Affairs Committee, June 25, *Congressional Quarterly* Database.

van Creveld, Martin (1991). *The Transformation of War.* New York: The Free Press.

Viviano, Frank (1995). "World's Wannabee Nations Sound Off." *San Francisco Chronicle,* January 31, p. A1.

Vogel, David (1995). *Trading Up—Consumer and Environmental Regulation in a Global Economy.* Cambridge: Harvard University Press.

Vogel, Steven K. (1996). *Freer Markets, More Rules: Regulatory Reform in Advanced Industrial Countries.* Ithaca, N.Y.: Cornell University Press.

Wæver, Ole (1995). "Securitization and Desecuritization." In Ronnie D. Lipschutz (ed.), *On Security* (pp. 44–86). New York: Columbia University Press.

Walker, R. B. J. (1992). *Inside/Outside: International Relations as Political Theory.* Cambridge: Cambridge University Press.

Walt, Steve (1991). "Renaissance of Security Studies." *International Studies Quarterly* 35, no. 2 (June):211–39.

Waltz, Kenneth (1979). *Theory of International Politics.* Reading, Mass.: Addison-Wesley.

———— (1971). "The Myth of National Interdependence." In Charles Kindleberger (ed.), *The International Corporation.* Cambridge: MIT Press.

———— (1959). *Man, the State, and War.* New York: Columbia University Press.

Walzer, Michael (ed.) (1995). *Toward a Global Civil Society.* Providence, R.I.: Berghahn Books.

Wapner, Paul (1996). *Environmental Activism and World Civil Politics.* Albany: State University of New York Press.

Weber, Eugen (1976). *Peasants into Frenchmen: The Modernization of Rural France, 1870–1914.* Stanford, Calif.: Stanford University Press.

Wehrfritz, George (1997). "The Uses of the Past: Historians and Archeologists Dig Up Evidence to Support China's Growing Nationalism." *Newsweek* 130, no. 1 (July 7):44–45.

Weigert, Hans W., et al. (1957). *Principles of Political Geography.* New York: Appleton-Century-Crofts.

Weinberger Caspar (1982). "United States Nuclear Deterrence Policy." Testimony before the Foreign Relations Committee of the U.S. Senate, December 14.

Weldes, Jutta (1992). *Constructing National Interests: The Logic of U.S. National Security in the Post-War Era.* Ph.D. diss., University of Minnesota, Minneapolis.

Wendt, Alex (1992). "Anarchy Is What States Make of It: The Social Construction of Power Politics." *International Organization* 46, no. 2 (spring):391–425.

Westing, Arthur H. (ed.) (1986). *Global Resources and International Conflict.* Oxford: Oxford University Press.

Wilmer, Franke (1993). *The Indigenous Voice in World Politics.* Newbury Park, CA: Sage.

Wingerson, Lois (1991). *Mapping Our Genes: The Genome Project and the Future of Medicine.* New York: Plume.

Wirls, Daniel (1992). *Buildup: The Politics of Defense in the Reagan Era.* Ithaca, N.Y.: Cornell University Press.

Wolf, Aaron T. (1995). *Hydropolitics along the Jordan River: Scarce Water and Its Impact on the Arab-Israeli Conflict.* Tokyo: United Nations University Press.

Woodall, Pam (1995). "The World Economy: Who's in the Driving Seat?" *The Economist,* October 7, special insert.

Woodward, Susan L. (1995). *Balkan Tragedy: Chaos and Dissolution after the Cold War.* Washington, D.C.: Brookings.

World Commission on Environment and Development (WCED; Brundtland Commission) (1987). *Our Common Future.* Oxford: Oxford University Press.

Young, Iris Marion (1990). *Justice and the Politics of Difference.* Princeton, N.J.: Princeton University Press.

Index

Agnew, John, 88
alienation, 44, 126, 182
aliens, 193n.12
Allison, Graham, 38–39
anarchy, 93, 97, 98, 103, 109, 132, 140, 193n.5, 195n.17; and markets, 140, 153–154; and morality, 139, 141, 145, 153; social construction of, 186n.19. *See also* Hobbesianism; State of Nature
Anderson, Benedict, 110, 193n.10
Andric, Ivo, 191n.4
Angell, Norman, 38
Annual Report to the President and the Congress (Secretary of Defense), 74
Arafat, Yassir, 194n.16
Aristotle, 155
arms race, 34

Aron, Raymond, 2
Atoms for Peace, 24
autarchy, 44, 89, 97, 154
authority: after, 157–160, 170, 173; of borders, 58–59, 135, 142–145, 154, 167; and citizens, 166, 178–179; diffusion, decline, and collapse of, 15, 118, 156, 157, 159, 165, 167, 179; of discourses, 65; and elites, 54, 165; establishment of, 27, 165; feudal, 139, 165; and globalization, 4, 118, 165, 168; and individualism, 4, 9, 166; moral, 134–135, 137, 139, 142–148, 153–154; new sources of, 135, 165, 171–179, 180; and security, 48, 52, 54, 61; of social contracts, 117;

221